1/20/58

MOSLEMS

ON THE

MARCH

BY F. W. Fernau

ernau *ilhelm*

TRANSLATED FROM THE GERMAN BY
E. W. DICKES

1954

NEW YORK: ALFRED A. KNOPF

MOSLEMS

ON THE

MARCH

PEOPLE AND POLITICS

IN THE

WORLD OF ISLAM

L. C. catalog card number: 53–9463

THIS IS A BORZOI BOOK,
PUBLISHED BY ALFRED A. KNOPF, INC.

FIRST AMERICAN EDITION

Published in Switzerland as FLACKERNDER HALBMOND: HINTER-GRUND DER ISLAMISCHEN UNRUHE, Copyright 1953 by Eugen Rentsch Verlag Erlenbach-Zürich

8484

Preface

THE MIDDLE of the twentieth century finds mankind caught in two world-wide conflicts. That between the Soviet Union and the Atlantic West is all too familiar to the peoples of Europe and America. It involves the issue of peace or war, so that the very existence of the individual is directly at stake. The problems of this conflict, the action it entails, and the possibilities of a solution are subjects of continual thought and discussion. The other issue, that of the emancipation of the peoples of Asia and Africa, seems to be treated as of secondary interest. Only at times of crisis is it given wider attention for the moment.

These two world conflicts are closely interconnected, and influence each other. But they demand separate consideration. The upheavals in the Near and Far East cannot be judged simply with reference to their bearing on the "Cold War," though that element is obviously important from the standpoint of the West. Such one-sided consideration would run the risk of obscuring the longer view and confusing temporary expedients with genuine solutions.

What is happening among those alien peoples is a process *sui generis,* of world-wide historical importance, and not merely incidental to the conflict between the Soviet Union and the West. It raises questions that call for at least as much resourcefulness and vigilance, at least as broad and imaginative treatment, as that of the relations with the Soviet Union. Failing that, this chapter of history might one day call irrevocably for the comment: "Too little and too late."

The expansion of modern Europe passed in a mighty wave over the ancient civilizations of Islam, Hindu India, and China. At the beginning of this century there came a turn of the tide. At first the movement was slight and uncertain. Not until after the Second World War did the flood, in a succession of dangerous crises not yet ended, breach the dikes. The non-European peoples of the Old World are demanding liberation from European tutelage. They are demanding not only political and economic independence but the right to order their own lives, the right to settle for themselves what they choose to do or not to do. That is the great common element. It must not be confused with the "united front of the colonial peoples." The Far Eastern civilizations and Hindu India are civilizations of Asia, in the specific historical and philosophical sense of the word; while Islam is neither Asian nor Western. It is intermediate between "Asia" and "Europe," and also—a fact that must not be overlooked—intermediate between Europe and black Africa. For the very reason of this intermediate position, the path chosen by the peoples of Islam may become of critical importance to the future development of the whole world. If they shut themselves off in hostility to the West, the bridges leading from Europe to Asia and Africa will have been blocked.

It would be a costly mistake to assume that in our day the West can still dictate the course to be followed by the Islamic world. But there is probably still time for a friendship based on common interests. That calls for knowledge and understanding. The present work aims at placing before the reader with a general interest in the subject the broad features of the Islamic community, and introducing him to the perplexing events of the immediate past. If it succeeds in so making some contribution to the needed knowledge and understanding, its purpose may be regarded as achieved.

A word may be added on the spelling of foreign names. This book is addressed to the layman and not to the Oriental expert. No attempt, therefore, has been made at a scientific transliteration of the Arabic alphabet. The spelling likely to be most familiar to the ordinary reader has been chosen. Turkish names have been given in conformity with the new Turkish alphabet.

Contents

Contents

x

Maps

(The maps for this book were originally prepared by SONJA SCHWIRZER; for the American edition they have been revised by RENA M. KANE.)

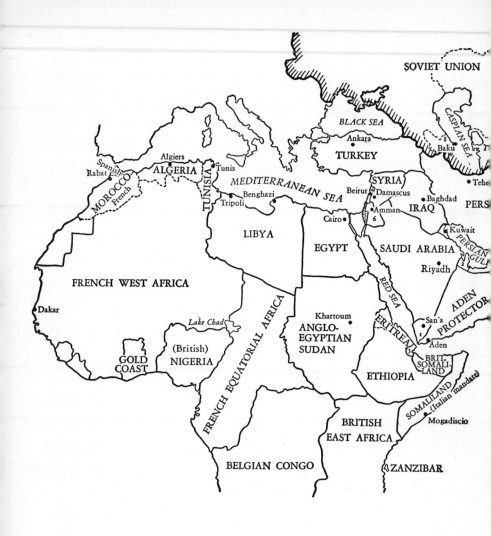

POLITICAL DISTRIBUTION OF THE MOSLEM WORLD

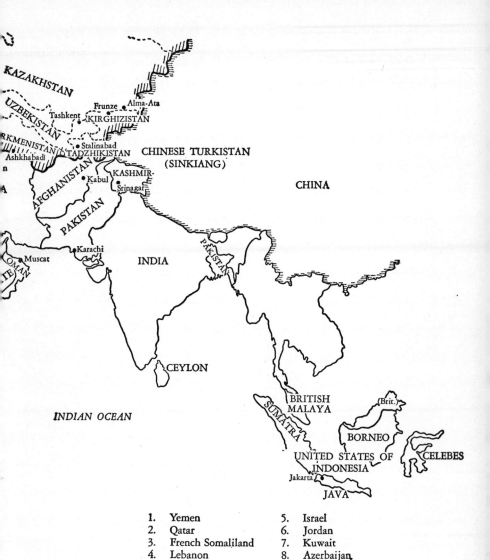

KAZAKHSTAN

UZBEKISTAN

Frunze • Alma-Ata

Tashkent • KIRGHIZISTAN

RKMENISTAN • Stalinabad

Ashkhabad TADZHIKISTAN

CHINESE TURKISTAN
(SINKIANG)

AFGHANISTAN • Kabul KASHMIR

CHINA

• Srinagar

PAKISTAN

Muscat • Karachi

INDIA

PAKISTAN

CEYLON

INDIAN OCEAN

SUMATRA

BRITISH
MALAYA

(Brit.)

BORNEO

CELEBES

UNITED STATES OF
INDONESIA

Jakarta

JAVA

1.	Yemen	5.	Israel
2.	Qatar	6.	Jordan
3.	French Somaliland	7.	Kuwait
4.	Lebanon	8.	Azerbaijan

Part One

THE

ISLAMIC

INTERCONTINENT

CHAPTER ONE

Deserts, Water, World Routes

THE YELLOW HOUSE OF ISLAM

A GLANCE at the map of the world might tempt one to a hasty generalization: that the spread of Islam is in inverse proportion to the distribution of the world's rainfall. But there is no such law; the fact is no more than a geographical coincidence. Western map-makers generally use shades of blue to indicate regions with adequate or ample rainfall, and of yellow for those with less than twenty inches of rain in the year. North and south of the tropics, in both hemispheres, one may see on the map more or less extensive yellow surfaces. These are the dry zones of the earth —the southern regions of the continents of South America and Africa, and large parts of Australia, in the Southern Hemisphere; in the Northern Hemisphere a strip in the northern part of the New World extending to the Rocky Mountains, and, greatly exceeding all the other arid regions in extent, the largest dry zone in the world, passing

3

like a girdle across the continental mass of the Old World from the Atlantic coast of North Africa to the western borders of China. The Arabian peninsula forms almost exactly the centre of that great girdle, North Africa its western end, and Central Asia the eastern end. The breadth of the yellow girdle varies between one and two thousand miles; its length is about six thousand. With its area of ten to twelve million square miles, it takes up roughly one third of the Old World. Its area may be compared with that of the African continent, which is eleven million square miles. The dry zone is essentially a continental mass, remote from the sea; on the two sides of the Arabian penisula the Red Sea and the Persian Gulf cut deeply into it.

From the arid yellow belt three regions tinted light to dark blue, indicating ample rainfall, are sharply marked off—Europe in the north-west, tropical Africa in the south, and the monsoon region of Asia in the south-east. Between the Urals and the Altai the dry zone passes right up to the regions with an Arctic climate. A line drawn from Dakar to the Somali peninsula may serve as the southern limit of the dry zone in Africa. In India the dry zone extends along the Indus, while a narrow strip of light blue following the long Mediterranean coastline indicates the rainy country edging the yellow of North Africa and Arabia.

The yellow girdle from the Atlas Mountains and from Senegal to the river Indus and the Altai is the home of Islam; or, more precisely, the mother country of Moslem humanity. For in the course of centuries the Moslem faith made great and lasting conquests outside the dry zone, so that today a good third of all the Moslems have their homes in monsoon Asia and Negro Africa, some of them widely separated from the compact mass of the main region. But these are permanent offshoots of the Islamic world. Islam came into existence on the soil of the yellow region, and

4

there its destinies have been decided and are being decided to this day.

In the Islamic dry girdle all life is a pursuit of water. Isolated sources of water dot the vast region with many small oases, remote from each other, like islands floating on an ocean of deserts. "Deserts," in this connexion, does not simply mean boundless stretches of sand, but also includes steppes, mountain wildernesses, and, in general, uninhabitable regions of every sort. The Sahara (Arabic for "reddish brown") and the Arabian peninsula form between the Atlantic and the Persian Gulf the greatest single mass of such wildernesses known on earth. Similar regions appear again and again in Central Asia between the Caspian Sea and the western border of China. The interior of Anatolia is barren and thinly inhabited, and still more so is the centre of the vast Iranian plateau. Not only the deserts, but vast mountain chains inimical to transport destroy the cohesion of the interior of the Islamic girdle. In the extreme west are the Atlas Mountains, in the centre the mountains of Lebanon and the Taurus and Zagros mountains, and in the east the Hindu Kush and the immeasurable mass of the Central Asian plateau.

Embedded in sand, steppe, and rock lie the great and small oases. Together they cover barely ten per cent of the surface of the Islamic girdle. Adequate rainfall is received almost exclusively by the countries of the Mediterranean coast, apart from islands of humidity by the Caspian Sea or in southern Arabia. Elsewhere where the rain fails, there remain only the rivers as donors of water. Along the river oases of the Nile, the Euphrates, and the Tigris, as well as of the Indus, arose some of the most ancient cultures of mankind. In the empty spaces, too, of Central Asia great rivers —with no outlet into the ocean—conjure up oases like fabled treasure.

5

Everywhere the natural conditions amid which Islam has developed tend to the gigantic, whether in mountain or river or wilderness. There are few transitions or mitigations. Anyone who looks out over the Nile valley from the Pyramids sees the sharpest possible demarcation between the deep green of the cultivated land and the pale yellow of the desert. The western European learns measure and moderation from the natural conditions amid which he lives; the Moslem does not. The harshness and the overwhelming scale of nature, however, deter men from rashly reaching out to the stars.

In the extreme west of the Islamic world the Maghrib (Arabic for "West") leads a separate existence of its own. It is a great island between the sand of the Sahara and the waves of the Mediterranean and the Atlantic. The desert comes so close to the Mediterranean through the deep incision of the Gulf of Sidra that it leaves only a narrow communication with the eastward lands. The European knows the Maghrib best by the names of its sections— Morocco, Algeria, and Tunis. The Arab geographers usually include Tripolitania in it. If the desert region to the south is left out of account, the Maghrib amounts in all to about double the extent of the Apennine peninsula.

Two oasis regions that have been familiar to the civilized world for thousands of years give its character to the central part of the Moslem girdle. The long river-oasis of the Nile, resembling a palm whose roots lie deep in the heart of Africa and whose crown fans out widely in the Egyptian Delta, maintains its waters from the regions of tropical rains in Abyssinia and the central African lakes. The second oasis has been named, from the semicircle it traces round the Arabian Desert, "Fertile Crescent." The crescent consists of two very dissimilar portions, the rain-fed coastal strip of Syria and the almost rainless country adjoining the two rivers Euphrates and Tigris, whose flood waters bring it the blessing of fertility. The irrigation of Mesopotamia faces the technicians, however, with difficult problems, because the flooding of the Euphrates and the Tigris, after the melting of the snows in the mountains to the north, takes place in the spring, whereas the inundation of the lower Nile valley takes place in the more favourable season of late summer. The Arabian peninsula itself, of little less extent than the whole of India, is an enormous barren country of sand and stone, sprinkled with oases. Only in the southern border, in the highlands of Yemen and Oman, does the monsoon bring rain and fertility.

Anatolia and Iran spread a mountain roof over the Arabian basement of the house of Islam. Their highlands, with little rain, partly areas of salt steppe and desert, are bordered by fertile strips and creviced mountains. While the Anatolian peninsula, pushing far out into the Mediterranean, emerges directly from the dry girdle, the Iranian highland bears the genuine characteristics of Asian space and solitude. Considered as a whole, the Anatolian-Iranian zone resembles a gigantic mountain fortress, completely protected at every point. In the east it is bordered by the valley of the Indus, some thousands of miles long, with a climate and conditions of existence that still clearly indicate the yellow zone.

Beyond the Hindu Kush ("Hindu Killer"), which rises to 23,000 feet, stretches the wide "country of the Turks," Turkistan. It extends from the Caspian Sea to the border of the Gobi Desert, and within its frontiers, which, indeed, no one can define with any precision, there would almost be room for the whole of Australia. The Altai region, the cradle of the Turanian peoples, divides with its foothills Western from Eastern Turkistan. Here lies the Pamir, the "Roof of the World," and all Turkistan has sometimes

7

been described as the empty centre of the Old World. There are inland waters and fertile oases, but they seem lost in the vast space shut in by the mass of the continents. Turkistan is open in the direction of Siberia; and the basin of the Caspian gives convenient access to the lowland plains of eastern Europe.

The principal outer lands of Islam are in the Sudan, in India, and in south-east Asia. The broad strip crossing North Africa which the Arabs call Bilad es-Sudan ("Country of the Blacks") also has all the marks of the yellow dry zone. The Niger and the Senegal, Lake Chad, and the Nile supply the means of linking the western and eastern Sudan. In the north the Sahara and in the south the jungle draw almost rectilinear natural frontiers. While it may be said of the Sudan that it is virtually identical in character with the original Islamic region, that is not true of the Moslem countries of south-east Asia. In those regions Islam has penetrated into natural conditions that are the direct opposite of those of its original home. Bengal, the Malacca peninsula, and the islands of Java and Sumatra, all countries with Moslem majorities, are among the rainiest regions of the world. Their inhabitants, surrounded by tropical luxuriance, know nothing of the inexorable contrast of desert and oasis.

OUTLINE OF SOCIAL CONDITIONS

ABOUT two hundred million human beings inhabit the Islamic girdle of countries from Morocco to Turkistan. This is only a rough estimate, for reliable statistics of population do not exist, and even the results of the censuses held in some countries must be accepted with caution. Assuming a total population of two hundred millions, we get an aver-

age of barely twenty persons to the square mile, compared
with ten times as many in Europe, India, and China. It
might be inferred that the Islamic world has no overpopu-
lation troubles, were it not that the average figure gives an
entirely false picture owing to the natural conditions of
the arid zone. Only one tenth of the original Islamic homeland consists under present conditions of cultivable land,
so that the two hundred millions are confined in reality to
an area smaller than that of western Europe. This gives
a density of population comparable with that of Europe
and the Far East. But the sharp differences in distribution
of population, with thickly populated oases next door to
vast unpopulated wildernesses, give the Islamic world a
structure, in the matter of settlement, very different from
that of Europe and of the countries of the monsoon in Asia.

The impact of European civilization on the world of the
Moslems has produced almost everywhere, sooner in some
places, later in others, a rapid increase of population,
where disorders and decay had produced in the past a low
level that in some places had approached depopulation.
Comparable statistical details are available for Egypt.
Napoleon landed in 1798 in a thinly populated country with
only two and a half million inhabitants. A century later
the population had grown to ten millions, and now there are
nineteen million Egyptians, in a country in which there
had never before lived more than six to seven million people. In a century and a half the population of Egypt has
been multiplied by eight. Egypt certainly offers a particularly striking example, but the tendency is the same in
the other Moslem countries. The annual increase of population (excess of births over deaths), amounting to one to
three per cent, is exceptionally high. In some regions—for
instance, among the Arabs of Palestine or in the Lebanon
—the figure is among the highest in the world. This rapid

increase of population seems, however, to have passed its peak, the rate of increase now slowly diminishing. In Egypt it has fallen from 2.35 per cent at the turn of the century to no more than 1 per cent at the present time; in Turkey the rate fell between 1935 and 1947 from 2.14 to 1 per cent. In spite of this unmistakable reversal, the increase of population continues to be considerable, and if the present-day estimates are confirmed, the population of the Islamic world is likely to grow by fully ten per cent in the next ten years.

In general the increase in the cultivated land has failed to keep pace with the growth of population, and in some countries at least this must be regarded as one of the deeper causes of popular unrest. The question whether the Islamic Orient is already approaching the limit of its economic capacity or could offer the means of living to many million more people has been given very different answers. No general estimate can be given. Egypt is the only country of the Orient of which it can be definitely stated that it is greatly overpopulated. In regard to some other regions it has been calculated that there are substantial reserves of cultivable land, though the experts differ in their forecasts. The optimists are expecting miracles from irrigation and technical progress; in practice their high-flown plans generally meet quite quickly with very formidable obstacles. The picture of the Islamic Orient as a sort of slumbering fairyland, waiting only to be awakened by the magic wand of Progress, contains a grain of truth mixed with a good many bigger grains of technological fantasy. In some oasis regions human and technical organization may produce miracles of fertility, as is shown by the classic example of Egypt. In general, however, the dry zone of Islam has been poorly provided for by nature, more poorly than Europe and far more poorly than the luxuriant tropics.

As far back as our historical knowledge goes, social conditions in the dry zone have been dominated by the contrast between cultivable land and desert. The peasants settled in the oases and the wandering Bedouin meet often in friendly barter, and more often in deep hostility. The history of the ancient Orient is a long chain of such intercourse, and the incursion of the Arabs into the civilization of Eastern Rome and Persia was only one more link in a similar chain. The same process has recurred countless times in the Islamic period on a larger or smaller scale.

The different forms of existence in oasis and desert are paralleled by different social systems. The Bedouin nobles are the heads of simple tribal system; the many gradations of the social pyramid in the oasis countries produce an upper class of landowners, merchants, and scribes (Ulema) : in Islam the Ulema take the place of the clergy. The mass of the population is formed in the vast desert steppes by poor Bedouin, and in the cultivated oases by depressed fellaheen, bound to the soil. The traditional social order of the Islamic Orient remained substantially unaltered until its contact with modern Europe.

After decades of ferment produced by foreign intellectual and social contact, the picture of Oriental society has become still more confused and unbalanced. While many elements of the traditional social order continue, there have grown up alongside them a mass of social innnovations and new ideas that reproduce almost the whole of the changes Europe experienced step by step in the course of centuries. Quite apart from the fact that nearly one tenth of all the Moslems have suffered from the merciless workings of the Bolshevik social revolution, in the rest of the Islamic world the great differences in the degree of modernization have created gulfs between the various peoples, gulfs that make it almost impossible to sketch a social outline of general validity. Within the nations themselves, the short span of a few generations has been insufficient to achieve a harmonious mingling of new and old. As a rule the social development of the Islamic East has inevitably been interpreted in terms borrowed from the conditions in the Western world. It must be borne in mind in this connexion that such terms as Democracy and Socialism, Liberal and Conservative, have behind them a background entirely different from that of Europe and America in such countries as Persia, Morocco, or Pakistan.

The nomad life is continually retreating in face of the modernization of the state and the growth of trade and industry. But though the new national states endeavour to set limits to the unruly element of the tribes within their borders, there is repeated evidence that the old dualism of tribe and state has not yet lost its political and social importance. The border tribes of Afghanistan and the large tribal populations of Persia and Iraq hamper the inner consolidation of the state. North Africa offers many striking examples of the difficulty of reconciling the modernism of the town population with the traditional order of the tribes. This may be seen in the Sudan, in the realm of the Senussi of Cyrenaica, and in the hostility of the Berbers of the Maghrib to the Arab element of the towns. Often national differences add to social tensions, as is shown by the problem of the Kurds in Asia Minor.

The settling of the Bedouin that is occupying the attention of governments is closely connected with a larger problem, that of land reform. Some three quarters of the inhabitants of the Islamic girdle are tillers of the soil. Their very number is evidence enough of the importance of the question of agrarian landownership. Our knowledge of the agrarian structure of the Islamic Orient depends largely on estimates, for the state of agrarian law and land registration does not enable exact details of land distribution to be obtained. An unmistakable element is the predominance of great estates, whether in the hands of individual families and ruling houses, of the state, or of the *wakf,* the widespread form of religious foundation. In Egypt about half of the cultivated land belongs to great landowners; and half of the rural population is in the employment of the landowners, the other half being largely made up of owners of diminutive holdings insufficient for subsistence. These conditions exist in the main, with little variation, in the other Islamic countries. Turkey offers the only exception of any importance: its land distribution does not show the same gross inequalities, and the Turkish peasant is closer as a rule to the peasant type of the Balkans than to the fellaheen.

It is widely supposed that the class of landowning pashas exercises dominant political influence in the countries of Islam. That view must not be accepted without reserve. Turkey is again the only exception. In the other countries the power of the pashas is sometimes very considerable, but in some cases it is already visibly diminishing. Nowhere is it any longer taken for granted as generally as it was only a few decades ago. Generally speaking, the Oriental pasha has no more in common with the European conception of landed nobility than the fellah has with the social type of the European peasant. The economic power of the landowners is largely of purely commercial origin. The proverbially rich pasha class of Egypt owes its rise to the cotton of the Nile valley, which only became an element of world trade in the course of the past century. Moneylending and speculation often contributed substantially to the origin and spread of large landownership, as, for instance, in Syria. Recent technological advance in agriculture has sometimes had the undesired social effect of increasing large landownership, because only the wealthy landowner

13

is in a position to buy machinery and implements, and not the debt-ridden fellah. Land is the traditional investment of the possessing class. It is often found that the landowner takes no interest in the farming of his estate, living in town on his ground rents and devoting himself to politics or business. Thus very often, though not in all cases or all countries, the pasha becomes a member of the urban community. It must not be overlooked that the landowning class has given many a gifted statesman to the young states of the Orient.

The fellaheen are generally regarded as a mass of country people living in inarticulate poverty and ignorance; but they show not only dull indifference but instances of strong vitality and many natural gifts. What is really going on in the villages is difficult to determine and yet of immense importance. Sooner or later incalculable social forces may be revealed in the mass of fellaheen, once the consciousness spreads that the system of landownership was not given its existing shape once for all.

The towns have been growing with alarming rapidity. This, too, is a consequence of contact with the West. The revival of the Oriental activity as intermediary in world trade and world transport, the beginning of industrialization, the discovery of oilfields, and even the creation of modern systems of administration, have had their influence on the advance of urbanization. The population of the large cities increased by leaps and bounds during the Second World War. Cairo grew beyond the two-million limit; the population of Teheran doubled, and the same process was to be seen from Karachi to Casablanca. Millions of people migrated to the towns, where war industries promised ample employment and good wages. After the war, when the opportunities of earning in the overpopulated great cities suddenly shrank, the drawbacks of this migra-

be said is that the Moslem peoples are pursuing the same
social path; only the stages they have reached along that
path are very far from each other.

KEY TO WORLD POWER

IN THE centre of the Egyptian capital, Cairo, looking over the
Ezbekieh park, is a world-famous hotel; or rather it stood
there until, one day in January 1952, it was wrecked by a
furious mob. An Englishman named Shepheard had had
the idea of opening it—nearly thirty years before the Suez
Canal was opened to international traffic. The fame of
Shepheard's Hotel reflected for generations the intercourse
between East and West. Among the names entered in
Shepheard's register are those of African explorers, royalties, ambassadors, and viceroys of India, names familiar to
the whole world. Globe-trotters used to say that you need
only stop long enough on the terrace of Shepheard's and
you would see passing everyone you had ever met anywhere else. No doubt that was an exaggeration, but there
was this amount of truth in it: that nowhere in the world
is so varied a collection of people from every part of the
world to be found as in the great cities of the Islamic Orient.

The Islamic girdle forms a vast stretch of intercontinental land. It is embedded between the two great settled
and civilized regions of the Old World, Europe in the
west, India and China in the east. In the south it borders
on tropical Africa, which until late in the nineteenth century was unknown territory, a true Dark Continent, but
whose entry into world history has since taken place; in the
future it will attract far more attention. All communications between Europe or the Far East and Africa cross the

Islamic world, except by sea or the far north. It is quickly evident that the political picture of the world today has little use for the customary divisions between Europe, Asia, and Africa. Neither the Bosporus nor the Urals, still less the Suez Canal, forms a limit today between political units. Islam would traditionally be regarded as an Asian and African element, and often enough it is summarily coupled with Hinduism and Buddhism among the "cultures of Asia," whereas in reality its spiritual foundations have much more in common with the West than with those of the cultural world of the Far East. To regard Islam as an outpost of "Asia" in the struggle with Europe is to go wrong at the outset. Except for its remote tropical lands, the world of the Moslems stands out clearly and unmistakably from its environment: it is a separate world. On the world map the connected territory of the Moslem peoples shows itself as the long-drawn-out "intercontinent" of the Eastern Hemisphere.

It was one of the outstanding viceroys of India who said that the world's game of chess would be decided in Turkistan, Persia, and Arabia. It was a fixed idea of the British viceroys of India that India was in the forefront of Russian designs of expansion, and Lord Curzon's dictum must be regarded as concerned primarily with the whole Islamic intercontinent. In the first thousand years of Islam the Moslem realms were strong enough to take advantage of their central position and to keep the initiative in world policy. The West, India, and China were on the defensive or pursued isolationism. A change came in the eighteenth century, and since then the home of Islam, the centre of the Old World, has been the arena of the disputes of foreign states. An intercontinent cannot withdraw into splendid isolation as China and also India were able to do through long periods of history.

In the age of a true world policy the Great Powers have become aware that the key to world power is to be found in the Islamic intercontinent, and particularly in its central portion, which Europeans commonly call the Near and Middle East. A continental power that can extend the realm

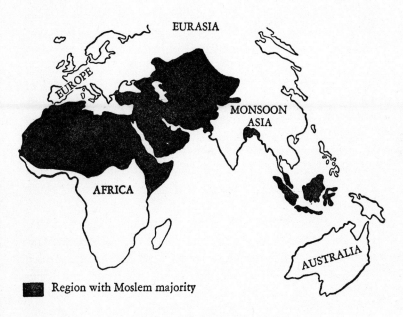

Region with Moslem majority

1: THE ISLAMIC INTERCONTINENT

of its dominance to the Persian Gulf, the Nile, and the Indus might be able to subject the whole land mass of the Old World to its will. A naval power might be unable to maintain any longer the equilibrium on the continents that was indispensable for its security, if it ever permitted the strongest continental power for the time being to gain possession of the single house-key that is shared by

Asia, Africa, and Europe. The Islamic intercontinent has the character of a universal house-key of that sort. It borders the southern and eastern Mediterranean, from whose shores the vulnerable points in Europe may be reached. Moslem peoples control the means of access to India—not only the Khyber Pass, which is generally but mistakenly regarded as the only gateway to the gigantic peninsula of India, but also the Hindu Kush and the corridor between Indus and Ganges, which is strewn with historic battlefields. The barrier of the Caucasus is largely guarded by Moslems, while at the extreme north-east end of the Islamic intercontinent, between the Gobi Desert and the high mountains, is a much-travelled pass into the interior of China. The only route to the heart of the Dark Continent that is not dependent on the control of the seas lies between the Suez Canal and the Nile valley. If we also take into consideration the offshoots of Islam in south-east Asia, we find that all access to the Indian Ocean except the time-wasting route round the south of Africa or Australia is past countries inhabited entirely or mainly by populations belonging to Islam—via Aden and Suez, the Persian Gulf, or the Straits of Malacca. Since the days of Napoleon I there have been many changes in the perspectives of world policy from which the Islamic intercontinent has had to be considered, but its key position remains an irrevocable fact. The Islamic intercontinent has from of old been a turntable for world trade and communications. Access to the valued merchandise of China and India was possible for the peoples of the West only if they came as friends or foes past the borders of the interposed countries of the Moslems; for the Moslems possessed the monopoly of the land routes for world trade. The continental trade of past times, confined to small quantities of valuable goods, followed a few paths indicated by nature. The silk caravan routes from China converged on Turkistan, whence they continued across the Iranian plateau to the Mediterranean and the Black Sea. Goods from India were brought by the merchants of the Orient either through the Persian Gulf to the trade centres of the Levant or through the Red Sea to Egypt. The coasts of North Africa were the point of departure for the caravan trade with the interior of the Dark Continent.

Modern world trade has been unable to do anything to alter the fundamental fact that the Islamic intercontinent is the indispensable means of access between Europe and the Far East. For a time it seemed as if the Moslem Orient would lose some or all of its function of intermediary in world trade. For the Atlantic navigators had discovered the route to India round the south of Africa, and Russian merchants and Cossacks had opened trade and communications with the territory, unknown till then, of Siberia. When the Islamic block had been flanked in this way, it seemed as if the old trade routes of the Orient would no longer be needed. The Islamic intercontinent suffered a long period of economic decay, while the peoples of the West, for the first time in history, were placing the oceans at the service of mankind as means of commercial transport. In addition to this, the Osmanli, who had conquered a large part of the Islamic world, showed little interest in commerce—one more reason for the merchants of Europe to take advantage of new routes, free from the Moslem monopoly of communications. For some five centuries the Islamic intercontinent, the natural intermediary, lay idle, deserted by the growing world commerce, until its old function was restored through the cutting of the Suez Canal. The canal, which converted the Mediterranean and the Red Sea into a single long channel between the oceans, not only had great influence on East-West commerce but also created strategic opportunities which were not without effect on the balance in world policy between land and naval powers.

In the twentieth century the conquest of the air has consigned the period of inactivity of the Islamic world entirely to the past. The airplane is bringing the old lines of continental trade and communication back to their former importance and prestige. Those who want to go by air from the West to South Africa or India, Indonesia or Hongkong or Australia, have to cross the countries of the Moslems. Tripoli and Cairo, Beirut and Damascus, Dhahran and Karachi are familiar stations for the traveller by air today. Only a few generations after Ferdinand de Lesseps carried out his idea of a waterway between the Mediterranean and the Red Sea, the "Suez Canal of the air" has been brought into being and is being rapidly developed. And while contemporaries find it difficult to gauge the full future importance of this process, they are already witnessing the redirection of their ideas of the only recently discovered oil wealth of the Moslem world along a new and fascinating course.

It is true that the oil of the Orient was made the subject of political negotiations before the First World War; but it has only recently been discovered that the Islamic intercontinent possesses about half of the estimated world reserves of oil. We are now witnessing only the beginning of a development that demands an entirely new assessment of the Islamic girdle. Up to now the growth of world communications had little or nothing to do with the economic development of the Islamic countries themselves, because it was concerned with more distant objectives, with the raw materials of tropical Asia and Africa. The cotton cultivation of the Nile valley and Turkistan was at first only an exception to the rule that the central Islamic region had little to offer from its own economic resources.

22

The oil discoveries must not now be allowed to lead to a hasty jump to the other extreme, with the assumption that the Islamic intercontinent will prove to be an inexhaustible treasure-chamber. The effect of the oil industry on the prosperity of the Islamic zone is not to be overlooked, even at this early stage; the methods of administration and exploitation of the newly discovered mineral wealth are as yet undetermined. But the special character of the oil as a raw material, what is called its strategic character, bracketing it with coal and steel, is bound to influence and change the Western powers' estimate of the Near and Middle East in ways that cannot yet be foreseen. Only gradually will a due place in the political and economic view of the world be found for the recognition that the house of Islam possesses in the oil levels of its basement what is probably the mightiest source of energy yet discovered in the world.

CHAPTER TWO

Builders of the House of Islam

THE CALIPHS OF THE PROPHET'S LINE

IN THE north-west of the Arabian peninsula a mountain barrier separates the Red Sea coast from the high lands of the interior. The Arabs call this region the Hejaz ("the Barrier"). It is the mother country of Islam. At the time when the Emperor Justinian was holding his magnificent court in Byzantium, and when western Europe was still suffering from the aftereffects of the Teuton invasions, Mecca, the principal city of the Hejaz, was known as a wealthy trade centre, whose merchants furnished the costly merchandise of India to the countries of the eastern Mediterranean.

The community of Mecca was a merchants' oligarchy, comparable with the Italian mercantile republics of the Middle Ages. The ruling class came from a single widely ramified tribe, the Koreish (Quraysh). From one of the less wealthy landowning families of that tribe, known from its ancestor Hashim as the Banu Hashim, came Mohammed ibn-Abdullah, the Prophet. The rulers of the city suspected that Mohammed's religious zeal covered subversive activities, so that the Prophet finally withdrew to the city of Yathrib, north of Mecca, which thereafter was called Medinat-en-Nabi ("City of the Prophet"); the name was later shortened to Medina. The Moslems date their calendar from the year of that flight (*hijra,* hegira), A.D. 622. The hegira was, indeed, the turning-point, for in Medina Islam discarded the guise of a small sectarian body. Mohammed, who not only founded a faith but had the capacity of a great statesman, gave his followers the institutions and the laws of an independent community. In the end even the proud merchant rulers of Mecca could no longer resist the Prophet's influence, and at Mohammed's death, in 632, the law of Islam reigned throughout the Hejaz.

When Mohammed died, as spiritual and temporal head of the young Moslem community, he had made no decision as to his successor. It may be that the new state, like so many of the communities created by the Arabs before it, would have fallen to pieces if a small body of active and politically gifted men had not taken in hand the continuation of the founder's work. In Mecca there was great confusion after his death, and a number of pretenders to the succession came forward. In the end the Prophet's father-in-law, Abu Bekr, was proclaimed and recognized as Caliph ("Successor"). Within a few years Islam overcame the disunity and segregation of the Arab tribes, and, thanks to elements among which the economic needs of the Bedouin played no small part, the new united Arab community launched attacks against the realms of Byzantium and of the Great Kings of Persia. No more than ten years sufficed for the conquest by Arab warriors of Syria and Egypt, Iraq and Persia. The families of the Koreish tribe provided Arab expansion with most of its political and military leaders. Among them was the strongest figure and one of the most eminent statesmen of Arab history, Omar ibn el-Khattab, the second Caliph. The family to which Omar belonged was one of the minor families of the Koreish. Omar, however, not only was one of Mohammed's closest associates but was connected by marriage, like Abu Bekr, with the house of Hashim, a daughter of his having become the wife of the Prophet.

From the very beginning the rise of the Arabs was accompanied by bitter feuds among the leading Arab families. The oligarchy of the Koreishites was torn by violent discord between families, which lasted right down to modern times in the Islamic and especially the Arab world. The family chronicles of the Koreish are therefore of the utmost value for the understanding of Arab politics to this day. The Umayyads *(Banu Umayya)* were among the most eminent families of pre-Islamic Mecca. At first, with a few exceptions they were bitterly opposed to the Prophet, until in the end they too came over to the victorious Islam. It was only natural that the Umayyads, by whom the Hashimi Prophet's family may well have been regarded as upstarts, considered the highest dignities in the Arab realm as their due. In the end they attained their ambition when one of them, Muawiya, who was Governor in Syria, secured recognition as Caliph. The capital of the Arab realm was now transferred from the Hejaz to Damascus, in Syria, where a succession of caliphs of the house of Umayya ruled for ninety years.

Not all the Hashimi passively accepted the seizure of power by their rival. The opposition was grouped at first round the descendants of the fourth Caliph, Ali ibn Abi Talib. Moslem views of Ali, who was a cousin of the Prophet and became his son-in-law, are divided. What is beyond controversy is that he profoundly influenced the further development of the Islamic community, because it was from him and his party that the most important permanent rift in Islam came. The downfall of the Caliphate of the Umayyads was due, however, not to Ali's family, but to another branch of the Hashimi, the Abbasids. All that is known of the founder of their line, a certain Abbas, is that he was an uncle of the Prophet. His descendants carried on subversive propaganda in the eastern Persian provinces of the realm of the caliphs, adroitly taking advantage not only of religious and social grievances but of the discontent of the Persian element with the overlordship of the Arabs. After their overthrow of the Umayyads, the Abbasid caliphs created Baghdad, by the Tigris, as the new capital, after Medina and Damascus the third and last capital city of the caliphs. The rule of the Abbasids lasted five hundred years. But the power of the Caliphate had disintegrated, and the unity of the Islamic state had become no more than a fiction, long before, in the middle of the thirteenth century, the Mongol invasion swept away the glories of Baghdad. In fact, if not in form, the fall of Baghdad marked the end of the caliphs of the Prophet's line.

No more than a hundred and twenty years after the death of the Prophet Mohammed, the outer limits of the Islamic intercontinent were approximately as they are today, though at that time the territories covered by Arab expansion were as yet far from being assured bases of Islamism. In the west the Arabs had penetrated as far as the Atlantic and the Pyrenees; in the east they had reached the Indus and the steppes of Turkistan. In 711, after their armies had conquered all North Africa as far as the Strait of Gibraltar, Tarik, an Islamized Berber commander, crossed to the mighty rock on the south coast of the Iberian peninsula, which bears his name to this day—Gibraltar ("Tarik's

Rock"). Arab generals pushed on, without meeting serious resistance, into the south of France, and advanced up the Rhone valley as far as Lyon. They soon had to evacuate French territory, but they maintained their hold in Spain for eight hundred years. In Central Asia the Arab power came to terms with the Emperor of China; the Arabs reached the Indus valley through the Persian Gulf.

After the Arab conquest of North Africa, that region soon developed an independent existence. Its geographical separation from the centre of the Arab empire is sufficient explanation of the fact that in the western regions of North Africa the power of the Caliph never had much reality. The Maghrib thus served often as refuge and centre for sectaries, rebels, and the discontented. The only Umayyad who escaped from the fighting with the Abbasids fled to the West and founded a Caliphate of his own in Spain, in Córdoba. The obduracy of the Berber tribes of the Maghrib frequently showed itself in independent movements in politics and religion, for though most of the Berbers were converted to Islam, they were never really assimilated in the Arab world empire. Several times assistance was given by Berber princes to the political unification of the Maghrib, including Moslem Spain. But the power of the Maghrib realm was at all times shortlived, giving place to anarchy. In the late Middle Ages the glory of the Maghrib departed, after it had illuminated one of the most famous epochs of Islamic spiritual life. In the same year in which Christopher Columbus discovered the Western Hemisphere, Spain was lost to Islam for ever. The North African coastal lands came into some measure of dependence on the Ottoman sultan. Morocco, however, never gave allegiance to the rulers of Constantinople. In the middle of the sixteenth century Arab dynasties, one of which reigns to this day, replaced the rule of the Berbers in Morocco. The families of

28

the new rulers had only come in recent times from Arabia. They were reputed to be descendants of the Prophet and his daughter Fatima, and therefore bore the title of "sherif." The sherifs of Morocco successfully resisted all the efforts of the Turkish sultans to impose on them the overlordship of Constantinople. Thus Morocco, the extreme west of Islam, remained down to the twentieth century an isolated outpost on the shores of the Atlantic.

Egypt, on the dividing line between the west and the east of the caliphs' empire, retained a special status. The Arab invasion meant no more for the country at first than a change of governor: Egypt remained for a long time a province of the Caliphate, as in the past it had been a province of the Byzantine Empire. Its alien lords, who made the Nile valley the point of departure for their political plans, later raised Egypt to the eminence of an Islamic Great Power. Islamic Egypt enjoyed its first period of splendour when the ruling house of the Fatimids, whose name indicates Syrian origin, brought both Syria and the Maghrib under their rule. From that period date the founding of the city of Cairo and the beginning of the famous teaching centre of al-Azhar. After the Fatimids another alien, the Kurd Salah-ed-Din (Saladin), took advantage of an opportunity that had long been offered by the command of the lower Nile valley. The Egypt of Salah-ed-Din may be described as the foremost power of the Islamic world of its time. It ruled over the northern Sudan and Cyrenaica and over much of Syria. The Kurdish dynasty became the victim of its own Guards, drawn from Turkish slaves (Mamelukes), whose officers soon preferred to appoint the sultan from their own ranks. The alien warrior caste of the Mamelukes ruled Egypt for six hundred years. In the course of that period they had to submit to Egypt's becoming a province of the Ottoman Empire, but in the country itself they maintained their power almost untouched. The oligarchy of the Mameluke beys was not brought to an end until the beginning of the nineteenth century—by another alien, an Albanian, Mohammed Ali.

The rise of the empire of the caliphs began the great period of Arab rule. The purely Arab character of the empire at its founding remained virtually undiminished until the time of the last of the Umayyad caliphs. The Arabs, who in the conquered countries lived mainly in segregated military settlements, formed the ruling class, and the aristocracy of the empire, consisting of the leading Arab families, watched jealously over the purity of their Arab blood, mixing as little as possible with their subjects. The conquests of the Arabs, though made under the banner of a "holy war," did not take the form of a widespread campaign of conversion to Islam. Islam then took the character of a national Arab religion; it was the firm cement that held together the many very self-willed Arab tribes. At first the Arab rulers were entirely uninterested in any mass conversion of subject peoples to the faith of the Prophet, because the empire of the caliphs was financed by the extraction of tribute from non-Moslems, and Moslems were exempt from taxation. Only the later caliphs showed favour to mass conversions to Islam, with the inevitable result that the method of financing had to be changed.

Under the Abbasids the epoch of the national Arab realm came to an end; Islam became a world religion. The Abbasids were themselves of distinguished Arab blood, but the movement with the aid of which they came into power had its origin in the Persian parts of the realm, and the new rulers therefore relied mainly on the Persian element. Baghdad, the Abbasids' capital, was built at no great distance from the old capital of the Persian Great Kings. Outstanding statesmen of Persian origin were frequently responsible for the business of government, and they carried on the administration of the empire in the spirit of the Persian Great Kings. During the Abbasid period the Arab way of life amalgamated with the manifold spiritual inheritance of the Orient into a new civilization, that of Islam. The Arab ruling class entered on the same terms as the newly converted peoples into the great Moslem community.

A world language and the fundamentals of a constitutional system were the permanent legacy of the Arabs to Islamic civilization. The inviolable authority of the Koran must be accounted the principal reason for the fact that for more than thirteen centuries the Arabic written language has remained virtually unchanged, a unique case among the living languages of civilized mankind. Arabic is spoken as their mother tongue by at most one fifth of the Moslems, but the knowledge of the language of the Koran is still widespread throughout the Islamic world. The Arabic script is used by all the peoples of Islam, from the Malays to the Negroes of the Sudan, with the exception of the Turks and of the Moslems living in the Soviet Union. The codification of Islamic law was not the work of the Arabs alone, but that achievement bears unmistakable marks of the Arab genius; it is an achievement that is not inferior to that of the great creators of Roman law.

CARAVANS AND MERCHANTMEN

IN THE fourteenth century—that is to say, at a time when the world of Western Christendom was confined to the region between the Ebro and the Vistula—an Arab scholar of Tangier, Ibn Battuta, undertook a journey through the lands of the Moslems. After travelling through the greater part of the then known world, this Marco Polo of Islam set down his impressions in a book that is famous to this day. Ibn Battuta found coreligionists on the Volga and in East Africa, in Indonesia, in China, and on the banks of the Niger. Islam has not remained within the political frontiers of its great territorial conquests in the Orient, but has penetrated through missions into regions remote from the centre of the Islamic world. It is true that Islam, with its little concern for ecclesiastical organization, has no such thing as any centrally conducted missionary activitiy. The mission work is that of individual persons and groups, as every Moslem is authorized and expected to spread his faith. Islam thus followed in the footsteps of the Arab traders and was spread through the agency of caravans and merchant vessels. Religious brotherhoods also played a very important part in this missionary work, which will be referred to later. Often enough the missionary proceedings were decidedly warlike, but, for all that, there is justification for describing this side of Islamic expansion as "peaceful penetration." Behind it stood no political or military state activity, and it continued without interruption even when the mother country of Islam had fallen into impotence and subjection to foreign conquerors. The peaceful penetration had its greatest success in Africa and in the East Indies. Only in recent times has there been news of the regular training and sending out of Moslem missionaries, as in Pakistan and Egypt. That is a new development, whose results remain to be seen.

The interior of Africa has been open to Islam from two directions: from North Africa and from the Indian Ocean. As early as the tenth century the Moslems of the Maghrib, mostly Berbers, reached the Niger and the Senegal by the caravan routes of the western Sahara. In 1077 Moslem Berbers founded Timbuktu, on the bend of the Niger, and that city remained thenceforth the commercial and spiritual centre of the Moslems in the western Sudan. Between Morocco and the western Sudan there has always been active intercommunication. A Berber tribe from the Senegal started the movement of the Murabitun (Amoravides), which spread quickly over the whole of north-west Africa, and over Spain for a time; it created the city of Marrakesh as its centre. The eleventh and twelfth centuries saw the penetration of Islam into the central Sudan. There Hamitic tribes, experienced in war and commerce, formed the upper class, and the Negroes the mass of the population. The Hamitic rulers, converts to Islam, made the spread of the faith by peaceful and warlike methods their aim, often fanatically pursued. Pre-eminent in this were the merchants of the Haussa tribe; the warlike Fulbe, also of Hamitic race, set up a number of Islamic sultanates in the Sudan. The conversion of the Sudan to Islam was a work of centuries, and is still incomplete.

Gradually the Moslems pushed from west to east in the upper Nile valley. At the beginning of the nineteenth century this eastward-moving mission was balked by the conquests of the Egyptian khedives, whose armies pushed from Egypt up the Nile valley and subjected to Egyptian sovereignty what became known as the Anglo-Egyptian Sudan. By the end of the century Islam had reached a line running roughly from Dakar to Khartoum and Massawa, coming to the borders of the jungle of the Guinea coast and the Congo basin. The penetration continued in the present century, so that on the upper course of the Nile there has finally been formed an incipient conjunction with the new Islamic lands in East Africa.

Arab merchant vessels were sailing along the coasts of East Africa in the earliest centuries of Islam. The Indian Ocean tempted the inhabitants of southern Arabia to adventurous trading voyages, especially as the monsoon winds offered good opportunities for sailing ships. Before long the Arabs were sailing to the settlements on the coast of East Africa, and even to the Far East. Zanzibar, Mombasa, Dar-es-Salaam, and Mozambique were originally Arab trading settlements. For a long time the Arabs penetrated very little into the interior. When the Portuguese discovered the sea route round Africa, there came a long and bitter trade war between them and the Arabs all over the Indian Ocean. But in the end the Portuguese failed to deprive the Moslems of their East African trade. In the eighteenth and nineteenth centuries the sultans of Oman, on the south coast of Arabia, consolidated the Arab position in East Africa. The island of Zanzibar, whither a branch of the ruling house of Oman transferred its capital in 1832, became a wealthy transshipment centre for the Arabs' African trade. The European colonial regime brought no reduction of the influence of Islam in East Africa, but on the contrary gave it access to the interior. Since then, however, Arab emissaries have been outnumbered by Indian immigrants as the propagators of Islam. Just as in large parts of the Islamized Sudan the language of the Haussa traders became the general means of intercommunication, so the Moslem influence in East Africa helped to bring a similar common language into general use; it is known all over the world as Kiswahili, "the language of the coast-dwellers."

Unquestionably Islam has done valuable civilizing work in Negro Africa. In many places in the past the shadow of the slave-hunt lay over its advance, but the Moslems may point in this matter to much that European colonization has to answer for. At the present day two fifths of the inhabitants of the African continent have been converted to Islam. In the great Moslem block of North Africa the only break is made by the Coptic Christendom of Abyssinia. Islam is

34

not passive in Africa, but continues to work toward the centre of the continent, where it competes with the missionaries of the Christian churches for the seventy to eighty million Negroes who remain pagan. The outer world has given little attention to this quiet Islamic expansion, whose political importance to the future of Africa is only gradually being revealed. But as the independence movement among the colonial peoples of the Dark Continent grows, the fact that the whole northern half of Africa as far as the tropics is now a part of the wider Islamic world becomes of growing importance in international politics. Although the teaching of the Prophet has often taken strange forms among the Negro population, the association with the centres of Islamic life is active enough, and the unrest that has taken hold of the Islamic intercontinent is thus spreading far into colonial Africa.

Arab navigators pushed round the southern tip of India and through the Straits of Malacca as far as the shores of China. They were not the first foreigners to pursue trade and spread civilization through the waters of south-east Asia. Before them India had had active spiritual and commercial contact with those regions. More than five hundred years passed after the first appearance of Moslem traders before Islam gained a firm footing in south-east Asia. From the small coastal settlements and factories there grew, as time passed, a mighty south-east Asian block of sixty to seventy million Moslems. They are mainly Malays, and Malay has become the language of trade and communication in that remote Islamic region. After some of the rulers of the Malacca peninsula had turned to Islam, the new faith spread to the islands of Java, Sumatra, and Borneo and even to parts of the Philippines. When the first Europeans came to south-east Asia, they found already a varied collection of Moslem Malay sultanates. The dominance of Islam, however, in Indonesia was established only in the time of the Europeans.

The conversion of south-east Asia to Islam takes a place of its own in the history of the Islamic world. The Portuguese had taken pains to cut off the relations of the Malay Moslems with their co-religionists, but later the Dutch permitted traffic between Indonesia and the Islamic homelands. Many Arab emigrants from the south coast of the Arabian peninsula settled in Java and Sumatra. Large numbers of Indonesian pilgrims came into touch in Mecca with the Moslems of all the world, so that there was no lack of spiritual intercourse. It is true that in the alien environment of south-east Asia Islam changed or lost a good deal of its original form. In Indonesia the Moslem missionaries were not meeting with more or less primitive tribes as in Negro Africa; they had come to a zone already influenced by the Indian intellect. The Malays of the East Indies are therefore, though mainly Moslems, a group of a special character within the Moslem community, and their political and economic interests are closely bound up with the destiny of the Far East.

Moslem caravans and merchantmen also came in early times to China. In the eighth century the authorities of the Chinese Empire permitted Arab and Persian merchants to settle in certain ports, especially Canton. The Arab oversea trade in China does not seem to have been coupled with any missionary enterprise worth mention; the Moslem communities confined themselves as a rule to their trading activities. The origin of the Moslem population of China, running into millions, may be traced to the overland trade through the interior of Asia, which brought China into touch with the advancing Moslems along the silk caravan routes of Turkistan; it may also be traced to the Mongol period. But China was too remote, and the assimilative influence of Chinese culture too strong, for the immigrant or newly converted Moslems to provide Islam in China with such triumphs as in India and Indonesia. Thus Chinese Islam has remained a remote and something of a forgotten Diaspora. China has, however, had a limited share in the events of the Islamic intercontinent in Eastern Turkistan, whose Moslem population is of Turkish origin.

TURKISH WARRIORS, PERSIAN POETS

WHILE the magnificence of the Caliph's court at Baghdad was still disguising the decay of the great Arab Empire, the rumour was growing that the peoples of Central Asia were once more migrating in masses. The Turkish migrations, which continued for almost a thousand years, meant for Islam the beginning of a second great access of power after the period of the Arabian caliphs. These Turkish migrations were a link in the long chain of migrations and conquests of the "Turanian" peoples of the interior of Asia —Huns, Hungarians, Bulgarians, Kalmucks, and finally Manchus. The last traces of most of these peoples have disappeared, but the achievements of the Turks left permanent marks on the world.

It is supposed that the primeval home of the races of which one tribe—the Turks—gave its name to the rest, was at the foot of the Altai Mountains in Central Asia. The word "Turk" is said to mean "power," "strength." The Turkish tribes came into contact with Islam in the tenth century, and from then on they adopted the new faith; and it may fairly be said that the conversion of the Turks to Islam had much the same effects for the Orient as the conversion of the Teutons to Christianity had for the West. Turkish migration was not an assault of innumerable masses: small companies of warriors adventured in separate waves, independently of each other, into the east of the Islamic world. Turkish warriors took in hand the destinies of the decaying Abbasid state; among them was the famous Seljuk tribe. Turkish sultans at the head of Turkish prætorian guards became the all-powerful mayors of the palace of the caliphs. Turkish principalities were formed everywhere in the eastern parts of the realm; Turkish emirs were entrusted with the guarding of the frontier in Asia Minor against Christian Byzantium.

It was in the age of the Turkish migrations that the literary art of the Persians made its brilliant contribution to the cultural heritage of the Islamic world. The Turkish princely courts often played the part of a Mæcenas for Persian poets and thinkers. It was in the capital of a Turkish sultan that Firdausi wrote his *Book of Kings,* the Persian national epic. In Konya, in Asia Minor, the Persian mystic Jalal ed-Din Rumi produced his works, and the poetry of Saadi gained the favour of the potentate of his native city, Shiraz. Still better known in Europe than the works of that poet are the verses of Omar Khayyám ("the Tentmaker") and the poems of Shams ed-Din Mohammed, who was given the name of el-Hafiz ("the One Who Remembers") because he had learned the Koran by heart in early youth. Under the influence of the great poets the new Persian language gained the elegant form that enabled it to assume and maintain the foremost place throughout the east of the world of Islam. When, late in the fifteenth century, the classic period of Persian literature came to its end, the Persians had won the right to be counted among the great peoples of world literature.

Far in the interior of Asia, in the tents of Mongol tribes, the storm gathered which in the end opened the way for a new order in the world of Islam, bearing the imprint of the

Turks. The Mongols, distant relations of the Turks, were nomad cattle-breeders, living in a number of separate groups of tribes, east of the Altai, on the fringe of civilization. Islam had not reached them, nor had any other of the great religions of the East. It is not known what were the underlying forces that brought about the union of the Mongol tribes under Temuchin, the new Great Khan (this was probably the meaning of the words Genghis Khan). In the twelfth century Genghis Khan set his united Mongol tribes moving on the long path of world conquest. Before he died he followed the Mongol custom by dividing his empire among his sons. Genghis Khan's race did not only bring suffering and devastation to the civilized world; he imposed on an immense region that included China, Central Asia, and eastern Europe the iron discipline of the *Pax Mongolica.*

A grandson of Genghis Khan laid Baghdad in ruins in 1258, and the Mongols were halted only at the gates of Egypt. To contemporaries the Mongol assault must have seemed the worst disaster that Islam had ever suffered. It could not then be foreseen that in a short time the Mongol conquerors would be absorbed in the Islamic civilization and in the Turkish nationality. The Moslem Turks entered into the heritage of the Mongol Empire west of the Altai. This applies equally to Central Asia and to the empire of the Golden Horde on the Volga. When finally in the fourteenth century Timur, a descendant of the Turkified Mongol tribe of the Berlas, followed once more in the footsteps of the Great Khan, conquering and laying waste the whole region between Moscow and Delhi, Samarkand and Damascus, he did so under the banner of the Prophet. After the various Mongol hordes had overrun the north and east of the Islamic intercontinent, they left behind them a heritage of three great Islamic empires, two of which, the creations of the Osmanli and of the Indian Great Moguls, were the product of the state-building capacity of Turkish tribes, while the third, the Persia of the Safavid shahs, was certainly closely connected with the Turkish migration.

Unnoticed by its contemporaries, a small Turkish tribe, suffering from the pressure of the Mongols, had migrated from Central Asia and finally, toward the end of the thirteenth century, had gained a footing in the neighbourhood of the Anatolian town of Eskishehir. There it formed one of the many Turkish dominions on the border between Byzantium and Islam. The life of the first historical personality of this tribe, Osman, has been overgrown by legend. His name has gained world-wide fame as that of the tribe and ruling house of the Osmanli. The members of the line of Osman were a strong race. The first sultans carried the rule of their small state over the whole of Anatolia, crossed the Straits of Gallipoli, and conquered the Balkans. In 1453 Greek Byzantium, beleaguered on all sides, was carried by storm by the conqueror Sultan Mehemet. After that the Osmanli brought under their rule the whole of western Islam, so that the sultans of Constantinople were lords of North Africa and the Fertile Crescent, the shores of the Black Sea, and south-eastern Europe as far as the middle Danube and the Carpathians. In 1520 the Turks appeared for the first time before Vienna; it was the army of Soliman the Magnificent, the most famous of the Osmanli rulers. From 1683, when the Turks attacked the capital of the Habsburg Empire in vain for the second time, date the two and a half centuries of Ottoman decay. It is tempting to draw a parallel between the fate of the Habsburgs and that of the Osmanli. The first ancestors of the two houses, Rudolf von Habsburg and Osman, belonged to the same period; so do the Emperor Charles V and the Sultan Soliman I, each of whom could say that the sun never set over his territory. The First World War brought the downfall of both houses, after Habsburgs and Osmanli had incorporated a good part of West and East in their realms.

The warring Osmanli underwent the same process as the Arab ruling class of the Caliphate. The Osmanli were absorbed into the civilization of the regions they had conquered. When Constantinople became the centre of the Turkish Empire, the Turkish shell was quickly filled with the spirit of the Byzantine imperial house. With the unlimited powers of a despot the sultan controlled the hierarchy of the officials and officers of his empire, and in a way even the Byzantine type of ecclesiastical hierarchy had its influence on Islam: the Mufti of Constantinople gained the position of spiritual head of the Ottoman Empire.

One circumstance did more than anything else to alter the national Turkish character of the rule of the Osmanli. This was the system of enrolment of young Christians, the so-called *devşirme*. The recruited youths were converted to the Moslem faith and brought up at the expense of the state. They were then assigned to the public service, helping to form the body of officials and the officers' corps. In this way a large number of grand viziers and other dignitaries came from the subjected Balkan peoples, especially Albanians and Bosnians. Through the *devşirme* were also recruited the famous troops of the Janizaries, who formed the nucleus of the armies of the Osmanli and until their end played often enough the classical part of prætorian guards in the politics of the sultan's realm. Far from attempting to pursue any national Turkish aim, the Osmanli wove the family of peoples subject to them into a supranational community, whose traces may be recognized if we look just a little below the surface of the Near East.

India was the scene of the second historic achievement of the Turks. In 1483 Mohammed Zahir ed-Din was born to a petty prince in Central Asia; later he was given the Persian nickname of Baber ("the tiger"). When we learn that the "tiger" was descended on his father's side from Timur and on his mother's from Genghis Khan, it is not surprising to find that the young Baber had inherited his ancestors' instinct for power. At nineteen years of age Baber crossed the difficult passes of the Hindu Kush, marched past Kabul into the open country of the Punjab, and defeated the armies sent against him at the historic gateway to the Ganges valley. Baber became the founder of the line of the Great Moguls, whom it might have been better to call the Grand Turks of Delhi, in imitation of the Grand Turks of Constantinople. The spread of Islam in India did not begin with the Great Moguls; it was in full swing centuries before the arrival of Baber. But the Great Moguls furthered the process and gave it permanence. The rule of Baber's successors lasted some four centuries. In 1858 the last of their dynasty was dethroned and exiled by the British.

The rule of the Moguls is remembered as the climax of Indian Islam. Turkish conquerors set the boundaries of the Moguls' power; Persian was the official language of the Mogul realm, and Persian culture was dominant at the imperial court in Delhi. The communications between the Mogul Empire and the rest of the Islamic world through the north-west frontier of India were always sufficient to maintain the exchange of ideas and personal contacts. But the longer the Moguls' rule lasted, the more those intruders succumbed to the influence of the Indian atmosphere. The conquered Hindus often rose to high place and great power in the Mogul Empire.

The zeal for the faith varied considerably during the

Mogul rule. The Emperor Akbar, whom many, though not the Moslems, regard as the greatest figure in the dynasty, was decidedly a freethinker. He made a vain attempt to create a new mixed religion, and even took up a thoroughly hostile attitude to Islam. His great-grandson Aurangzeb, on the contrary, was an active and unbending champion of Islam.

Neither the Moslems nor the Hindus gained the upper hand throughout India. Even Islam's long period of un-opposed political dominance gave it a lasting hold over less than half of the Indians. There remained, however, a strong and convinced Moslem minority, which found in the memory of the great period of the Moguls the strength for a new revival.

It was reserved for Persia to give its special note to the era of the formation of the great Islamic realms that dis-tinguished the late Middle Ages. A religious order, not a tribe of warriors, started the new Persian realm. In the con-fusion of the Mongol period it was regarded as nothing unusual or in any way striking when the pious sheikh Safi ed-Din, from Ardabil, a town in Azerbaijan, claimed to be descended from the Prophet and began to gather disciples. The order of the Safavi (Safavids) seemed at first only to offer another example of the way the plagued Moslem people sought refuge in religious associations. The control of the order remained in the hands of the founder's family. The Safavids carried on active propaganda in Azerbaijan and the surrounding regions, and acquired such influence that they were described as almost a theocratic state. In the sixth generation of the descendants of Safi ed-Din, Ismail, one of the greatest personalities of the history of Islam, felt strong enough for higher things than the leadership of a religious order. He broke the power of the Turkish tribes then ruling in his native province, and, as a child of eleven,

43

assumed in Tabriz, the capital of Azerbaijan, the title of king (shah). For the first time since the Islamic conquest, Persia regained her individuality as a state. The foundations laid by Ismail have remained intact to this day.

In present-day terms the Safavids have the appearance of the founders of the Persian national state. But this is a misleading definition that needs certain limitations. In their rise to power the Safavids had the aid of Turkish tribes. How far they were themselves of Turkish blood is not easy to say. In any case, in their time Azerbaijan was inhabited and ruled by Turkish tribes. Turkish remained the language of the Safavids, until Shah Abbas the Great introduced Persian as the official language. The rulers' bodyguards were Turks. Gradually the Persian element made its way, imprinting its own character on the Safavid realm. An important part was played in this by the fact that the Safavids made Shi'i Islam the state religion of Persia. This step strongly and decisively marked the place of Persia in the Moslem community. The Safavids are hardly likely to have thought of deliberately associating themselves with the rich tradition of pre-Islamic Persia. But unmistakably there was a revival, under cover of the Shi'a, of ancient Persian ideas of a state church and of the divine right of the ruler. The Shi'a also permanently united the mixture of peoples produced on Persian soil by the various invasions of Arabs, Turks, and Mongols. Thus it made an important contribution to the continuance of the new Persian realm, while Persia's western and eastern neighbours did not survive the shocks of the nineteenth and twentieth centuries. It is true that the adoption of the Shi'a as the state religion had the further consequence of isolating Persia from the rest of the Moslem world.

After two and a half centuries of uninterrupted rule, the last hour of the Safavids struck. Nadir, a general of the Turkish Afshar tribe, deposed Shah Ismail's last successor in 1929 and made himself Shah of Persia. Nadir was one of the last of the great Turkish conquerors. He made Persia for a few years the strongest power in the Islamic world. He also tried to make an end of the Shi'i "heresy" of the Safavids and to bring Persia back into the fold of Islamic catholicity. He failed in this, and his political innovations were no more enduring. Nadir's star came and disappeared like a comet in the Persian sky.

Migrations and conquests of Turkish peoples brought Islam once more an expansion hardly less than that of the time of the Arabs—in Central Asia and India, in Anatolia and the Balkans, on the Volga, and in the Crimea. Most of this expansion brought permanent gains to Islam. Some territory on the borders of Christian Europe was lost later, but on the whole the Islamic intercontinent found its final shape in the Turkish period.

After the Central Asian sources of the Turkish migration had dried up and the new conquerors had expended their strength, the world of Islam sank back into lethargy. The eighteenth century brought the Moslem peoples an epoch of growing anarchy. The three Islamic powers on whose shoulders rested the order of the intercontinent were afflicted by internal weakness or even suffered dissolution. In India the Great Moguls had to defend themselves against their insubordinate feudal princes, against a revival of Hindu hostility, and against the growing influence of the Europeans. In Persia there was a growth of internal dissension, while in the eastern part of the fallen Safavid Empire the first signs became visible of an independent Afghan state. The Ottoman Empire was irrevocably in retreat in face of Europe and in process of becoming the Sick Man of the Orient. The border regions of Islam in Central Asia and in the extreme west had lost all serious political importance.

The decay of the power of the Islamic world was unmistakable; but a cultural and economic low level seemed also to have been reached. In the conviction that a new inner impulse was needed, there spread within the Moslem community a demand for reform, for the removal of religious overgrowths and of social evils. At first this had little to do with European intervention; in the eighteenth century there was still very little European influence in the Islamic world. Through their own development the peoples and realms of Islam had become ripe for a new age.

CHAPTER THREE

The Moslem Community

ONE SEVENTH OF MANKIND

THE total number of Moslems in the world is estimated at 320,000,000 to 350,000,000. Roughly, therefore, every seventh human being is one of the faithful of Islam. Three quarters of the whole community of Moslems live in Asia, and the remaining quarter in Africa. Europe today has only a few million Moslems on its soil, mainly in Albania and Yugoslav Bosnia. Altogether there may be 4,000,000 to 5,000,000 Moslems in the Balkans. The picture is altered a little if we include Turkey, which politically regards itself as a part of Europe and geographically represents a bridge between the continents, and if we also include European Russia. In that case Europe's share of Moslem humanity will come to some ten per cent.

But these figures of distribution according to the traditional geographical units tell us really very little. Of much more significance is the fact that the Islamic community is distributed most eccentrically. Only a quarter of the Moslems live in the Near and Middle East—that is to say, in the countries of which we habitually think when talking of the Islamic world, and which have always formed the spiritual and political centre of Islam. The main body of the Moslem community has shifted in the course of time to the border of the Moslem world. The Indian Moslems, numbering nearly 100,000,000, are the strongest group, amounting to three tenths of the Islamic world. Next come the Indonesians, 60,000,000 to 70,000,000 in all. These two great communities together make up half of the Moslems. Outside the Islamic intercontinent there are a further 40,000,000 and more of Islamized Negroes. Apart from these populations in south-east Asia and Negro Africa, there remain four great groups to be distinguished by speech, culture, and nationality: Arabs, Turks, Iranians, and Indian Moslems. The differentiation within the Moslem community in modern times is based on these four groups.

The Arab world forms a connected continental mass from Iraq in the east to Morocco in the west. Its boundaries along the interior of Africa are difficult to define, as the process of Arabization in this quarter is not yet ended. The northern limit along the Turkish and Persian language regions is more or less definite. Altogether there may be 50,000,000 to 60,000,000 people whose mother tongue is Arabic; of these there are 19,000,000 in Egypt, 10,000,000 in the countries of the Fertile Crescent, 7,000,000 to 8,000,-000 in the Arabian peninsula, and the remainder in the Maghrib and the Sudan. All such figures as these, however, call for a general reservation. They can be no more than quite rough estimates, as the peoples within the great community of the Moslems are still far from being as sharply and permanently marked off from each other as in Europe.

Before the time of Islam the Arabs were confined to the

Arabian peninsula itself and the inner margins of the Fertile Crescent. What we find now on the map as the Arab world is the result of the great expansion of the seventh and eighth centuries, with certain later accretions. The unity of the Arab world depends on the common language and on Islam. Whatever views may be held as to the political strength of the so-called Pan-Arab movement, the bond of community of language, which embraces also the 2,500,000 to 3,000,000 Arab Christians in Egypt and Syria, is an incontestable reality. The different dialects have diverged so widely that a Syrian and a Moroccan would have great difficulty in understanding each other. But the written and printed Arabic is exactly the same language in Baghdad, Cairo, and Algiers. The consciousness they share of being the parents of Islam, together with the memory of the great period of the Arab caliphs, gives the Arab peoples a further plain indication of their unity.

The degree of Arabization varies greatly in the different parts of the Arab world. Outside the Arabian peninsula, the countries of the Fertile Crescent have received the strongest admixture of Arab blood. In Egypt the pure Arab element has always been much less numerous; outside the towns the mainly Hamitic character of the population has persisted under the Arab conquest just as it withstood the earlier invasions of the Nile valley since the time of the Pharaohs. Still less has been the effect of the Arab campaigns in the Maghrib. During the first centuries the indigenous Berber population was thoroughly predominant in the ethnographic picture, the number of Arabs remaining negligible. The Berbers were not turned into Arabs or driven into the mountains on a large scale until the Fatimids of Egypt, in the eleventh century, sent a punitive expedition of two great Arab Bedouin tribes, the Banu Hilal and the Banu Suleiman, into north-west Africa. Even then the Berbers remained formidable neighbours of the

Arabs: they made a stand in the mountains, in the western Sahara, and on the frontiers. Their proportion of the population is largest in Morocco and smallest in Tunisia. In general the degree of Arabization of the Maghrid falls as one goes from east to west and from the coast southward into the interior.

It is more difficult for the observer to visualize the collection of Turkish-speaking peoples than the Arab mass. The Turkish migrations share with the Arab expansion the common feature that a few conquerors imposed their language far and wide on subjugated peoples. The penetration of the Turkish peoples extended farther in the countries in which Islam had set foot either not at all or only to a small extent; it proceeded hand in hand with conversions to Islam after the Turks had adopted Islam and had themselves become zealous militants for the faith. Between the tenth and fifteenth centuries Central Asia, Anatolia, and large parts of Caucasia, Persia, and eastern Europe were Turkified. Gradually new regions of Turkish-speaking peoples extended from the western border of China to the Balkans. Three groups are distinguished within the Turkish world by their historical origin and their regions of settlement. The southern Turks were the first to come into contact with Islam and had the most lasting influence on the development of the Islamic world. They are also the numerically strongest group among the Turks. The Seljuks and other tribes of the early period of the Islamic Turks, whose traces have since disappeared, belonged to the southern Turks. Of the peoples of southern Turkish origin the most outstanding at the present day are the Osmanli Turks, who maintain the only independent Turkish state; the Azeri Turks in Azerbaijan; and the Turkomans south-east of the Caspian Sea. The second Turkish group is made up mainly of the Turkish peoples of Central Asia— Uzbeks, Kazaks, Kirghizes, and the Turks of Eastern Turkistan. The region occupied by this Central Asian group corresponds to the realm which Genghis Khan assigned, in his partition of the Mongol Empire, to his son Jagatai; on this account the Central Asian Turks are still known as Jagatai Turks. Finally, the northern Turks—Volga Tatars, Bashkirs, and Turks of the Crimea—are a relic of the Mongol rule. These last peoples are the remnant of the "Golden Horde" who for several centuries held together the western part of the Mongol heritage.

The total number of the Turks is probably between 45,000,000 and 60,000,000. Of these, 25,000,000 to 30,000,000 are southern Turks, 15,000,000 to 20,000,000 Central Asian Turks, and 7,000,000 to 9,000,000 northern Turks. Under Soviet rule there have been great compulsory shiftings of populations, so that the present picture of the Turkish world can only be indicated with reservations. There are roughly the same number of Turkish-speaking Moslems as of Arabs. The Turkish world today lacks, however, the geographical compactness of the Arab region. It also lacks the common written language, though the close relationship between the various Turkish languages, which at all events enables educated persons to understand one another, might have paved the way for a common written language. Geographical separation and differences of language are only partly the work of nature; they are largely due to the influence of alien interests, which have been actively at work to prevent the close cohesion of the Turkish world. In any case, Islam, relationship of language, and modern nationalism have together developed a sense of community in the Turkish family of peoples.

When Islam came among them, the Iranians were the indigenous element in the whole of Central Asia. Iranian-speaking peoples inhabited the high land named after them as far as the Euphrates and Tigris, and also Western Turkistan. Of these peoples the Persians were able, at the time of the incursion of Islam, to look back upon remarkable political and cultural achievements. We need only point to the great days of the Persian Achæmenides and the Sassanid kings. Neither the Arabs nor the Turks possess a pre-Islamic tradition of the greatness of that of the Persians. The Iranian peoples were won to Islam, but only partly to the alien nationality of their conquerors. Thus Iraq, which once was Persian, acquired Arab characteristics, and Central Asia and Azerbaijan Turkish. Elsewhere the Iranian element generally held its own, so that the two states of the high land, Persia and Afghanistan, bear the Iranian stamp. The credit for this belongs mainly to the tenacity of Persian culture and the Persian idea of the state. Thus the Persians have been almost alone in determining the part played by the Iranian element in the Moslem community.

Some 30,000,000 people may be regarded as belonging to the Iranian-speaking family. Next in importance after the Persians come the 8,000,000 to 9,000,000 Afghans, whose region of settlement extends beyond the borders of Aghanistan into north-west India. Of Iranian origin are also the Kurds, the Baluchis, and the Tadzhiks—the last remnants of the Iranian population of Central Asia.

The 90,000,000 to 100,000,000 Indian Moslems belong to two categories. Alien conquerors and immigrants came to India in wave after wave from the original Islamic territory. Of the first appearance of the Arabs on the soil of India little trace remains; they were followed by the main stream in the time of the great Turkish migration. These Islamic immigrants are represented most strongly in the valley of the Indus, which is most closely connected territorially with the rest of the Islamic world. But the descendants of the Turkish, Iranian, and Arabic immigrants together make up only the smaller part of the Indian

Moslems of today. The majority are descended from Hindus who were converted to Islam. The members of the lower castes of Hindus welcomed the new religion, which asserts the equality of all the faithful. And the circumstance that for centuries the Moslems held in their hands the political power in India aided proselytism.

On the basis of the conditions existing before the partition of India, the Moslem share of the total population of the subcontinent may be set at about one quarter. It is not possible to draw an indisputable dividing line between the territories inhabited by Moslems and Hindus, but two main geographical centres of Islam may be recognized in the Indian subcontinent: the north-west, and Bengal. More than half of the Indian Moslems live in Bengal; 23,000,000 live in north-western India. In these two regions the Moslems form the majority of the population. Even after the partition of 1947, which gave the Indian Moslems their own state of Pakistan, by no means all the Indian followers of Islam could be included in that new state. It has been estimated that at the moment of partition there were some 50,000,000 Moslems in Pakistan, 40,000,000 remaining in Hindu India. Since then there have been some changes in the relative numbers. According to the census of 1951, there are 65,000,000 Moslems living in Pakistan, forming eighty-six per cent of the total population of that state.

Indian Islam owes its unity simply and purely to the faith and to inherited Moslem doctrine. It has neither a compact territory nor any bond of common speech or common nationality between its followers. It remains to be seen what effects on the further development of Indian Islam the founding of the new Moslem state will have.

STRUGGLE OVER THE CALIPHATE

ISLAM makes no distinction between the religious and the secular life of its community. It knows nothing of the Western conception of state and church. Islam further recognizes only faithful and infidel, and pays no attention to the divisions between nations or castes or classes. It proclaims the equality of all who bow to the teaching and the law of the Prophet, and knows nothing of priestly intermediaries between God and the faithful. Consequently the community of the Moslems is both a religious community and a state system. Both elements are established in a Constitution, the various parts of which the Moslems include in the Arab name *Shari'a* ("right way"). As the Shari'a claims to govern every field of human life, it is a comprehensive law, at once canon and civil and municipal.

The law and the Constitution of the Moslem community are the product of the work of several centuries. When the Prophet died, the political and social order of the Moslem community had not yet been established. But as the Moslem believes that the whole of the law was revealed to the Prophet by God, all sources of the law must be traced back in some form to Mohammed. Of these sources there are four. The principal one is the Koran, because according to Islamic dogma it sets down God's direct revelation and not mere personal views of the Prophet. At the Prophet's death the Koran had not been compiled. Only under the first caliphs was it given, at Medina, the textual form that is universally binding today. The Koran did not give answers, however, to all questions. The endeavour was made to fill the gaps by recalling sayings and acts of the Prophet, in order to draw from them answers to obscure questions of law. The collection of traditional sayings of

54

the Prophet, the so-called *Sunna,* is the second source of
Islamic law. Koran and Sunna rely directly on the Prophet
for their authority; the community of the faithful has authority also to determine by general agreement the purport
of divine revelation. In practice this element of legisla-
tion depends not on the whole community but on the body
of those qualified by their knowledge of doctrine, the *Ulema.*
Thus, in the cases in which neither the Koran nor the
Sunna gives guidance the law may be laid down by anal-
ogy or by the agreement of the community *(ijmá').* Theoretically the two last-named sources of law could be availed
of as means for adjusting the Constitution of the Moslem
community to changed times; in practice the work of the
Shari'a is regarded as virtually complete, in view of the
body of doctrine accumulated by the learned in the law
under the caliphs. The result of those labours lives on as
the Sunni form of Islam. It is not a very well-chosen appel-
lation, because the Sunna is not by any means the main
subject of controversy with the Moslem groups who have
gone their own way; but the term is in general use. At the
present day nine tenths of the Moslem community belong
to Sunni Islam. The percentage shows how largely the
spiritual unity of Islam has been preserved through thirteen
centuries.

In the Caliphate Constitution the Moslem community
has received the directives of its state system. At the head
of the community is the caliph. To him the defence and
expansion of Islam are entrusted. He has to lead the Moslems in the "holy war" *(Jihad).* The Moslems' duty to
fight for their faith was spoken of by the Prophet himself;
it is based on the Islamic principle that the world is divided into the "House of Islam" *(Dar-ul-Islam)* and the
"House of War" *(Dar-ul-Harb).* Theoretically the two parts
of the world are permanently in a state of war. It is true

55

that this conception may be interpreted rather as Islam's political claim in the world than as fanatical intolerance; for the law of Islam allows Christians and Jews, whom it calls "Possessors of the Book," the right to practise their religion without hindrance so long as they submit to Moslem rule and pay the prescribed tribute. The spread of Islam by means of the "holy war" has long been no more than a theoretical objective, but the removal of alien rule over Islamic countries remains a fundamental duty of Moslems. The "holy war" has passed from the offensive to the defensive.

The caliph is a secular ruler without the least authority to amend or interpret the Shari'a. He is not equipped with the attribute of spiritual infallibility. It is therefore entirely mistaken to liken the caliph to the pope of the Roman Church. Islam has neither a supreme spiritual head nor any ecclesiastical organization. The place of a clergy is taken by the Ulema, the muftis, the cadis, and other persons versed in the law, who are alone authorized to interpret the Shari'a. The opinion of Islam on particular questions is expressed in the common view of the majority of the Ulema; the caliph has nothing to do with it. Thus the counterpart of the Vatican would in any case be the Ulema as a whole; the caliphs would correspond to the mediæval emperor of Christendom. This is but a rough comparison, but it may help to indicate the outlook of the Moslem community.

The law requires that the caliph shall be chosen from among members of the Koreish tribe, to which the Prophet belonged. The caliph should also possess sufficient secular power to enable him to fulfill his duties as protector of the community. Only the four first caliphs met all the requirements of their office. The Umayyads and the Abbasids fulfilled the condition of Koreish origin; but they set themselves in conflict with the original Caliphate Constitution by introducing a hereditary office of caliph. Thus at the end of the Abbasid rule in the thirteenth century the Caliphate was actually carried to the grave, never to rise again in its ideal form. Descendants of the Abbasids continued to assume the title in Egypt, but they had no secular power. The legend runs that the Turkish Sultan Selim had the title conferred on him by one of these shadow caliphs; but there is no truth in this. The Turkish sultans were not even Arabs, and certainly not of Koreishi blood. As the most powerful rulers in the Islamic world of their day, they assumed the title of caliph, but they were never recognized by the whole of the Moslem community. Later attempts to make the Osmanli a sort of spiritual head of world Islam were in entire conflict with the tradition of the Caliphate Constitution. In 1924 the National Assembly of the Turkish Republic deprived the line of Osman of the Caliphate. The Sherif of Mecca, Hussein, who was a Hashimi, and therefore a direct descendant of the Prophet, seized the opportunity to proclaim himself Caliph. The step was a dismal failure. Quite apart from the internal modifications of the Moslem community, none of the Moslem rulers would today be in a position to fulfill the conditions implicit in the office of caliph.

The only lasting division within Islam arose from deep differences of view in regard to the political structure of the Moslem community, and was not concerned with differences in regard to dogma. About ten per cent of the Moslems seceded permanently from the great majority of Sunnite Islam. The conflict over the nature of the Caliphate broke out in the period immediately following the death of Mohammed. Thus the formation of sects in Islam was not the final result of a lengthy development, but took place at the very moment when the Moslem community was in process of formation. A section of the Moslems—today they would perhaps have been called Radical Democrats—held

57

the view that anyone among the faithful should be eligible as caliph, no matter what his line of descent, and that it should be possible to depose the caliph if he was not properly performing the duties of his office. They did not accept the existing system of the Caliphate. This extremist movement, that of the so-called Khariji, was the cause of a great deal of unrest during the first centuries of Islam, but now has only a few million supporters in southern Arabia and East and North Africa. Since its early days it has discarded its radical tendencies.

Much greater were the effects of the agitation of the Legitimists of the earlier Islam. They would have nothing to do with any election of the caliph, and wanted the highest office in the Moslem community to be filled strictly through the succession of the direct descendants of Mohammed. They considered the condition of legitimacy to be best fulfilled by the family of Ali, who was a cousin of Mohammed and had married the Prophet's daughter Fatima. Accordingly Ali's party was formed and given the name of Shi'a Ali, or "partisans of Ali"; from it came the many groups of Shi'i Islam. Not until later were particular religious features associated with the political legitimism of the Shi'is, under the strong influence of the outlook of the former Persian regions of the Caliphate, in which Ali's party had received most support. The Shi'is do not recognize the Caliph of Sunni Islam. They call the supreme head of their community *Imam* ("Director"). The imams, who must be descended from Ali, are given the attributes of infallibility, omniscience, and freedom from sin, and are elevated to the position of intermediaries between God and the community. This deification of the imam reveals most clearly the profound breach between the Shi'a and the Caliphate Constitution.

According to Shi'i doctrine, the series of imams broke off

at an early date. The last of the imams lives in seclusion until the day of his return to the body of worshippers. The idea of the Imamate is to be found once more in the modern constitutional law of Shi'i Persia. At the beginning of the twentieth century the first Persian Parliament was opened "in the presence of the Imam in retirement," and the Persian Constitution is expressly made valid until the "return of the Imam."

The sectarianism that characterizes the Shi'a has produced a confusing mass of further particularisms, so that the great majority of the sects whose names continue to appear in the news of the Islamic world have a Shi'i background. The various groups of the Shi'a are at issue over the question which is the legitimate succession of imams. The greater the distance of the generations from the time of Ali, the greater, of course, became the number of descendants who thought they had a claim to the high office of imam. As early as the time of Ali's great-grandson the Zaydi seceded, gaining supporters in the Yemen; they are now the ruling dynasty in that remote Arab state by the Red Sea. In the seventh succession of imams two rivals claimed to be the legitimate successor; one of them, Ismail, gave rise to an astonishing number of attempts at secession. Ismail is followed by the strange community of the Druses in Lebanon and Syria, which has many particular beliefs. The terrorist sect known as the "Assassins," with their evil reputation, have the same origin. The name of the sect is a European corruption of the Arabic word *hashish:* it was said that the leader of the sect used hashish to reduce his followers to a state in which they would give unconditional obedience, even to his commands to commit murder for political or religious reasons. The spirit of those Shi'i terrorists lives on in our time in the acts of the Persian association of Fedayan-i-Islam ("martyrs of Islam"). No

59

one would dream that the Aga Khan, the pet of society journals, comes from the same stock of the Imam Ismail as the terrible Assassins of the Middle Ages, with whose violence he and his followers have not the least thing in common. The Aga Khan is the supreme head of an Ismaili Shi'i sect, and is held in divine honour by his followers. The grandfather of the present holder of the title was given it by the Shah of Persia, and was made Governor of a Persian province; not only that, but he was given one of the Shah's daughters in marriage, so that the present Aga Khan has in his veins the blood of past rulers of Persia. The Shah's son-in-law who at first was so loaded with honours was soon compelled, however, to flee from Persian intrigues; he went to Bombay, where the Aga Khans now have their headquarters. There is no room to pursue here all the ramifications of the Shi'is. Much the largest and most important of their communities is the one in Persia, where the Shi'a is the state religion. This group ends the succession of the imams with the twelfth link, and is therefore called the "Shi'a of the Twelves."

Roughly ten per cent of the Moslem community are Shi'is. They include most of the population of Persia, about half the Moslems of Iraq, and eight to nine per cent of the Indian Moslems. The majority belong to the Shi'a of the Twelves. The members of the other Shi'i communities number only a few millions. Small communities of Shi'is are also to be found scattered throughout the Islamic world. Altogether the Shi'a probably counts between 30,000,000 and 35,000,000 followers, compared with nearly 300,000,000 of the faithful who are united under the broad roof of Sunni Islam. Sunnis and Shi'is were long filled with fanatical hatred of each other. This hatred had a particular political background in enmity between the Sunni Osmanli sultans and the Shi'i shahs of the Persians, an enmity that produced many wars. In modern times common troubles and common difficulties have brought these two enemy camps of the Moslem community closer together. Among the upper classes, if not yet among the masses, the sense of Moslem solidarity has bridged the gulf of confessional differences.

THE WOOLLEN CLOAK OF THE DERVISHES

THE community of the Moslems has not been spared tension between the guardians of the law and movements that have grown up among the mass of the faithful, the laymen. Present-day Islam cannot be understood without a knowledge of the long series of these dissensions. The ideas, the names, and the external forms of Islamic popular movements of the Middle Ages reappear in the political disputes of the twentieth century. It may suffice to indicate here the example of the Moslem Brotherhood of our day, in which conceptions dating from the early days of Islam, given a new and changed content, inspire slogans of the modern political struggle.

After Islam had spread through countries in which Christian and Persian religious teachings had sown the seed of mysticism and asceticism, there soon appeared among the Moslems the first mendicant friars, who thought they found the true path of Islam in renunciation and surrender to God. They wandered about the country districts clothed in plain woollen cloaks, a fact that gave them and the whole popular movement which they started the name of Sufis (*suf* is Arabic for wool) and Sufism. Most of the Sufis came from the lower classes of the new Moslem community. For centuries Sufism was a burning question for Islam. The Ulema had no liking for this mystical trend among the "laity." But they succeeded in keeping the movement of Sufism within the broad stream of Islamic unity.

The religious feeling of the Sufis laid the foundation for the rise of the first brotherhoods of Islam. These brotherhoods did inestimable service to the spread and permanence of Islam. Their work has left particularly deep traces in Africa, where their influence is paramount to this day in some regions. The brotherhoods built fortified monasteries in the Islamic mission fields; they watched over the safety of commerce and communications, opened Koran schools, and sometimes formed states of their own. They were also successful in amassing wealth through the caravan trade. Their form of organization is always the same. A sheik (called *pir* in the Persian-speaking region), furnished with great authority, is the head of the brotherhood (or, as it might be called, the order). The members are called in Arabic *ikhvan* ("brother"), and in Persian *dervish* ("mendicant" or "mendicant friar"). At times the number of dervishes must have been extraordinarily high. Today it has fallen greatly. But there are still some fifty brotherhoods, with 8,000,000 to 10,000,000 members, in the Islamic world. The influence of these orders extends considerably farther among the Moslem community than the figures might indicate.

The oldest of the still existing and widespread brotherhoods was founded in the twelfth century in the Caliph's city of Baghdad by a certain Abd-ul-Kader el-Gailani, probably a Persian. The members of this order are called Kadirites, after the founder. A modern successor of Abd-ul-Kader, formerly Prime Minister of Iraq, Rashid Ali el-Gailani, became known throughout the world when in 1941 he became involved in war with the British. It was characteristic that the political party of which Rashid Ali was one of the leaders associated itself with the idea of an order by calling itself the National Brotherhood.

The Turkish period saw the founding of many orders,

and the orders of dervishes have long had a special place
in the Ottoman Empire. The head of the Mevlevi Brotherhood had the privilege of investing the new Sultan with
the sword, while the Order of the Bektash was entrusted
with the care of the souls of the Turkish Janizaries. Later
the Bektash, who liked to describe their religious teaching
as a liberal Islam, developed their principal basis among
the Moslems of Albania. Finally, the brotherhood movement found rich soil in the Maghrib. At the end of the
eighteenth century the mysticism of the Sufis found there a
new impulse through the Berber Ahmed et-Tijina. The
brotherhood named after him quickly spread not only
through Morocco and Algeria but into the western Sudan,
where it soon found the French colonial authorities help-
ful in working with it. The brotherhoods have adjusted
themselves to the life of the Moslem community. They
have not turned their backs, like the sects, on the Sunnite
parent house of Islam, nor have they generally pursued
the path of political subversion.

Persians, Turks, and Berbers meet most frequently
among the founders and followers of the Sufi orders. It has
therefore been sought also to recognize in Sufism traits that
indicate a rejection of the rigid and unimaginative form
of Arabian Islam. Under the woollen cloak of the dervishes, mysticism and the cult of saints have found their
way into the house of Islam. The guardians of the true
faith put up with these popular embroideries of doctrine
as the only way of serving the unity of the Moslem community. At the height of the influence of the Sufi orders
the Arabs were weak and in perplexity after suffering the
loss of their political power in the Islamic world. In the
long run, however, there came inevitably in the Arabian
homeland of Islam the call for a reform and purification of
the Moslem community.

63

There also grew up in the field of mystical ideas the weed of Islamic world revolution. It was nourished by the hope that the Mahdi would one day appear to redeem the world from its evils and to set up once for all the rule of Islam over all mankind. The Mahdi (literally, "He who is guided aright") is the figure of the great Islamic redeemer. In the original doctrine of Islam this figure had not the place given it in later times, but the doctrine of the Mahdi is not without the cloak of legitimacy. According to the general belief, the true Mahdi must trace his descent back to the Prophet; this claim none of the very many Mahdis who in the course of Islamic history have believed themselves to be called have omitted to put forward. Mahdis' activities have always spread in epochs of confusion and decline. Thus a revolutionary propaganda of world redemption accompanied the struggle of the Abbasids against the Caliphate of Damascus. The Fatimid rulers of Egypt also owed their rise to similar propaganda. Most of the Mahdist movements, however, spread no farther than their local place of origin. Even the most famous "redeemer" of modern times, the Mahdi of the Sudan, was only able to set up a shortlived African Kingdom of God. It is true that his appearance bore political fruit at a later date, the rule of the Mahdi becoming retrospectively interpreted as a sort of national tradition of the Sudan and brought forward in advocacy of the self-determination of that African region.

RIVAL REFORMERS

IT IS in the nature of Islam that religious and political movements of its followers cannot be clearly distinguished from each other, or not in any case without much more difficulty than in any other of the great religious communities. The various symptoms of Islamic unrest would be easier to interpret and to trace back to a common origin if the purely political nationalism borrowed from the West had not struck root among the peoples of the Moslem community. The interlocking of nationalism with Islamic modernization, two very different elements, complicates present-day events beyond all possibility of simplification.

Efforts at modernization in Islam go back to the eighteenth century. In the course of time they followed two main directions. Puritanical reformers—the older of the two types—sought their ideal in the original form of the Moslem community. The others, the laicists, pursued with more or less resolution the path of the separation of state and religion. They are, therefore, twin brothers of modern nationalism. The puritans were strongly influenced by contact with Europe. Without such contact the laicists might well have been inconceivable.

The forgotten Arabia, the cradle of Islam, is also the source of the puritan reformation. That movement dates from the middle of the eighteenth century. The demoralization and decay of the Ottoman Empire was an abomination to many Arabs of the Holy Places of Islam, among them the young Mohammed ibn Abd-ul-Wahhab, a student of theology in Medina. Abd-ul-Wahhab was born in the Arabian district of el-Hasa, in which the derricks of the Arabian-American Petroleum Company have been erected in our day. He soon began to preach an uncompromising puritanism, and succeeded in persuading one of the princes of central Arabia that the time had come for the purification of Islam by the sword. The reformer Abd-ul-Wahhab and the ruling house of the Sa'uds entered into an alliance, strengthened by family bonds, from which sprang the Arabian conquests of the so-called Wahhabis. Fortune, however,

65

did not always favour the Sa'uds and their Wahhabis. They suffered long-continued failure, which only began to be retrieved when in 1901 the young Abd-ul-Aziz ibn Sa'ud, by a daring coup, regained the lost territory of his predecessors. Step by step King Ibn Sa'ud brought almost the whole of the Arabian peninsula, including the two holy cities, under Wahhabi rule. The Kingdom of Saudi Arabia is the only present-day Moslem state in which the puritan reformers have sole control of the state.

The Wahhabis, whose spiritual influence has spread far and wide in the Islamic world, have made an important contribution to the broad stream of efforts at reform. The last word has not yet been said about this Islamic reformation—if this term may be used here to include every tendency. The movement has different features among the Bedouin from those in the urban civilization of the oasis countries; this is sufficiently explained by the difference in the manner of life and in social conditions. In the Bedouin countries militant orders have accepted the reformers' ideas. These puritan orders closely follow the model of the Sufi brotherhoods, without, of course, their mystical element, the total elimination of which in Islam is precisely the aim of the Arab reformers. King Ibn Sa'ud has created a Wahhabi brotherhood. In doing so he was moved partly by the aim of collecting the nomads into fraternal colonies and so inducing them to enter upon a settled existence.

The widest international interest has been aroused by the puritan Order of Mohammed Ali ibn es-Senussi. Its founder, an Algerian who is said to have come from a family of the old Spanish-Arab aristocracy, came into contact with puritan ideas in Mecca about 1830. He retired to Cyrenaica, where the Order of the Senussi became the nucleus of the Kingdom of Libya, founded in 1952. The brotherhoods have also assumed controlling influence in the internal development of the Anglo-Egyptian Sudan, so that they must be described as a strong political force in that country, now approaching self-determination. It is also incontestable that in the Arab Bedouin countries the reform movement has had a large share in the awakening of a new political consciousness, sometimes leading to the formation of states, though under primitive social and spiritual conditions.

The more complicated structure of the Islamic countries with an old civilization makes the struggle between various ideas much more obstinate and unpredictable. The groups of reformers have found their principal centres in Egypt and India. In both countries the effort for a modernization of Islam is closely connected with the political, economic, and intellectual penetration of modern Europe into the Orient. The Moslem intelligentsia discovered with alarm the internal and external weakness of their world and sought means of bringing new strength to the Moslem community. The first warnings came from a very remarkable Moslem personality, Jemal ed-Din el-Afghani. Nothing definite is known of this man's origin except that he grew up in the Afghan capital, Kabul. His restless life lasted roughly through the period of the reign of Queen Victoria. He became an adviser to the Turkish Sultan and to the Shah of Persia; he taught at the Azhar University in Cairo, and he also lived many years in the Western world. Finally he was laid to rest in the Nijantaj cemetery in Istanbul. Jemal ed-Din, a man thoroughly acquainted with every field of Islamic knowledge, was above all an inspiring political propagandist. He has been called an Islamic revolutionary, because he preached a struggle with every means, not only against alien rule but also against despots and against crumbling regimes among the Moslems themselves. Jemal ed-Din gained extraordinary influence in the Islamic world; but he was one who stirred men's minds rather than a revealer of new paths.

Only his most important disciple, the Egyptian Mohammed Abduh, was able to develop and deepen the ideas of his teacher into a complete body of thought. This man, the greatest thinker among the modern puritan reformers of Islam, came from an Egyptian fellaheen village. He soon came into conflict with the Ulema, the great majority of whom would have nothing to do with any sort of reforming ideas. For a time Mohammed Abduh had to leave his country, but during the last years of his life he filled the high office of supreme Mufti of Egypt. He died in 1905, nine years after his teacher, Jemal ed-Din. Unlike his friend and teacher, Mohammed Abduh did not believe that the path of revolution could bring salvation to the Moslems; he considered that the great need of modern times was for a spiritual and political reform of the Moslem community.

The teachings of Mohammed Abduh are the basis of the so-called Salafiyyah. The word virtually means "ancestral tradition"; it was coined by the master himself. His ideas were developed and spread throughout the Islamic world only after Mohammed Abduh's death. The Salafis of the Moslem spiritual centres are the counterpart of the Wahhabis of the desert. The very name shows that the Salafis do not mean by reform of Islam simply Europeanization; they believe that the authentic Islam of the first caliphs represents the state system and the way of life that can cope with modern questions as with all else. They are entirely against substituting for the Moslem community the European conception of the "nation" and breaking it up accordingly. And in that respect they are definitely opposed to the "Westernizers." At the same time the Salafis are opposed to the conservative elements of Islam, and put forward certain proposals for social reform. Thus Mohammed Abduh

68

himself was a resolute defender of popular rights against absolutism, and his successors have even taken over and made their own the demand, unheard of until then in Islam, for women's emancipation. It is therefore impossible to dismiss the Salafi movement as reactionary, though the reformers have also made the demand for a return to the authentic Islam. The anti-reform majority of the Ulema distrust these tendencies and often sharply condemn them. There have been excited debates at the Azhar University between the reformists and the conservatives. The fact that the idea of Islamic puritanism has tended to lead the masses of the peoples along other paths that might end in violence and subversion is another matter: that course could result only from a distortion of the teachings of Mohammed Abduh and his disciples.

The Salafiyyah aims at modernizing the Moslem community without injuring the soul of Islam. Only in this way does it consider that it can serve the defence of Islam, which remains its supreme aim. To the Indian reformers also the maintenance of the Moslem community by its own efforts is the absolutely essential objective. The spiritual environment of Indian Islam differs substantially, it is true, from the Arab tradition, and British rule has brought the Indians into closer association than any other Moslem peoples with modern western Europe. This explains why the great Indian reformist thinkers are inclined to adopt a liberal interpretation of Islam rather than puritan rigour.

The founder of the Indian Moslem reform movement, Sir Sayyid Ahmed Khan, was an Indian civil servant. He was born in 1817 in a family with a long tradition of service to Islam. The family had migrated from Arabia to India in the time of the first Great Moguls and had given the Moslem rulers in Delhi a succession of capable administrators. Ahmed Khan brought back to India after a long stay in England the strong impression that the Moslems must make use of Western science and Western ways of thinking if they were not to be hopelessly submerged. The anxiety grew especially great among the Indian Moslems when they found themselves greatly outnumbered by the Hindus. With the aim of intellectually equipping his co-religionists, Ahmed Khan founded the Anglo-Oriental University of Aligarh, which later became famous. The methods of teaching were modelled on those of Oxford and Cambridge. The criticism of the conservative Ulema, suspicious of such innovations, was disarmed by inducing some Islamic princes who could not be suspected of a lust for innovation to become patrons of the Aligarh University.

Needless to say, Ahmed Khan and the Indian reformers rejected the radical hostility to Europe of Jemal ed-Din el-Afghani. They were not afraid of collaboration with the British masters of India, and one of the most celebrated Moslem reformers, Amir Ali, actually became the first Indian member of the British Privy Council. In the person of the thinker and poet Sir Mohammed Ikbal, the Indian reform movement extends down to the recent past. Ikbal thoroughly absorbed the European spirit in England and Germany. He did not infer that there was a need for radical Westernization, but sought to build a bridge to modern times by adopting the primeval democratic form of the Moslem community, which he believed to have existed in its purity in the time of the Prophet himself and of the first four caliphs. Thus the "Islamic democracy" of Mohammed Ikbal comes very close to the ideal conceptions of the Egyptian reformist thinkers.

The Indian reformation has gained great political importance in so far as it has awakened in Indian Islam the consciousness of a special "national community." The Aligarh University has also formed a modern class of leaders among the Moslems, a class that later should enable them to set the new state of Pakistan on a safe course. Many of the men now in high positions in Pakistan owe their training to the Aligarh University. Sir Mohammed Ikbal is regarded as the great herald of the Indian Moslem state. He did not live to see the success of his political ideas; for it was nine years after his death that the Pakistan he foresaw, the heir of a great Islamic past, was created.

The work of the puritan reformers gradually elicited a wide response among the middle and lower classes of the Moslem peoples. This Islamic movement, with its mass support, is reminiscent in some respects, if we regard simply its political and social features and not its doctrinal content, of the Sufism of the Middle Ages. Both movements reflect a wide current of lay opinion within the Moslem community. It is true that the Sufi propaganda had not the command of the technical apparatus of modern mass organization of which the new movement is able to avail itself. A quantity of popular literature about the Prophet and the great leaders of Islam aroused enthusiasm for the idea of protecting the Moslem community from the very great influence of aliens and for restoring the greatness of the past. In the twenties of this century there came into existence, scarcely noticed at first by the non-Islamic outer world, a number of Moslem leagues and associations with this aim. As is the nature of Islam, the religious element was mixed as a matter of course with political and social aims, and the new societies often made use of the vocabulary of the brotherhoods and dervish orders. They tried to revive Islam in the form of an entire ordering of human society, thus acquiring a certain relationship, though only superficial, with the totalitarian movements of Europe. This was clearly to be seen in the varied career of the so-called "Young Egyptian Party," led by the lawyer Ahmed Hussein, which discovered Socialist features in the Constitution of the Shari'a, and finally lost itself in a maze of nationalism, Socialism, and Islam.

Of much more importance is the mass organization of the "Moslem Brotherhood" *(el-Ikhwan-el-Muslimun)*. Its founder was an Egyptian teacher with extraordinary oratorical gifts, Hasan el-Banna. In its best times the Brotherhood is said to have had more than a million members. It has its paramilitary formations, and binds its members to implicit obedience of its leader, just as in the organization of the orders. Its program includes much of the ideology of the Salafi reformers, and it is therefore worth while to refer in detail to its statutes, dating from 1948. The Brotherhood demands in its statutes a constitution that might be described as a caliphate republic, because the president, to be elected for life, is to be proclaimed caliph of the Moslems. The Moslem peoples are to unite in an Islamic league, "which shall join in work for world peace by preaching the universal principles of Islam." Among the slogans of the Brotherhood we meet with sentences like "the Prophet is our leader," or "the Koran is our Constitution." Thus the Caliphate Constitution is curiously poured here into a modern mould. The program of the Moslem Brotherhood of Egypt may be mentioned as typical of the great number of similar organizations spread over the whole Islamic world. The "holy war" makes its appearance again in the postulate that the fight against all who are declared to be enemies of Islam must be the duty of members, whether these enemies are Moslem "traitors" or infidel intruders in the Islamic house.

The influence and strength of the various organizations of militant Islam are largely unascertainable by the outsider. Often the public begins to learn of their existence only when they emerge dramatically from their seclusion. This was what happened when the assassination of the

Persian Prime Minister Ali Razmara, the consequences of which left the world in breathless suspense, was brought into association with the activities of the Shi'i league of the Fedayan-i-Islam. Groups of similar origin and tendency have been held responsible for the assassination of King Abdullah of Jordan and of Liaqat Ali Khan, Prime Minister of Pakistan. In all these cases the victims were good and pious Moslems, not independent thinkers, still less "infidels." It has been suggested that these and other outrages point to the underground existence of a Pan-Islamic conspiracy, but there is no clear evidence of this.

The Egyptian and Indian reformers are pursuing the same aim, the self-preservation of Islam in the modern world, by different methods. Another reform movement aims at a radical change in the conception of the Moslem community, confining Islam to the purely religious sphere. The model for such efforts is the laicism of Europe, which has made the principle of the separation of church and state a maxim of the modern state system and social order of the West. Only in a single Moslem country, Turkey, has the laicist ideal been radically carried into effect. The creators of modern Turkey grew up in the atmosphere of European nationalism. Kemal Ataturk therefore countered the total Islam of the puritans with an equally total Europeanization of the community. A long succession of laws in the 1920's and 1930's fundamentally altered the outward life of the Turkish Moslems. It must be borne in mind, however, that that great Turkish statesman was able to throw, and did throw, the whole power of an authoritarian State into the support of his laicist reforms. The Turkish People's Party, which until 1946 had been the state party of the Turkish Republic, included the complete separation of state and religion among its principles, and so raised laicism to an inseparable component of the so-called Kemalist Constitution.

Since the death of Ataturk, Turkey has remained a laicist state, and it intends to remain so in the future. Since the war, however, certain modifications have proved unavoidable. It became clear that the sudden dethronement of Islamic tradition was not proceeding without injury to the community, and especially to the younger generation. Then it was found that the mass of the Turkish people clung tenaciously to Islam, and, indeed, that a renascence of Islam was to be observed. When in 1946 the authoritarian regime gave place to the multi-party system, the political leaders had to take account of the hold of Islamic tradition over the people to prevent any approach to a counter-reformation against the achievements of Ataturk. The Turks have not turned their backs on the Kemalist principles, but they have modified the laicist reform in some respects. The Turkish example has found friends all over the Islamic world, and laicism has become an influential movement in the Moslem community. But nowhere has the Westernization of public life proceeded so far as the dictatorial reformer of Ankara carried it.

In the parts of the Islamic world under Soviet rule, religion and state have been rigorously separated; but this is not a genuine reform springing from the spiritual development of the peoples affected.

In Persia, Riza Khan, although as Shah he used a strong hand in his reforms, had to proceed a good deal more cautiously with Islam than his Turkish fellow ruler. It is doubtful whether he had any intention of pursuing the same radical laicism as Ataturk. Indonesia and Syria have embodied laicist principles in their Constitutions. In Egypt there was published in the middle of the 1920's an eagerly discussed pamphlet maintaining that Mohammed was not the founder of a state, and that the separation of religion and state had justification in the doctrines of Islam. A defence of laicism on those lines

74

is certainly disputable, and the supreme council of the Egyptian Ulema lost no time in declaring that the author was an "enemy of Islam."

The controversy between the puritans and the Westernizers is still in full swing, and the outcome of the struggle is quite unpredictable. Even where one of the two tendencies has been able to develop fully, the last word has not yet been spoken, and compromises have to be made day after day. For a long time it seemed as if the Westernizers were marching invincibly forward, but since then Islam has reappeared with unbroken power on the political plane. Its hold on the masses has proved much stronger than was suspected by many people who had formed their judgment from the Westernized façade of the great cities. Quietly and tenaciously the struggle goes on with varying fortunes between the two extremes of spiritual development, in Parliament, in conversation, in literature, and at the universities. Two souls are fighting each other in the Moslem's breast. The Westernizers are condemned by their opponents as "enemies of Islam"; the puritan zealots are execrated as "reactionaries." While the puritan reformists want to make the religious element the criterion for the political system, the laicist Westernizers are landed by the logic of their line of thought on the shores of the national state.

At the present time there are two integrating forces in the Moslem community: Islam and nationalism. In theory they are mutually exclusive; in practice both are at work everywhere. So it is that such a conception as that of "Islamic nationalism" has a seductive appearance of simplification, for which the complicated developments in the Moslem world seem to call. "Islamic nationalism," however, is an interpretative expedient applied from without, with nothing in its favour beyond the fact that both Islam and nationalism are up in arms against alien domination and alien influence. For in this connexion the advocacy of Westernization must not be assumed to imply political friendliness to the Western world. The Westernizing nationalist is just as actively hostile to imperialism as the Islamic crusader for the faith. But—and this is entirely cloaked by the conception of "Islamic nationalism"—the two currents are fed from altogether different sources, and part at once when they have no common enemy. That is not all. Until the end of the First World War the Moslems could look upon the West as a single unit from St. Petersburg to London and New York. There were only slight shades of difference between the Western education that a Moslem received at a British, a French, or a Russian university. Since the Bolshevik Revolution of 1917 the once uniform "Europe" has stood before the Moslem in two shapes; it has been irrevocably split into two camps, whose quarrel has unsettled the peoples of the whole world. It is not easy for the Moslem to find his way about in the world of the 1950's, and he cannot justly be blamed if he reveals an inner unrest similar to that which the West itself is unable to overcome.

ISLAMIC POLICY

CURRENT opinions differ very widely about the political unity of the Islamic world and the significance of Islam in international relations. Some people are inclined to contend that Islam still possesses a genuine capacity for the unification of its peoples and states. While they regard Pan-Islamism as the propaganda of a limited group, they point out that the inner framework of the Moslem community and its relations with the outer world are determined today entirely by the nation and the national state. There is another body of opinion in violent contrast to this, regarding the Islamic clamp as strong enough to hold together a political Moslem block. The advocates of either view can bring forward a quantity of serious arguments in support of it, so that it seems as if the unifying and dividing elements in the community of Islamic peoples are of much the same strength and effectiveness.

Jemal ed-Din el-Afghani, the tireless reformer and propagandist of the last century, is generally regarded as the first source of all the movements that have helped to produce the Islamic unrest of the present day; he is also described as the spiritual father of modern Pan-Islamism. The title is justified in so far as it was he who for the first time insistently appealed for the unity of Islam in its historical settlement with modern Europe. Since then Pan-Islamism has figured on the long list of the modern "pan-ideas," alongside Pan-Slavism and the appeals for Pan-Europe and Pan-Asia and the rest. This has created the impression that Pan-Islamism is a product of the nineteenth century. The Moslem will have nothing to do with that view. Actually the idea of political unity existed from the first in the community of the followers of Mohammed: strictly this community is "a state that demands loyalty from its subjects." The puritan reformers have accordingly taken the so-called Pan-Islamic postulates as axiomatic. They recall a fundamental trait of the Moslem body of believers, the sense of a fraternal bond uniting all Moslems, without distinction of race, class, or nation. Islamic brotherhood, wrote an Indian Moslem who in other respects is not by any means to be included with the puritans, is comparable with patriotism, with the difference that its sanction for unity of law and constitution in the community is drawn not from race or geography, but from divine revelation. Strictly, therefore, "Pan-Islamism" is a pleonasm.

Thus we have to go back in history to the short period

of the first caliphs to find the political unity of Islam achieved. Later the Islamic world was always split up into a number of state systems, often violently hostile to one another. Regarded in this perspective, political Pan-Islamism has certainly something of an artificial character. This became very clear when the Osmanli Sultan Abdul Hamid II tried to revive the title of caliph, which his predecessors had not bound up with particular ambitions. He had a special political motive: to hold together the peoples of the Ottoman Empire (which was threatening to fall to pieces) under the banner of the Prophet. An article was therefore added to the Osmanli Constitution of 1876 to the effect that the sultan, as supreme caliph, was the protector of Islam. Abdul Hamid's efforts to revive the Caliphate met with a varied reception. Outside the Ottoman Empire it was welcomed in many quarters, especially in Indian Islam, where a new and strengthened Caliphate promised valuable aid for the self-support and emancipation of the Indian Moslem community. Abdul Hamid failed, however, to bind his Arab subjects, with whom he was mainly concerned, more closely to Constantinople through the device of the Caliphate. In the First World War the Arabs revolted, under the leadership of one of the most distinguished descendants of the Prophet, against the Ottoman Caliph. The attempt to preserve the outlived political system of the Islamic Orient by means of the Caliphate had come to grief. Nor was any more success achieved when at the end of the First World War a Caliphate movement spread among the Indian Moslems, aiming at bringing aid to the Turkish Sultan in his weakness.

Abdul Hamid's Pan-Islamism proved a peculiar growth. As it was entirely impossible for the Sultan Caliph to unite the whole Islamic world under his rule, the ruler of Constantinople tried to institute a spiritual form of caliphate. He had seen from the example of the French and Russians that a protectorate over widespread religious communities might be followed by political influence. Following the example of the Christian Great Powers, Abdul Hamid set out to make himself Protector of all the Moslems. He found no excessive sympathies for this fantastic innovation among his own believers, but some of the European Great Powers agreed to allow the Sultan Caliph certain spiritual rights over the Moslems under their rule. But Abdul Hamid's dream of a sort of Islamic papacy remained no more than an episode.

Later the Indians especially, for reasons easy to understand, showed an interest in a spiritual unification of the Islamic world. But Islam would have to undergo radical changes if the ground was to be prepared for the general recognition of a spiritual centre of world Islam. Accordingly Mohammed Ikbal, the pioneer of the idea of Pakistan, once thought of proposing that a Pan-Islamic legislative assembly should be convened to undertake, on the strength of the unanimous will of the faithful *(ijma')*, the reform of the Constitution of the Moslem community. So far no move of this sort has got beyond the stage of preliminary discussion. All that these movements show is that Moslem solidarity, the fraternal sense of the faithful, has a vitality that is revealed by the search for new forms for its expression. Now that the epoch of the great Islamic empires has been definitely closed in the twentieth century, the development of the division of the Moslem community into national states is continuing in the political field. This development seems still to be far from its end.

At the beginning of 1952 there were twelve independent states with a Moslem majority in their population. The number is increased to thirteen if we add the Republic of Lebanon, whose population is half Moslem and half Christian. Eight of these thirteen states are of Arab character:

Egypt, Jordan, Syria, the Lebanon, Iraq, Yemen, Saudi Arabia, and finally the latest arrival, Libya. The remaining Moslem states form a long chain along the southern border of the Eurasian continental mass: Turkey, Persia, Afghanistan, Pakistan, and Indonesia. The rapid growth of the family of independent Moslem states is shown by the simple fact that six of those now existing, or almost half, attained their independence during the last decade. The wave of state-formations on the soil of the Islamic intercontinent has not yet come to a stop. Already there have appeared on the horizon the outlines of two new African Moslem states. By 1960 Somaliland, under Italian trusteeship, is to be so far advanced that it will be qualified for independence, and it is expected that the Anglo-Egyptian Sudan will be granted sovereign status still earlier. Finally, what is fair for the Sudan and Somaliland, Tunisia and Morocco will consider only fair for themselves.

Apart from the fact that the majority of their population are followers of Islam, the common characteristics of the Moslem group of states are rather few. In this connexion the term "Moslem state" does not imply that the life of the state is determined by the principles of the Islamic Constitution. Islamic law, the Shari'a, is enforced in only three states: Afghanistan, Saudi Arabia, and Yemen. Islam has the character of a state religion in only eight of the Moslem states; Turkey, Syria, and Indonesia are expressly described in their Constitutions as laicist states. The Lebanon dispenses as a matter of course with a state religion. The forms of the states of the Moslem world pass from the theocracy of Yemen to the parliamentary democracy of Turkey, through plenty of gradations. Pakistan is a Dominion of the British Commonwealth; Egypt, Turkey, Indonesia, Syria, and the Lebanon are republics; all the other Moslem states are monarchies, some absolute, some constitutional.

Only one Moslem throne has endured from the Middle Ages to modern times: that of the Shah of Persia, which from the sixteenth to the twentieth century has been transmitted by inheritance. It is true that this has reference only to the institution, not to the dynasties, and not to the world-famous Peacock Throne, which was brought from Delhi in the eighteenth century among the booty of the conqueror Nadir Shah. Since 1925 there has reigned on the Peacock Throne the dynasty of the Pahlavis. The Pahlavi shahs belong to the Shi'i state religion; this in Persia is a rigorous and understood requirement. For that very reason, apart from any others, the relations between the Persian rulers and the kings of Afghanistan, their neighbours, can never have been very cordial. Since their state has existed, the Afghan rulers, strict Sunnis, have belonged to various families of the powerful Afghan tribe of the Durrani. They have borne the title of king only since 1923.

The princely houses of the Arab world are a picturesque and instructive reflection of Arab-Islamic history. With the exception of the rulers of Yemen, who since the Middle Ages have incorporated the leadership of a Shi'i sect, the Arab kings have acquired their titles and thrones in the twentieth century. It is true that the family traditions of some of them go back far into the Islamic past. The Hashimis who rule in Jordan and Iraq had held for six centuries the high dignity, respected throughout Islam, of sherifs of the holy city of Mecca. They bear the name of the Prophet's family, because they are descended from Mohammed's son-in-law Ali. But the imams of Yemen and the Senussi King of Libya also claim to have the blood of the Prophet in their veins. King Ibn Sa'ud, on the other hand, does not bear the title "sherif" or "sayyid," as the descendants of Mohammed are entitled to do. The founder of his line belonged to the Bedouin aristocracy of central Arabia. Thus he is unquestionably of pure Arab blood. The kings of Egypt had much greater power and distinction than their Arabian cousins. But the founder of their line, Mohammed Ali, was not an Arab, but a Turkish officer of Albanian origin, who came to Egypt in the stirring days of Napoleon's campaigns in the Orient.

To complete the account of the princely families of the Arab world, mention must be made of the dynasties of the Maghrib. The sultans of Morocco and the beys of Tunis have not at present the rank of independent rulers, but they look back on an unbroken dynastic tradition of longer duration than most of the other sovereigns of Islam. The sultans of Morocco have reigned since the sixteenth century, the beys of Tunis since the period remembered in Europe as the epoch of Louis XIV. The rulers of Morocco place their pride as Arabs in the title of sherif; the origins of the princely house of Tunis are to be found in the warrior caste of the Ottoman Empire. Thus descendants of the Prophet and of daring conquerors are alike to be found among the Moslem rulers of the twentieth century.

Between thirty and forty per cent of all Moslems live under alien, non-Moslem rule, mainly in Africa, Central Asia, and India. The great colonial empires of the French and the Russians have more Moslem subjects than any of the independent Moslem states, with the exceptions of Pakistan and Indonesia. If only because of its challenge to their own position, neither French nor Russians have any liking for political Pan-Islamism, though it must not be overlooked that France, which has for centuries been closely associated with the Islamic Orient, enjoys a very different status among the Moslems from that of the Soviet Union. French dominance extends mostly to the extreme west of the Islamic intercontinent, and Russian to the north-east. Six of the federal republics of the Soviet Union are situated geographically on the borders of the Islamic intercontinent and have a Moslem majority among their population: Azerbaijan, in Caucasia, and the five Central Asian republics of Turkmenistan, Uzbekistan, Kazakhstan, Kirghizistan, and Tadzhikistan.

The relations of the Dominion of India with Islam are of a special nature. The thirty to forty million Moslems living in Indian territory make the Dominion a country inseparably associated with world Islam. India's aim, as that of her creators, is to be not a Hindu state but the state of the Indian nation. In the international field she represents both her Hindu and her Moslem citizens; Pan-Islamic agitation cannot be pleasant for her, and she tries to work against it by placing in the foreground of her action and propaganda the common interests of the peoples of Asia. A significant example of this was the way India worked to secure the friendship of the Moslem world in the Kashmir dispute.

Since the British withdrawal from India in 1947, Great Britain's direct rule over Moslem peoples has been confined to the colonies in Africa and in south-east Asia; but through their close association with Pakistan and their political interests in the Near and Middle East the British still have influence over the development of the Islamic world. Great Britain has not always shared the definitely hostile attitude of the other colonial powers to the Pan-Islamic tendencies; on the contrary, British policy has often given evidence of the view that the uniting force of Islam may offer means of stabilization in the Near and Middle East.

Many manifestations of the Moslem sense of community may be adduced, in great matters and small. They are obvious in strictly religious affairs. The pilgrimage to the Holy Places in Arabia, one of the five main duties of the Moslem, brings together tens of thousands of the faithful every year from all parts of the world. After the war, on the suggestion of Pakistan, the Pan-Islamic idea was given practical effect in the field of economic co-operation. In November 1949 there assembled in the capital of the Indian Moslem state the first Islamic Economic Conference, attended by industrialists, businessmen, and engineers from the Moslem countries. This organization is inspired by the idea of developing from Islamic fundamental principles a program of economic and social justice. The practical purpose of the conference, however, is shown by the fact that it was not allowed to be swamped by theoretical discussions, but tackled such concrete questions as the creation of a Pan-Islamic Air Company and a Pan-Islamic Bank. A more political character is borne by the Islamic World Congress (el Mu'tamar el-Alami el-Islami). Its beginnings date back to the Arab-Jewish conflict in Palestine. It met for the first time in 1931 in Jerusalem, to discuss the protection of the Islamic shrines in Palestine. The Congress meets at irregular intervals; it has hitherto been presided over by the former Mufti of Jerusalem, Amin el-Hussein. The Mufti, an Islamic dignitary belonging to a distinguished Palestinian Arab family, studied at Azhar and was later an officer in the Turkish army. In the modern Moslem community his personality is surrounded by party hatred and allegiance. He might be called the modern spiritual heir of the first herald of Pan-Islamism, Jemal ed-Din el-Afghani. It should be expressly mentioned that the Pan-Islamic activity that finds expression in these efforts is not an affair of governments but of private organizations and private individuals.

It is a long-familiar fact that events in one Moslem country exercise men's minds in the remotest corners of the Islamic world. This is just as much a fact in the twentieth century as in the time of the caliphs. Anyone who strikes a note in Morocco or in the Sudan must be prepared for the Islamic strings to be set in vibration as far as Pakistan and Indonesia. Thus Islamic brotherhood is a living reality in the broad masses of the whole Moslem community, ignoring state frontiers. It is a reflection of popular feeling. The forum of the United Nations is offering governments clear evidence of Moslem solidarity. The Moslem States have ten votes in the General Assembly of the United Nations, or eleven if we include the Lebanon. The world organization remains closed only to Jordan and Libya. In the body of member states of the United Nations, sixty in all, eleven votes are a substantial force. It may be objected that Turkey can only be included in the "Moslem group" of the international parliament with the utmost reserve. But in many cases the vote of India offers a substitute. Apart from the special case of Turkey, as soon as the question arises of the self-determination and independence of a Moslem people, there is unity among the delegations of the Moslem states.

But does all this indicate any considerable probability of a political Moslem bloc? What has actually come is a series of regional coalitions on the soil of the Islamic intercontinent, such as the Arab League of 1945, and before it the Oriental Four-Power Pact of 1936, into which Turkey, Persia, Afghanistan, and Iraq entered. But while such regional groupings strike the Islamic note sometimes more loudly and sometimes less, they are not primarily Moslem alliances, but have reference to the national interests of the states involved or to common demands of a particular geographical region. Even the Arab League cannot deny that it includes this element, though it makes much of the historical identity of the Arab element with Islam. Turkey carries the laicism of its internal politics into its external relations, treating all coalitions and alliances "on a religious basis" with unconcealed mistrust. Shi'i Persia is neither suited to a Pan-Islamic leadership nor willing to undertake it. Pakistan is the most inclined to set its foreign policy on an Islamic basis. It not only is the most populous Moslem state, but owes its existence entirely to the bond of a common faith. Thus it is not surprising that Pakistan has shown eager initiative in many fields of Islamic collaboration. But the Pakistani too are aware of the political limits of Moslem unity; in their own conflict with Afghanistan and in the Kashmir question they are gaining instructive experience on that matter. In the description of international coalitions and movements, therefore, the attribute "Pan-Islamic" should be used only with the greatest caution. On the international plane the limits between Pan-Islam and nationalism lose definition, just as in the internal modernization of Islam the various reform movements overlap. At the present time the division of the Moslem community into separate national states remains the dominant fact. When the Afghan Government set up political claims against its fellow-Moslem neighbour Pakistan, it felt it necessary to meet the charge of falling short in Moslem solidarity. It issued a statement in self-justification, based on this definition of the present-day relations between a national state and the Moslem community: "Political Pan-Islamism cannot imply more than mutual respect and mutual understanding among Moslem states, and lasting friendship and sympathy for others' problems." In this sense the Moslem community represents a present-day factor in world politics.

CHAPTER FOUR

Alien Rule and Independence

THE PARTITION OF THE ISLAMIC WORLD

IN 1798 Napoleon Bonaparte, First Consul of the French
Republic, landed in Egypt at the head of his troops. A few
years later he concluded a military alliance with the Shah
of Persia and sent a French mission to Teheran. He was interested only indirectly in the Orient; his aim was to strike a
blow in India at his mortal enemy, Great Britain. This Cor-
sican genius had clearly foreseen the strategic key position
which the Islamic intercontinent was to assume in the approaching age of world politics. From then on, the countries
of the Moslems were to be one of the principal scenes of the
struggles between the European Great Powers. In face of the
superiority of modern Europe the Moslem states were impo-
tent. They had to accept the fate of every vacuum between
the high-pressure regions of power. For a full century after
Napoleon's initiative in the Orient, the whole of the Islamic
intercontinent, with the exception of a relatively small ves-

tige, was partitioned between the European Great Powers. The political and economic intervention of foreign powers was followed by the so-called Europeanization of the Islamic Orient. The upper class among the Moslem peoples learned to think in terms of nation and sovereignty, democracy and constitutional government. From the beginning of the nineteenth century the new nationalism put forward its double demand for independence from alien rule and for constitutional and social reform.

Napoleon's Oriental aspirations were not a matter of chance. Until the sixteenth century the Moslem powers had taken the lead in the world, but then the initiative passed gradually from the Moslems to the Europeans. The Atlantic peoples began the conquest of the oceans, the Great Russians spread from the Moscow region over the illimitable continental mass of Eurasia. When the Portuguese had discovered the sea route round the Cape of Good Hope, it became possible to evade the monopoly which the Arabs had maintained as middlemen in the trade between Europe and the Indian world. On and around the Indian Ocean there came the first competition between the enterprise of western Europe and the Moslems. Western colonial rule was first established in Indonesia, the Islamic region farthest from Europe. The Portuguese were followed by the Dutch, the French, and finally the English. In India the navigators of Atlantic Europe found the Mogul Empire in process of dissolution. In the course of the eighteenth century British power gained a firm footing in the Indian subcontinent, and the security of India from then on became one of the principal concerns of the international policy directed from Europe—one is tempted to say actually the foremost concern. Meanwhile the Russians had slowly but unceasingly continued their pressure on the south-east. The conquest of Kazan and Astrakhan in the middle of the sixteenth century brought the beginning of Moscow's expansion in the territory of the Islamic peoples, and at the same time the beginning of the bitter struggle between Russians and Turks. In Napoleon's time the Russians were already close to the Caucasus and the steppes of Turkistan. The temporary alliance between the French and Russian rulers brought the first threat to the security of British India. When the curtain rose on the epoch of European dominance in the world, there were three claimants to the heritage of Islamic power: the British in India, the Russians in Central Asia, and the French in the Mediterranean.

Great Britain contented herself until the construction of the Suez Canal with indirect protection of her interests in the Near East. Under Lord Palmerston the Foreign Office held to the principle that the integrity of the Ottoman Empire and Persia offered the best guarantee against a threat to the vulnerable north-west frontier of India. The British Ambassador in Constantinople took the "Sick Man" by the Bosporus under the wing of British power. The picture of the *Pax Britannica* of the nineteenth century is rounded off only by the fact that the European balance of power found its logical continuation in the Near East. During that period the British wished to see the minimum disturbance of the *status quo* in that quarter.

In 1830 the French went into Algeria; British opposition barred their access to the eastern Mediterranean. Conditions in the Maghrib, especially in its centre, in Algeria, were very disturbed. European shipping in the Mediterranean was in continual danger from the Algerian Moslems, who had embarked on piracy as a new form of combat with the infidels. During the Osmanli period a corsair oligarchy had been set up on the North African coast. The supreme head of this Algerian corsair republic, whose associations with the Sultan of Constantinople had become quite superficial, assumed the title of dey, which seems to have been originally conferred on Turkish Janizary officers. The Dey was elected in each case for life. The rulers in Algiers gave great provocation to the representatives of European states. When the Dey vented his wrath on the French Consul one day by overt action, the French Government lost patience and resolved on a punitive expedition. In July 1830 French troops landed west of Algiers. This was the beginning of French rule in the Moslem Maghrib. The subjection of the Algerian hinterland took the rest of the nineteenth century. From their first landing in Algeria, the French felt bound to consider the neighbouring countries, Morocco and Tunisia, from the point of view of the security of their newly acquired Algerian possession.

In the north-east of the Islamic intercontinent Russia pushed on steadily on both sides of the Caspian Sea. Persia was compelled after two wars to cede her Caucasian provinces, and by about the middle of the nineteenth century the Caucasus was entirely in Russian hands. The whole of Turkistan came under the administration of czarist nobles. Here, too, the Russian expansion took place partly at the expense of the weak Persian realm. The Russian Governor General of Turkistan took up his residence in Tashkent. The two central Asian principalities of Khiva and Bukhara remained in existence as vassal states of Russia, much as many principalities within British India continued to exist under the protection of the British raj. In the 1880's Russian expansion came to an end along a line that still forms the frontier with Persia and Afghanistan. The Russians had cut out of the Islamic world a colonial empire comparable in size, though not in population, with the British possessions in India. The Russian Czar had become ruler over many millions of Moslems. Relatively little attention has been paid as a rule to this side of European expansion, because colonial policy tends to be discussed only in terms of oversea territories. In Moslem eyes Russia's continental expansion is simply a variant of European imperialism.

Until the opening of the Suez Canal the Arab-Osmanli-Persian nucleus of the Islamic world had been free from alien domination, since it had been preserved by British diplomacy in the glass case of the balance-of-power policy. The canal entirely changed the strategic-political position of that great region. European trade and communications with the Far East now no longer took the long route round the Cape of Good Hope, but cut through the midst of the Arab world. Foreseeing the international problems bound up with any such revolution in communications and commerce, the Foreign Office had long opposed the cutting of the canal. When the canal was completed by a Frenchman, Ferdinand de Lesseps, Palmerston foresaw that it would involve Great Britain in unpredictable liabilities in the Arab countries and would conjure up for British diplomacy the nightmare of a "second Bosporus." After 1869, the year of the opening of the canal, the maintenance of the integrity of the Ottoman Empire was no longer a sufficient protection of British world interests. Thirteen years after the first ship had passed through the canal, British troops occupied Egypt—"temporarily," it was then said. At the time of the British landing, Egypt was nominally a part of the Ottoman Empire; actually it enjoyed virtually complete independence. Mohammed Ali, the founder of the modern Egyptian state and dynasty, had secured from the Sultan of Turkey in 1841 the hereditary dignity of viceroy in Cairo. He had conquered wide territories in the upper Nile valley, the present-day Sudan; he had extended Egyptian influence to Syria and the Arabian peninsula, and had made Egypt for the time a Great Power of the Near East. His successors, who from 1865 onward bore the title of Khedive, were unable to maintain the country at the same level. The internal conditions in Egypt gave occasion for European intervention. Great Britain's action in the Nile valley was the first and the decisive step toward British hegemony in the Arab East. It was considered in London that no other Great Power must be allowed to gain a footing in the neighbourhood of the Suez Canal.

The occupation of Egypt was followed gradually by the definitive partition of the whole of North Africa. The occupation had been preceded by French military intervention, a year earlier, in Tunisia. The treaties of Bardo (1881) and La Marsa (1883) placed the sovereignty of the beys of Tunis under French protection. France now needed only Morocco to round off her colonial empire in North Africa. For the sake of a common policy in Europe, Great Britain came to an understanding with France about Morocco and with the Russians about Persia and Afghanistan. In return for recognition of the British position in Egypt, France was given freedom of action in Morocco. In 1912 France concluded a treaty with the Sultan-Sherif establishing her protectorate over Morocco, satisfaction being also given to Spanish interests on the north Moroccan coast. At the same time Italy, after a short war with Turkey, set foot in Libya on the North African shores facing her own. In the east of the Islamic world Persia was divided into a Russian and a British sphere of influence, and Afghanistan was recognized as within the sphere of British interest. When the First World War broke out, only the rump of the Ottoman Empire was free from the overlordship of European Great Powers.

The entry of the Sultan of Constantinople into the war on the side of the Central Powers introduced the last phase of the so-called imperialist age. Great Britain, France, and Russia agreed in the spring of 1916 on the future partition of the Ottoman Empire. A year later Italy secured the assent of the Western powers to a sphere of interest. The Bolshevik Revolution interfered with the execution of the Allied agreements, but the Peace Treaty of Sèvres (1920) broadly confirmed the partition of the actual Turkish territory into various zones of influence. Britain and France reserved to themselves the reordering of the Arabian territories. The two powers agreed that France should receive the Levant coast, and Britain southern Iraq, and that Palestine should be internationlized in some form. What then remained was to form an Arab torso-state under joint British and French protection. These plans were in open conflict with a series of agreements and promises made by the British Government both to the Arabs and to the Zionist leaders, to whom the Balfour Declaration of November 2, 1917 had promised a home for the Jewish people in Palestine, subject to the maintenance of the rights of the non-Jewish inhabitants.

It was finally agreed to try in the former Osmanli parts of the Arab world the new institution of League of Nations mandates. The French received mandates over Syria and Lebanon, the British mandates over Palestine and Iraq. The Balfour Declaration assumed, as a part of the Palestine mandate, the character of an international obligation. Looking back on it, we may regard the settlement in Palestine as much the most difficult problem that the peacemakers of 1919 left behind them in the Near East.

When the government of the Osmanli Sultan entered into war against Great Britain, the British declared Egypt to be independent of Turkey and made it a British protectorate. Persian territory had involuntarily become a battlefield for Turks and Germans against Russians and British; after the war the British Minister placed a comprehensive treaty before the Persians. Its acceptance would in practice, if not formally, have meant a British protectorate over Persia. The Persian treaty, the Egyptian protectorate, the Arabian League of Nations mandates, and the Peace of Sèvres, dictated to the Turks, mark the zenith of European domination in the world of Islam. This reordering of the Near East by Britain and France produced between 1919 and 1922 a wave of violent opposition from the Moslem peoples. From then on, the western European powers were forced onto the defensive in their positions. The question of the emancipation of the Islamic world could no longer be dismissed.

STAGES OF EMANCIPATION

THE work of the peacemakers of 1919 in the Middle East received its first heavy blow in the border zone south of the Russian realm. The weakness of the Russian central administration after 1917, the year of the revolution, made itself felt in the three Moslem states of that border zone, Turkey, Persia, and Afghanistan. The Bolshevik rulers in Moscow, still weak and apprehensive of intervention from the West, sought freedom from disturbance on their southern frontier. Under those circumstances the national wave of hostility in the Orient against the Western powers—above all, Great Britain—could only be welcome to them. In 1921 treaties of friendship were concluded between Moscow and the three border states, protecting the rear on both sides. At that time Turks, Persians, and Afghans all had at their head men who, however different from one another, were far above the average: Mustafa Kemal Pasha in Turkey, Riza Khan in Persia, and Amanullah in Afghanistan. Before long both the dictated treaty of Sèvres and the Anglo-Persian treaty were overtaken by events. Neither was ever ratified. Afghanistan exchanged the quasi-protectorate of British India for the rank of an independent kingdom. The British and Russian troops evacuated the Persian territory occupied by them. The new Turkey secured in the Peace Treaty of Lausanne the recognition of her unrestricted sovereignty and her existing possessions. Five years after the end of the First World War the external emancipation of the three northern Moslem states could be regarded as substantially achieved.

In the Arab world, conditions of relative power were different from those on the border of the Russian continental mass. The Western powers had no reason to fear that the events in Russia would have serious repercussions on the Euphrates or the Nile. Only slowly, therefore, could Arab nationalism wrest from them one after another of its demands. The process of Arab emancipation has thus been long-drawn-out, and is still uncompleted. The changes in the European position of Great Britain and France were reflected more or less in the attitude of the two powers to Arab nationalism. The first phase of Arab development was taken up with the Arabs' struggle against the mandates and the Egyptians' against the protectorate. As early as 1922 Great Britain agreed to end the protectorate over Egypt, but subject to such crucial reservations that Egyptian independence remained for the time purely formal. Anglo-Egyptian negotiations for the evacuation of the Nile valley and the Sudan have dragged on like a red thread through thirty years of Egyptian independence.

The mandate system in Arab Asia Minor met from the first with the most violent opposition, because the Arabs saw in it nothing but a camouflaged form of colonial rule. Only in Iraq did developments proceed more or less in harmony with the original conception of trusteeship. After several failures, in 1932 the League mandate was superseded by an Anglo-Iraqi treaty of alliance. Similar changes were under preparation in the latter half of the 1930's in the Levant states under French mandate. Owing, however, to opposition from the Right-wing politicians and the military in Paris, the treaties prepared with Syria and the Lebanon were not ratified by the French Parliament. The arrangement for

Palestine led in the years that followed to the bitterest conflicts. The British mandataries soon found themselves faced with an impossible task if they had assumed that they would be able to reconcile the Arab aspiration for self-determination with the Jewish demand for the building of the promised national home. At the end of the thirties the Palestine mandate had already been frustrated by that incompatibility, without the least sign of any compromise between the two peoples at issue over the soil of the small country.

The term "limited independence" perhaps best describes the degree of emancipation which the Arab countries (except Palestine) either had attained by 1939 or were at least able then to hope for before long. Any idea that colonial methods could continue to be followed to preserve the influence of the western European powers in the Arab world could be dismissed. A fresh search was proceeding for a possible form of reconciliation between the Arab aspirations for independence and the interests of the Great Powers. Long-term bilateral treaties of alliance seemed to be the means best suited to the changed times. Among these are the British treaties with Iraq (1932) and Egypt (1936). The treaty with Jordan after the Second World War must be regarded as a latecomer in that system. The common feature of the bilateral treaties is that they recognize the independence of the Arab partner, but incorporate the Arab territory between Nile and Euphrates militarily and in regard to foreign relations in the realm of British world interests. Great Britain retained the right to maintain bases in war and peace in the countries concerned. The treaties drafted between France and the Levant States were drawn up on similar lines. Compared with the conditions of 1919, the bilateral treaties unquestionably show a considerable advance on the road to the complete independence of the Arabs. But it had to be realized that this was only a necessary stage and not a settlement for all time. The duration of that stage depended on many factors within and without the Arab world, factors whose development could not be foreseen at the time of the conclusion of the treaties. The simple fact that the most difficult problems, such as that of the future of the Sudan, remained outstanding gave reason to expect that the demand for revision would be unlikely to be deferred until the expiry of the treaties.

In the twenty years between the two World Wars the outlines of new Moslem national states made their appearance above the ruins of the great Oriental empires. The national revolution of the Turks released astonishing forces of reconstruction on the soil of Anatolia. Under other conditions and in other forms, whose endurance remained to be seen, Persia and Afghanistan consolidated their internal framework. In the 1930's Egypt and Iraq entered the group of independent states in the Near East. It was to be expected that these two outriders would be followed by other Arab countries. The first steps were already being taken for co-operation between the various new states, as in the four-power Pact of Saadabad, entered into by Turkey, Persia, Afghanistan, and Iraq, and in the first treaties proclaiming the Arab sense of unity. When the Second World War broke out, the Near and Middle East was already in the midst of a gradual emancipation that at least held out the possibility of satisfactory further development. The course of the war was, however, to change the relative strength of the powers so greatly that the very basis of the pre-war status of the Islamic intercontinent was destroyed.

THE HARVEST OF THE SECOND WORLD WAR

In November 1914 Mehmet V, the Osmanli Sultan-Caliph in Constantinople, unfurled the green flag of the Prophet for a "holy war," in the vain hope of being able once more to cover up the internal weaknesses of his empire. A quarter of a century later, when the world tempest broke out a second time, there was no longer anyone who could have made the same attempt with a shadow of authority. The peoples of Islam had outgrown their old shell. Everywhere among the various Moslem peoples national movements had developed a full consciousness of their interests. The war between the Great Powers thus produced a very different response among the Moslems from that of 1914. Declared partisans of one belligerent group or the other came forward, but in general there was little disposition among the Moslems to throw in their lot with either group. Nothing else, indeed, was to be expected, in spite of all the efforts to gain the favour of the Moslems made by the busy propaganda of the belligerents. Widespread and strong as the desire was to shake off the colonial domination of the British, French, and Russians, there was too much fear of merely exhanging the old masters for a new one. The great majority of the Moslems therefore preferred to look on passively and await the outcome. The Turks resisted all attempts to persuade them to abandon their neutrality. Nothing would induce them to jeopardize the existence of their national state. Afghanistan, too, successfully kept out of the conflict, a course which, indeed, was easier for that remote country to follow than for others. Egypt and Iraq showed little eagerness to bring into application their treaties of alliance with Great Britain, as that country desired. Persia carefully kept out of the conflict as long as it was possible for her to do so. In the course of the last years of the war all the independent Moslem states, with the exception of Afghanistan, declared war on the Axis Powers, but that step was taken mainly in order not to lose the opportunity of joining the United Nations.

The farther the war extended, the more difficult it became, of course, to reconcile the desire to maintain neutrality with the harsh realities. The Islamic world could not escape from the fate imposed by its geographical situation. Gradually from the foothills of the Caucasus to Indonesia and to Morocco it was brought into the events of the war. Compared with the fighting in the Islamic world between 1941 and 1943, the campaigns in the Orient in the First World War seem no more than local operations of secondary importance.

There is much truth in the statement that the great decisive occurrences of the Second World War took place in the Islamic intercontinent. The intercontinental turntable represented by the Near East was of critical importance to both of the warring coalitions. So long as the Dardanelles were closed—that is to say, until the autumn of 1944—Persia was the chief and almost the only link between the Anglo-Saxons and the Soviet Union. Five and a half million tons of Anglo-Saxon war material reached the Red Army by the roads of Persia. The history of the war has still to assess the full importance of the Persian bridge to the resistance of the Soviet front. At the conferences of Teheran, Cairo, and Yalta (a Crimean town of Turkish character), the broad lines of Allied war and post-war policy were determined. It is a geographical chance that the three conferences took place in the Islamic world; but that chance has indisputably a deeper significance. The intercontinent was in every respect much the most sensitive nerve-centre of the wartime alliance between the Anglo-Saxons and the Russians. And not only was it the region of contact between the Allies, it kept apart the European and the Far Eastern elements of the enemy coalition. Only those who were still caught in the Europe-centred thinking of the nineteenth century could fail to realize that the pledge of victory in a modern, world-wide war lay in the hands of the belligerents who had control of the intercontinent. Between the Caucasus and the Volga, and between Alexandria and Tunis, the battles were fought that were the prelude to the final defeat of the Axis Powers. Clearly it was felt in the Moslem countries—for instance, in Turkey—that the expulsion of the Axis troops from North Africa was not merely the end of an episode in a local theatre of war, but marked the turning-point in the whole war.

The first year of the war had little effect on the Islamic world. It was dominated by apprehension that the German-Soviet Treaty might give the Russians freedom of action in the Orient. That assumption was not confirmed, and the Anglo-French preparations, which led to the organization of the so-called Weygand army in the Levant and gave rise to the catchwords "Caucasus" and "Baku," soon proved purposeless. Not until Italy's entry into the war and the armistice with France did the curtain rise over the Islamic theatre of war. The Axis states now saw themselves in possession of outlets in Libya and Ethiopia. German and Italian influence could now gain ground in the French Maghrib and the countries under French mandate in the Levant. In the course of 1941 the British embarked on a series of actions to clear away this dangerous nucleus of enemy influence in the Near East. The campaign in Italian East Africa between January and May 1941 disposed, to begin with, of the threat to the Nile valley from that quarter. In Iraq the British had come into conflict with the regime of Rashid Ali el-Gailani. In April they quickly brought to an end the rule of the Arab nationalists in Baghdad and replaced in the government the elements in Iraq that were ready to collaborate with Great Britain. Soon after that, British units marched into Syria and the Lebanon with the Gaullists. The High Commissioner of the Vichy Government had to yield.

The last of these Allied cleaning-up actions concerned Persia. With the outbreak of war between Germany and Russia and the British-Russian alliance that followed, the crisis came in Persian neutrality. In August 1941, after a short exhange of notes, the outcome of which was considered unsatisfactory, British and Soviet troops occupied large parts of the country. In this way communication between Britain and the Soviet Union was established and safeguarded. The entry into Persia ended the first round of the struggle for the central regions of the Islamic world. The Allies had removed the threat to their rear: the Axis Powers had been preparing a great pincers movement from Libya and the Caucasus front. The extreme south-east of the Moslem world also began to hear the sounds of war when at the turn of 1941–2 the Japanese started their offensive against the East Indies.

The year 1942 marked the climax of the great battle for the intercontinent. The Japanese quickly conquered Malaya and Indonesia, and within a short time one fifth of the Moslem world witnessed the collapse of European colonial rule. In the western part of the intercontinent the enemy armies began the fight for the Caucasus and the Nile valley. In late autumn the Allies won that struggle. The turn of events came in the "Moslem theatre of war" before Stalingrad and at El Alamein and Tunis. In the summer of 1943 the last of the German and Italian forces capitulated in Tunisia, and war operations in the countries of the Moslems were ended; the fighting continued, however, till 1945 in southeast Asia.

During the last phase of the war the capitals of the Near East saw already the first signs of the revival of tension be-

tween the Anglo-Saxons and Russia. Germany's political intervention in the destiny of that region had for the second
time been no more than an episode. Before and in both
World Wars it had brought British and Russians together.
After it had been ended, the rivalry between the continental
and the maritime world power, due to their permanent interests, resumed its place as the factor destined to exercise
in the long run the most enduring influence over the intercontinent. From 1943 onward the signs multiplied that the
Russians considered that the time was drawing near for the
resumption of old demands along their southern frontier.
Northern Persia, the Caucasian border, and the Straits were
brought up for discussion by the Soviet diplomats while the
war was still going on against Germany and Japan. The act-
ing Soviet Commissar for Foreign Affairs came to Teheran
with the demand for a north Persian oil concession. In Moscow Molotov informed the Turkish Ambassador that the
Russo-Turkish treaty of friendship of 1925 no longer corresponded to the "changed international situation." Those were
the last big events in the Near East in the chronicle of the
Second World War.

At the end of the war the Moslems were able to present
some bills to the Allies. To begin with, there were demands
of a general nature. The Allies had outlined their war aims
in the Atlantic Charter of April 14, 1941. Article Three admitted the right of all peoples to choose the form of government under which they wished to live. In wide circles of
the Islamic world this fresh confirmation of the right of
self-determination of peoples aroused hopes similar to those
raised twenty-five years earlier by President Wilson's Four-
teen Points. While the Atlantic Charter only proclaimed general principles, it certainly gave a considerable stimulus to
the aspiration of the Orient to independence.

In addition, however, to the formal but not binding Atlantic Charter, there were entirely concrete promises made in the war years by Britain and France. After the entry of the British and French troops into the mandated territories of the Levant in the summer of 1941, General Catroux issued in the name of the Free French a proclamation to the inhabitants in which he stated that he had come to make an end of the mandate regime and to bring freedom and independence to Syria and the Lebanon. The French were dilatory in the fulfilment of that promise, but in the autumn of 1943 national governments took charge in Damascus and Beirut. In 1946 the last Franco-British contingents withdrew. They left behind them two new independent Arab states.

In the peace treaty of 1947 Italy had to give up her African colonies. The end of the Italian colonial empire did not fail to make an impression on the Moslems of North Africa, especially after the General Assemly of the United Nations accorded independence to Arab Libya. A wartime promise played a part also in the long-debated decision on the Italian colonies: the British Government had given the Senussi of Cyrenaica a binding assurance that their country would not be placed again under Italian rule. In the creation of the United States of Indonesia much the largest part of the Moslems of south-east Asia gained their independence—one more event inseparable from the outcome of the Second World War. But all else was thrown into the shade by the development that followed the British promise to give India the status of an independent dominion. The result was not only the birth of Pakistan, the greatest Moslem state, but the invalidation of the principle of the security of India in British world policy: that principle, which had ruled the destinies of the Islamic world for two centuries, became meaningless when the British left India in 1947.

It may be maintained that the First World War gave the peoples of Islam the first signal for their emancipation, but nevertheless left the European hegemony virtually untouched. In the interwar period the issue between "imperialism" and "nationalism" remained mainly an internal affair of the colonial powers, a secondary issue in high policy. The Western powers had no need to fear that the process of emancipation would pass out of their control. As late as the summer of 1939 no one would have dreamed of denying that it was a long and undefined road that led to the independence of the Islamic world. The Second World War fundamentally altered the international position of the Moslem countries. Until 1939 the independent regions were isolated dots on the map of world Islam; ten years later the situation was reversed. Today the dependent countries are confined to a few regions of retreat. During and after the Second World War roughly forty per cent of the Moslems of the whole world exchanged dependence on Europe for independence.

The United Nations have given general recognition to the principle of the self-determination of peoples. Thus the emancipation of the colonial peoples has more or less been legalized. Anyone who raises objections to it in the future, whether rightly or wrongly, will run the risk of setting himself in an evil light before world opinion. Anti-colonialism is often described as an expression of the *Zeitgeist,* of contemporary opinion. It is not only that. The change of principle is, in fact, also a sign of a change of relative power. After the severe blood-letting of the Second World War, the western European powers no longer have the strength to control and guide the development of the Islamic peoples. They no longer have the material strength, and often they no longer have the political elasticity needed. That explains why the many attempts to continue an Eastern policy in the old style have been fruitless. Henceforth the power of the West depends primarily on the military and economic strength of the United States, whose relations as a world power with the peoples of Islam are still tentative. The age of the balance of world power between the Atlantic and Eurasian centres of power opens new perspectives for the peoples of Islam. Between the obstinate tenacity of the old and the painful ripening of the new, a flickering light comes from the Crescent.

Part Two

NATIONS
IN
FERMENT

CHAPTER FIVE

Disappointed Arab Hopes

SECRET SOCIETIES IN SYRIA

ARAB nationalism began with the Arabic book. Seldom has the printing press done such obvious and thoroughgoing pioneer work in arousing national consciousness as in the Arab world. During the centuries of subjection that followed the Osmanli conquest, the Arabs had neglected and almost forgotten one of their greatest intellectual creations, the Arab literary language. The various dialects were overgrowing the common heritage of the language of the Koran. Literary Arabic remained at the stage of the Islamic Middle Ages and seemed to be destined to a similar fate to that of Latin in the Roman world. In consequence the Arabs had gradually lost active association with the intellectual heritage of their age of glory. Indifferent to their great past, the various Arabic-speaking countries lived on in provincial narrowness. They might feel themselves to be Moslems or Christians, Druses or Shi'is, but

not Arabs. The beginning of the revival of the Arabic written language was made when modern printing presses in
Constantinople and Cairo, about a hundred and fifty years
ago, issued the first Arabic books.

But it was the work of missions from the West that
brought to fruition on the soil of Syria the seed of a
modern national consciousness. If we seek the birthplace
of Arab modernism we must go to Syria. By this is meant
not only the territory of the present Republic of Syria, but
the wider geographical term the name implies, including
all the country from the slopes of the Taurus Mountains in
the north to the Sinai peninsula. The countries of the
Levant, along the east coast of the Mediterranean, had
never entirely lost contact with the West, if only because
the Arab Christian communities of Syria were concerned to
keep the support of the Great Powers of Europe. Especially
the small Christian community of the Maronites in the
Lebanon, which had been united since the Middle Ages
with the Roman Church, was traditionally associated with
Catholic Europe. French orders, among them Jesuits, concerned themselves with the cultivation of relations with the
Maronites.

There also came to Beirut in 1820 from the mission sta-
tion in Malta the first emissaries of American Protestantism.
There were narrow limits to missionary success in a country that had been firmly won to Islam. Much greater was the
influence of the new arrivals on the general development of
the Arab mind. The Americans took with them to Beirut a
printing press; they printed Arabic schoolbooks, and in the
course of a few decades they built a considerable number
of schools, with about one thousand Arab pupils. In 1866
they ventured on the important step of the opening of a
university college. The Syrian Protestant College, which
later grew into the American University of Beirut, may

claim to have been the first of the modern universities in the Arab East. A few years after the Americans, the Jesuits went to work. The stern, solid building of the Université du S. Joseph in Beirut is their achievement. At these two universities in the Lebanese port a large part of the intellectual elite of the Arab countries are educated as doctors or lawyers, technicians or civil servants.

The first pupils of the foreign missionaries were naturally almost all Christian Arabs. The Moslems held aloof at first from the schools of the Christian aliens. Gradually, however, a reluctant realization of common Arab interests was able to bridge over the gulf between the separate religious communities of Syria. Soon Moslems and Christians were united in the groups in which the young Arab intellectuals studied and discussed the ideas that were pouring in from the West. This was something unique, and so it was probably felt to be by contemporaries. The literary gatherings in Beirut brought a romantic enlightenment and aroused a sense of the earlier greatness of the Arabs. People began to speak of the yoke of the alien Turkish rule, and eloquent poems were recited behind closed doors when friends met together in the evening. "Up, ye Arabs, and awake!"—this verse from the early days of Arab nationalism gave its name to the rising of the Arab peoples. The only way the Arab dreamers of freedom and independence could evade the vigilance of the Turkish authorities was by the formation of secret societies. In 1875 five students of the Syrian Protestant College joined together in the first secret society, concerned not only with literary discussion but with political aims. Posters were drawn up in denunciation of "Turkish tyranny," and supporters were sought in the big cities of Syria. But the police of Sultan Abdul Hamid made life so difficult for the Arab conspirators and so severely restricted their intellectual freedom that many of the Syrian

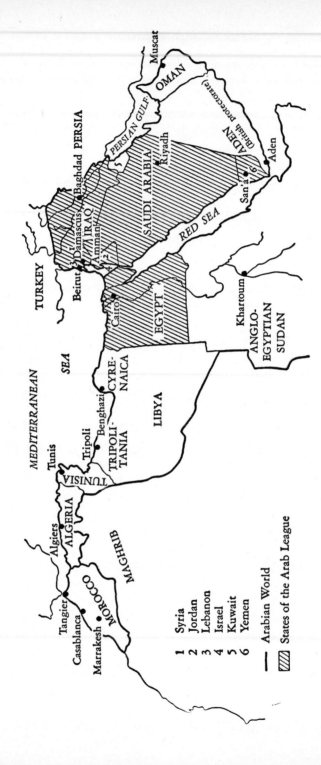

Muscat

OMAN

PERSIAN GULF

PERSIA
Baghdad

Riyadh

SAUDI ARABIA

ADEN
(British protectorate)

Aden

San'a

6

Damascus
Beirut
IRAQ
5
Amman
2
1
4

RED SEA

TURKEY

EGYPT

Khartoum

ANGLO-
EGYPTIAN
SUDAN

Cairo

CYRE-
NAICA

MEDITERRANEAN

SEA

LIBYA

Benghazi

TRIPOLI-
TANIA

Tripoli

Tunis

TUNISIA

ALGERIA

Algiers

MAGHRIB

Tangier

MOROCCO

Casablanca

Marrakesh

1	Syria
2	Jordan
3	Lebanon
4	Israel
5	Kuwait
6	Yemen

—— Arabian World

▨▨ States of the Arab League

2: THE ARAB WORLD

intelligentsia decided to go to Egypt, where they were no longer within the Sultan's reach. These Syrian émigrés founded great Arabic newspapers and periodicals and contributed a great deal to Cairo's becoming in Abdul Hamid's time the place of shelter for the Arab renaissance. The Takla brothers published the *Ahram,* which has become the leading Arabic newspaper in the world. Faris Nimr started another important newspaper, *Al Muqattam,* and to this day Syrians fill an important place in publishing in the Egyptian capital, which means that they exercise no small influence on public opinion throughout the Arab world.

At first the Arabs gave an enthusiastic welcome to the Young Turk Revolution in 1908, which made an end of the absolute rule of the sultan and introduced constitutional government. The Arabs, who made up half of the population of the Ottoman Empire, hoped for a certain measure of autonomy. At first all seemed to be going well, but bitter disappointment soon followed, and a breach between the Young Turks in Constantinople and the Arab nationalists became inevitable. By then, however, the Arab national movement had ramified so extensively that the police were no longer able to cope with it. New secret societies, much more powerful than the first effort in 1875, gathered together the active elements of the young nationalism. Three of these organizations paved the way for the later independence. Their external characteristics were always the same. The membership was kept within narrow limits; admission was granted only under the most rigid precautions. The great families of the Syrian towns and the Arab corps of officers of the Ottoman army filled the lists of the nationalist secret societies. Most of the names appeared again and again in subsequent decades, at first as adversaries of the Turks, later as opponents of British and French domination. We find the Arslan family of the Druses, the Nashashibi and the Abdulhadi of Palestine, the Aslai and Mardam of Damascus, a Nuri es-Said of Iraq, and many others who later became well known.

Al-Kahtaniya, the oldest of the three principal secret societies, dates from 1909. The name itself clearly shows the national spirit of this organization; for the choice of Kahtan, a legendary ancestor of the Arabs, was intended to be a link with early Arab history. The head of the society was an Egyptian by birth, Major Aziz Ali el-Masri. This officer had taken an active part in the Young Turk Revolution, and he long remained convinced that the continuance of the Ottoman Empire was the best solution for the Arabs so long as the Constantinople Government showed readiness to accord self-government to the various peoples of the empire. The program of the Kahtaniya therefore contained the demand that the Ottoman Empire should be converted into a Turkish-Arab dual monarchy. In the original view of the men round Major el-Masri, Arabs and Turks were to remain united through the personal link of the ruler. Only when Aziz el-Masri was driven to the view that there was no prospect of this did his ideas change to a more drastic Arab nationalism. He thought of trying to win over the Arab officers of the Ottoman army to his plans.

At the beginning of 1914 a secret association of officers was founded under the name El-Ahd ("The League"). The Iraqi element among the officers of Arab origin was particularly strongly represented, and one of the consequences of the founding of the Ahd was therefore that Iraq, which until then had had little part in the Arab awakening, was drawn into increased participation in the effort of the nationalists. Branches of the Ahd were formed in Baghdad and Mosul. This activity in Arab circles did not remain entirely unknown to the Turks, and Major Aziz el-Masri was arrested and kept in prison for a time by the Turkish police. This did not end the political career of Aziz el-Masri as an Egyptian-Arab nationalist. Shortly before the outbreak of the Second World War he found himself placed at the head of the Egyptian General Staff. This time he had to yield to the mistrust of the British, who secured his dismissal in Cairo. After the seizure of power by General Naguib, Aziz el-Masri, now an old man, made his appearance once more.

The most enduring influence on the national movement has been that of the civil secret society of the Young Arabs (El-Fatat). In 1911 it was started by some Arab students in Paris. At first the French capital remained the headquarters of this nationalist association; later it was transferred to Syria. The Young Arabs were recruited mainly from the leading Moslem families of Syria. The earlier secret society, the Kahtaniya, was brought to an end by the treachery of one of its members; El-Ahd, the officers' association, was confined to a relatively small circle; but the men of the Fatat were able in the critical years 1914–15 to transfer the policy of Arab nationalism from academic discussion to practical activity.

For a long time opinion was sharply divided among the Arab nationalists as to their attitude to the Turks and the Ottoman Empire. Although the Arabs were strongly opposed to the centralism of the Constantinople Government, many of them at first would not hear of the extreme step of the complete dissolution of the empire. But developments quickly and irrevocably made the idea of Arab autonomy out of date. When the Sultan entered the war on the side of the Central Powers, the leaders of the Arab national movement were already resolved to work for the complete independence of the Arabs. In this situation the enemies of the Ottoman Empire were the natural allies of the Arab nationalists.

THE DREAM OF THE ARABIAN KINGDOM

ONE day in May 1915 there took place in Damascus a strictly secret meeting. It was attended by members of the secret societies El-Fatat and El-Ahd and by the thirty-year-old Emir Faisal, the second son of the Sherif of Mecca. It was wartime, and the Turkish authorities, who were watchful in Syria, must not under any circumstances be allowed to discover what was being discussed between the nationalists and the Sherif's envoy. Some years before the outbreak of war the Turks had conferred on the ambitious Hashimi Hussein the dignity of Sherif of Mecca, though there had always been in Constantinople a little distrust of this man's intentions. The office of administrator of the Holy Places of Islam gave its holder, the Sherif, no great material power; but it conferred on him a degree of authority among the Arabs, and among Moslems in general, which an able man with political ambitions could turn to account. Hussein's intention was to use his office to further a policy that would place the Hashimi house at the head of the Arab national movement. His romantic conception of a great Arab kingdom, of which he dreamed as a descendant of the Prophet, had only a superficial relationship with the motives of the nationalism that had grown up in the cities of Syria. But the two had virtually the same course before them.

For his plans the Sherif needed an ally among the Great Powers. He sought and found one in the British representative in Cairo. There had been some contact between the

Sherif and the British before the war, and the state of war between Britain and Turkey brought Hussein his great opportunity sooner, perhaps, than had been expected in Mecca. Before entering into a formal alliance with the British, the Sherif wanted to make sure that the nationalists

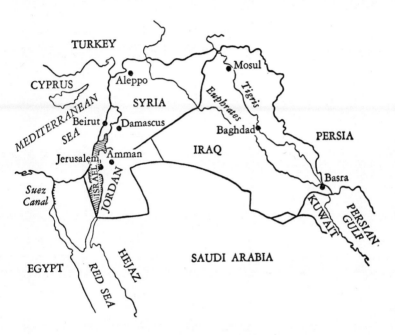

3: THE "FERTILE CRESCENT"

in Damascus were ready to move with him, and to learn what conditions they would put forward. Emir Faisal's task was to ascertain this and to secure agreement on common action. There was careful consideration in Damascus of the risks involved in open resistance to the Turks and co-operation with Great Britain. The Arabs' conditions were laid down in a comprehensive protocol, which one of Faisal's staff took safely to Mecca through the Turkish lines, sewn into his shoes. The Damascus Protocol may still claim to be of interest, because it shows the original aims of the Arab nationalist movement in a light that later developments have in many respects obscured. As the condition for a military alliance with Great Britain, the protocol demanded the guarantee of Arab independence between the Mediterranean and the Persian Gulf and from the northern frontier of Syria to the Indian Ocean. On that basis, found in Damascus, Sherif Hussein negotiated for six months with the British High Commissioner in Egypt, Sir Arthur Henry McMahon. Apart from some reservations in regard to the frontier, the latter formally declared his government's readiness to recognize and guarantee an independent Arabian state. The Sherif regarded these assurances as adequate and openly went over to the British side. In the summer of 1916 he gave the signal for the "Arab rising" on the flank of the Syrian front. In October 1918 the collapse of the German and Turkish armies gave the Emir Faisal admittance to the ancient caliphs' city of Damascus. Arab independence and unity seemed to be within reach. But Faisal's government in Damascus, the first high point of Arab nationalism, was only shortlived. Great Britain's commitments to her European allies outweighed the alliance with the Arabs in the scales of world policy. In face of the hopes of independence the League of Nations mandates of the Western powers brought bitter disappointment, and instead of union came partition into three mandated territories, Palestine, Syria and Lebanon, and Iraq.

The events connected with the Arab rising made so deep and so lasting an impression on the character of Arab nationalism that it is difficult to understand present-day conditions without a knowledge of those events. The Arab nationalists felt that they had been robbed of the reward for their alliance with Great Britain. The disappointment was so great that Arab nationalism became filled with bitterness against its original ally. The seed was then sown of complications and conflicts whose continued effect has kept the Arabian countries disgruntled, even now that the mandates belong entirely to the past, and independent Arab states have taken their place.

The Sherif Hussein died, an embittered man, in exile. The house of the Hashimis held fast to the ideas of the aged Hussein regarding the claim to the throne of a great Arabian kingdom as an unwritten law of the dynasty. Hussein's sons, Faisal in Iraq and Abdullah on the banks of the Jordan, followed in their father's footsteps. When Iraq attained independent statehood, first among the mandated states, it was regarded as the hoped-for Piedmont of Arab unity. Faisal died unexpectedly in 1934 and was widely mourned by the Arabs. The leadership of the Hashimis passed then to Abdullah. The ruler of Jordan steadily pursued the plan of a great Hashimi kingdom as long as he lived. It is true that Abdullah had not the prestige of his younger brother. Tirelessly but in vain he pursued from his palace in Amman his ambition for a Greater Arabia. Shortly before his death he was working for a union of Jordan and Iraq. He was assassinated in Jerusalem in July 1951, on the steps of the Mosque of Omar; the house of the Hashimis was then left without a leader of recognized authority. In the next generation the political ideas of the Hashimis changed. Two of Hussein's grandsons, King Ghazi in Iraq and King Talal in Jordan, came closer to the Arab nationalism of their time than to the dynastic ideas of their forefathers. Both of them reigned only for a short time. What path the new generation, the great-grandsons of the old Sherif, may pursue is hidden in the mystery of the Arab future.

The Hashimis meet with the keenest opposition in the very place where they found their first ally, Damascus. The old capital of the caliphs regarded itself as the predestined administrator of Arab unity, and the foremost families of the Syrian cities have claimed since the days of the Young Arabs the right of primacy in the Arab awakening. In the eyes of the Syrian notables Iraq was not the legitimate leader of the Arabs, and still less so was the poor state on the east bank of the Jordan. It was always difficult for the oligarchical pride of the great Syrian families to endure the idea of subordination to the Hashimi immigrants from the Hejaz. It is—or was—an Arab tradition to regard politics as a family affair. And that spirit was better served by the republican form of state than it could have been by a Hashimi monarchy. Damascus has therefore always been hostile to the Hashimi schemes. It was not without natural allies. Lebanon, a republic of wealthy merchant families, in which Christians and Moslems have settled down together, had little liking for the propaganda for a great Arab state, fearing a disturbance of the balance between Christians and Moslems. King Ibn Sa'ud, however, has given unwavering support to the Syrian republicans. There is a long-standing feud between the Hashimis and the al-Sa'ud family. Hussein and his sons never forgave the desert King for forcibly ejecting them from their ancestral homeland, the Hejaz. It was therefore not in the least in King Ibn Sa'ud's interest that the Hashimis should increase their power and perhaps be placed in a position to become a danger to his rule over the Arabian peninsula.

The negotiations as to the form of Arab union, carried on between the Hashimis on one side and Damascus and King

Ibn Sa'ud on the other, frequently pursued intricate paths. They become still further complicated by the fact that, quite apart from the interests of the Great Powers, they are affected by the internal struggle for power within the various Arab states, the deeper causes of which are to be sought in social changes and in the succession of generations. During the struggle for independence attention was generally diverted from internal problems. When, however, one state after another gained independence, the landowning oligarchy found its power threatened by the demand for constitutional and social reform. The example of their near neighbour Kemalist Turkey was not lost on the Arab peoples. The young intelligentsia, and such commercial middle classes as had been formed, had other ideas to put forward than those of the Young Turks and of the Arab rising. In the army, too, discontent with the existing system and opposition to it were voiced. It was in Iraq, the first of the states of the "Fertile Crescent" to gain independence, that the first murmurs of discontent grew loud and insistent. In 1936 a part of the army, in league with ardent reformist politicians, carried out a *coup d'état*. The political leader of the enterprise, Hikmet Sulaiman, obviously had a Turkish background. He was the brother of Mahmud Shevket Pasha, who had come into prominence in the Young Turk Revolution of 1908-9; he was then a Turkish army-corps commander in Macedonia. The rule of the new men in Baghdad was shortlived. Before they had had any chance to carry their ideas into practice, they had to make way again for the old political leaders.

It is generally considered today that this *coup d'état*, isolated at the time, was a first sign that the Arab peoples were approaching a turning-point in their development. The old guard of Arab nationalism were closely bound up with the conservative feudal order, which put up a determined defence of the privileges of the great landowning families and clung to power behind a façade of parliamentary constitutionalism. Thus there was produced an outward show of democracy, with a total lack of the reality that the peoples of western Europe had won after centuries of violent internal struggle. It was a clay-footed pasha-democracy, and one thrust was enough to expose its fragility. The thrust came in the end from the Arabs' defeat in the struggle for Palestine.

What produced the struggle for Palestine, the shadow of which threatens to cast a gloom over the Near East for a long time to come? Its early international history lies beyond the limits of the Islamic world. So far as the Arabs are concerned, it takes us back to the old Sherif of Mecca. "The portions of Syria lying to the west of the districts of Damascus, Homs, Hama, and Aleppo cannot be said to be purely Arab, and must therefore be excluded from the proposed limits and boundaries" of the future Arab State. So ran one of the main sentences in the note sent by the British High Commissioner, Sir Henry McMahon, to the Sherif on October 24, 1915. At that time Sir Henry's formulation, not a masterpiece of geographical precision, aimed only at taking account of French interests on the Levant coast. A fatal circumstance, however, was that later Palestine was brought into the controversial issue over the interpretation of the sentence, the question what was to be understood by "portions of Syria lying to the west of" the districts named. The Arabs held, in good faith, that Palestine was a geographical but not a political or administrative term; that it was therefore not covered by the reservation in the British note; and that consequently it belonged to the Arab territory whose independence was promised. Great, therefore, was the Arab surprise and agitation when it was later discovered that, in its assurance of a Jewish national home, the British Government had entered into a second obligation in respect of Palestine. The Arab nationalists were concerned for the inviolability of the state assured to them. They felt no hostility to the Jews; for a long time Zionist settlers had been living peacefully in the midst of the Arab population of Palestine and had won esteem. At the end of the First World War they formed some ten per cent of the total population. At that time an understanding between Arabs and Zionists did not seem unattainable. Emir Faisal met the Zionist leader, Chaim Weizmann, who assured him that the Jews had no intention of setting up a state of their own on the soil of Palestine. Ultimately Faisal consented to sign an agreement laid before him, in which, in the name of the Arab national movement, he recognized the Zionist effort for a Jewish home. The Emir added, in his own hand, that the condition for this was the fulfilment of the promise of union and independence made to the Arabs. As that condition was not fulfilled, the agreement between Faisal and Weizmann remained a dead letter. The world of today has almost forgotten that.

Two peoples were laying claim to the soil of Palestine. An elemental conflict of that sort contains its own dynamism. Jewish and Arab nationalism came into collision in the narrow strip of land between the Jordan and the Mediterranean, until any sort of reconciliation was beyond the bounds of the possible. This is not the place for a detailed account of the decades of this dispute—the first Arab-Jewish clashes, the great Jewish wave of immigration that followed the Nazi seizure of power in central Europe, the Arab rising at the end of the thirties, the Biltmore program of 1942, in which the Zionists announced the demand for a sovereign Jewish state, the withdrawal of the British occupying force, and finally the military decision between Jews and Arabs in the summer of 1948. The birth of the state of Israel was marked by armistice agreements and by no genuine peace. The Arabs and the new state in their midst face each other in armed suspicion.

The defeat of the Arab peoples was a pitiless revelation of their weakness. The external marks left by the Palestine war were deep enough. As a result of it seven to eight hundred thousand Palestine Arabs, some three quarters of the Arab population of the mandated territory, were made homeless. The refugee problem is a heavy burden on the political and economic system of Israel's Arab neighbours. But that is not all that has resulted from the events of 1948. Thoughtful Arabs set themselves to learn the moral of what had happened, and came to a devestating verdict on the ruling class of the Arab states. The Arab armies that had fought in Palestine returned with the feeling that the incapacity of the Arab governments had been the decisive factor in the defeat. The determination to change all that spread among the officers. The storm broke in Syria. The *coup d'état* of Colonel Husni el-Zaim in March 1949 shook the dominance of the conservative feudal oligarchy of Damascus.

Husni el-Zaim was but a precursor. His regime lasted no longer than six months. A succession of military coups followed in Syria, and issues between the Arab states were fought out on the soil of the Syrian Republic. At first the strong man of the Syrian army, Colonel Adibesh-Shishakli, remained for a long time in the background. Not until November 1951 did he go over to unconcealed military dictatorship. In July 1953 Shishakli, then forty-four years of age, held a well-organized plebiscite and secured election as President of the Republic of Syria. Shishakli incorporates the republican tendencies of the Syrian army, and this made him a vigorous opponent of the plans of the Hashimis. His declarations of policy reveal the Syrian claim to leadership in the union of the Arabs— at all events, the Arabs of the Fertile Crescent. In home policy the regime set up by the army stands for reforms which have an indisputable relationship to the Kemalism of the neighbouring Turkish Republic.

In Jordan much was changed when the kingdom no longer embraced only the desert lands east of the Jordan with their Bedouin population, but also the urban society of Arab Palestine, and in addition to that was inundated with refugees. In the Egyptian army, too, there was smouldering dissatisfaction with the irresponsibility and corruption of the ruling circles. The stone was set rolling, and the nationalism of princes and notables gave place to new forces from the depths of the Arab peoples.

FREEDOM AND UNITY FOR THE NILE VALLEY

MOHAMMED ALI, the great Viceroy and organizer, opened the way for Egypt to modern statehood, the first known to the Islamic Orient. But that powerful *condottiere* would probably have shrugged his shoulders in mystification if he had been called an Egyptian nationalist. Mohammed Ali knew nothing of any Egyptian nation. The ruling house he founded was of Balkan origin, and the upper class was a mixture from the varicoloured palette of the peoples of the Ottoman Empire, with the Turkish element strongly represented. And Egyptian nationalism could scarcely ripen in the heads of those foreigners. It came to fruition among the common people, in the villages of the fellaheen.

Ahmed Arabi was a genuine Egyptian, son of a fellah of the Nile Delta. He joined the army, and good fortune raised him to high rank in the corps of officers, which normally was closed to the sons of fellaheen. Colonel Arabi gave the signal for the first national revolution in Egypt. His aim was to end the mismanagement of affairs by the court and the foreign pashas. He was strongly supported by leading circles in the Moslem Azhar University, where in the eighties of the last century the spirit of Islamic puritanism was beginning to stir. At first the Khedive had to yield to the nationalist pressure, and reluctantly he made Colonel Arabi his Minister of War. But British military intervention saved him and the ruling class from their threatened fall. Arabi vainly resisted the British troops; he was defeated and banished in 1882 to Ceylon. "What Arabi did remains a true creation out of nothing—the Egyptian nation." That was a British verdict on the man whose attempt to give Egypt to the Egyptians led to the British occupation of the Nile valley.

The great problem for Egyptian nationalism was how to end British dominance. After 1882, indeed, even the internal development of the Egyptian nation could no longer escape the consequences of the fact that the British presence in the Nile valley was bound to affect Egypt's home policy. The arrival of the British on the scene could not but drive the nationalism of the Egyptians into other paths than those natural to the Arab countries that remained under direct Osmanli rule. The interests of the Arab national movement in Syria and of the Egyptian nationalists were divergent down to the time of the dissolution of the Ottoman Empire. The Arabs of the Fertile Crescent were driven more and more to the side of Great Britain, from whom they hoped to secure liberation from Turkish rule. Even after the British occupation, Egypt remained formally part of the Ottoman Empire. The Egyptians showed no inclination to interfere with this bond with Constantinople, however slight, because they regarded it as some sort of guarantee that the British would not finally annex Egypt. The continuance of the Ottoman Em-

Cairo • *Suez Canal*

EGYPT

Nile

RED SEA

Atbara

Khartoum •

Blue Nile

White Nile

ANGLO-
EGYPTIAN
SUDAN

Lake Tana

Sobat

BRITISH
SOMALI-
LAND

Bahr el Jebel

ETHIOPIA

SOMALILAND
(Italian Mandate)

BELGIAN CONGO

Lake Albert

Lake Kyoga

UGANDA

KENYA

Lake Edward

Lake Victoria

4: THE NILE VALLEY

pire therefore seemed to them a safeguard worth working for. In Constantinople the Egyptian nationalists sought for support, and they joined energetically in everything calculated to serve the unity of the empire and also the strengthening of the Islamic community, while they looked askance at the anti-Turkish activities of the Arabs of Syria. The most brilliant representative of that epoch in the history of Egyptian nationalism was Mustafa Kamil. He was not, like Arabi, a fellah, but an Egyptian townsman, a lawyer filled with the French spirit, a gifted tribune of the people in whose person the type of the Europeanized intellectual came into the Egyptian foreground; in speech and writing he exercised a wide influence. His early death, however, prevented the movement he started from assuming a concrete and permanent form. Mustafa Kamil's National Party (El-Hizb el-Watani) stood absolutely uncompromisingly for Egypt's national demands from Great Britain. In the shadow of the all-powerful Wafd the political heirs of Mustafa Kamil played for a long time only a very modest part. Not until the military revolution of July 1952 did the National Party emerge from its unnoticed existence. It took part in the government of Mohammed Naguib.

During the decades of British rule Great Britain's role of arbiter in Egypt was exercised in favour of the maintenance of the existing internal order. This continued to be so after 1923, when Egypt, having gained formal independence, provided herself with a Constitution. There then formed two poles of political life, the court and the Wafd. Between these stood the British, whose power remained the deciding factor behind all that happened. The first two kings of Egypt, Fuad and Farouk, clung obstinately to the absolute authority of the throne. Personal rule best corresponded to the ideas and the character of those two monarchs; they regarded the Constitution as a troublesome concession. They preferred to Parliament, whenever possible, the more or less disguised dictatorship of the "Palace." Round the Palace gathered all who were interested in the maintenance of the social *status quo*—the landowners, the wealthy bourgeoisie, and also an undesirable element, a circle of favourites whose only concern, very often, was to get rich quickly.

Against the inclinations of King Fuad to absolutism stood a tribune of the people in the person of the son of a fellah. In the Egyptian social pyramid the divisions between the classes sometimes seemed not so very watertight, and so not a few gifted men were able to rise from the poverty of the villages to join the urban intellectuals, and sometimes to go farther still. One of these self-made men was Saad Zaghlul. He had sat at the feet of a great teacher, a man filled with genuine idealism, the Islamic reformer Mohammed Abduh (himself a son of the fellaheen), and later he went to the University of Paris. The distance seemed infinite between the Islamic puritans of the Azhar and the French professors of the Sorbonne. But Zaghlul drew from both sources the same demand for the unrestricted sovereignty of the people—a double claim, because it was directed both against the alien British domination and against the arbitrary rule of the Palace. Zaghlul's prestige stood so high that in November 1918 he was made the leader of a delegation to put before the British the Egyptian claim to independence. The Arab name of this group of representatives was El-Wafd el-Misri ("The Egyptain Delegation").

The Wafd, which was to stand for the national demands of its country, felt itself to be the representative of the whole Egyptian people. Its original task was far removed from internal controversies, and men of the most varied political views belonged to the Wafd. In the years that preceded the proclamation of Egyptian independence the Wafd was led by Saad Zaghlul; that was the time of the outbreak of the second national revolution in Egypt. Not until the country started its constitutional existence did the Wafd become a political party, adding to its external concern that of a defender of the Constitution. The Wafd extended its party organization throughout the country, and its influence on the masses became and remained overwhelming. Even the many splits the party suffered in the course of time did little or nothing to injure the position of the Wafd. Saad Zaghlul, and after his death Mustafa en-Nahas, were surrounded with the nimbus of the tribune of the people. The leaders held firmly in their hands the organization of the Wafd, and therewith the background of its influence.

The Wafd watched carefully over its monopoly position in political life. It had dangerous rivals on two sides to fear. The more progress was made in the economic development of the country, the more ground was gained among the people by socialistic currents and by Islamic puritanism. It was impossible, however, for Left-wing parties to form, because every attempt in that direction fell victim, rightly or wrongly, to the suspicion of Communism. On the other side the mass organization of the Moslem Brotherhood took no part in the elections. So long as this continued, the Wafd party had no cause for serious anxiety about its monopoly. It should be mentioned, however, that the electoral system makes the parliamentary strength of the Wafd seem greater than its voting strength warrants. Thus in the elections of January 1950 the Wafd received nearly seventy per cent of the seats, but only forty-five per cent of the votes cast; it should also be mentioned that only three fifths of the electorate went to the polls. In Cairo only fifteen per cent of the electors voted, and almost every vote went to the Wafd.

King and Wafd eyed each other in hostility for just a generation. Apart from these two forces there were no political factors of any importance in Egypt itself. Sometimes the

British supported the Palace, sometimes they encouraged the Wafd, and their opinion as to which of the two was the better partner changed again and again. Surveying the epoch between 1923 and 1952, we find that Egypt was governed considerably longer by the Palace than by the Wafd. The various periods of Wafd government came to a total of only eight years. King Fuad and his son Farouk tried again and again to break the power of the Wafd. Each time, however, they were forced to recognize the hopelessness of the attempt.

The Wafd began its rise as a genuine popular movement. The reputation built up for the party by the incorruptible tribune Saad Zaghlul remained unsoiled among the masses. But as time passed, many of the Wafd leaders were caught in the network of corruption spread from the Palace over the ruling class. In spite of their rivalry for power, in the end the pashas of the Palace and the great Wafd pashas came to terms on the basis of the social order made up of feudalism and plutocracy. This became particularly evident at the time of the Wafd Cabinets of 1950–2. In both camps of Egyptian politics powerful financial interests were at work to preserve inviolate the possessions and privileges of the small upper class that had its rendezvous in the Mohammed Ali Club. The reformist Left wing of the Wafd Party was as entirely unrepresented as the more far-seeing politicians in Palace quarters who seriously thought of carrying out internal reforms. Thus in the end the leaders of the Wafd were associated with the destiny of a short-sighted upper class that was obstinately refusing to open the sluices for social advance as a measure of prudence. The Palace and the Wafd leadership shared the fruits of Egypt's *ancien régime.* Three great unknown elements held aloof: the Left of all shades (including members within the Wafd), the puritan Moslem Brothers, and the army, which since Arabi's revolution had been politically submerged.

The ground had already become uncomfortably hot under the pasha democracy when in October 1951 the Wafd Government under Mustafa en-Nahas denounced the treaties with Great Britain, not only deliberately emphasizing Egypt's decades-old national demands but also unwittingly undermining the foundations of the existing order. The fire in the streets of Cairo in January 1952 contained a grave warning that the fragile edifice of the regime was tottering. The King merely took the opportunity to dismiss the unwelcome Wafd from the government: he drew no further conclusions. But the days were counted for the Palace too.

In the spring and summer of 1952 Cairo was like a smouldering volcano. The tension was finally ended by the army. Exactly seventy years earlier Colonel Ahmed Arabi had taken the first—unsuccessful—step toward an Egyptian renascence. With the founding of the Wafd after the First World War a second and this time much broader wave of national feeling had swept over Egypt. It had carried the country a good way on toward complete independence and had then been followed by stagnation. The regime it had set up lacked the will for internal reforms and for the pursuit of realistic aims in foreign policy. It achieved nothing, caught between demagogy and reaction. It may be that the ruling powers calculated that the British, after all, would continue to protect the *status quo* in Egypt. They had rescued the Khedive's throne and the privileges of the upper class from Arabi's revolution. But in 1952 history did not repeat itself. The British garrison by the Suez Canal remained in barracks when General Mohammed Naguib suddenly changed the face of Egypt. The future will tell whether the 23rd of July 1952 did not bring the most critical change in the affairs of Egypt since the British landing in the Delta.

The coup of July 23 developed its own dynamism. At first the army was ready to give the old parties a chance, but the parties were unable to escape from the domination of the ruling cliques. If the regime overthrown was to be effectively denied any chance of restoration, there was virtually no alternative to the assumption of power, at least during a transition period, by General Naguib and the revolutionary officers, with the support of the army and almost unanimous popular approval. The deposition of King Farouk removed the political influence of the Palace. An agrarian reform was directed against the power of the oligarchy of the pashas. Finally the first phase of the revolution was ended by the proclamation of the Republic in June 1953.

The new Egypt was ruled by a committee of twelve—the general and eleven officers. It adopted the official title of "Council of the Revolution." These officers had been brought together in the course of years, and were still held together, by the spirit of a patriotic conspiracy. Signs of political discontent in the corps of officers may be traced back to the time of the Second World War. It was due at that time to resentment of British power and British activities. *Warning to Imperialism* was the title of the first secret circular, dated 1945. The movement began to advocate definite reforms only when the Palestine campaign of 1948 demonstrated to the army the irresponsibility and corruption of the ruling cliques. From then on there was a settled conviction that there could be no prospect of the liberation of Egypt until the regime associated with the name of Farouk was brought down and the people freed from a corrupt ruling class. To prepare the way for this, a committee of five young officers was formed; their number was later increased to nine. These were the "Free Officers" (ed-Dubat el-Ahrar). They entered secretly into contact with persons within and without the army, and they also made use of secret circulars. But too much must not be made of the activities of the "Free Officers." Farouk's police knew about them, but took no action for a long time. In

the summer of 1952 Farouk's action against them was im-
minent. The conspirators felt that they must act. It may be
that they were surprised at the rapid success of their coup.
The "Free Officers" became the masters of Egypt literally in
a single night.

The eleven officers of the Council are young—very young
for the duties that have fallen to them. Most of them are in
the thirties. Nine of them took part in the *Putsch* of July 23;
two joined them later. General Mohammed Naguib supplied
what was lacking to the young and rather inexperienced officers—maturity, and his popularity. Naguib was born in
1901 in Khartoum. His father had been an officer with the
Egyptian troops who some years earlier, under Kitchener,
had broken the rule of the Mahdi in the Sudan. As a boy
Naguib was at school in Khartoum. He studied for a commission in the army, and found time also to study civil and
constitutional law and to gain a knowledge of some foreign
languages. There is little else to tell of the career of Mohammed Naguib as an officer until the war in Palestine in
1948. From that time, at all events, he was known as an outspoken critic of the ruling powers in Cairo. Naguib's actual
position in the Council of the Revolution is not easy to
divine. To outside observers, and especially to foreigners,
he stands for the new Egypt. Most of the resolutions of the
Council are adopted after free discussion. But certainly not
all of the twelve members carry the same weight in the Council. Lieutenant Colonel Gamal Abd-en-Nassir is described
as the second man in the regime, the next after Naguib. He
was the actual leader of the "Free Officers" and the organizer
of the *coup d'état*. Both laicist social reformers and the
Moslem Brotherhood seem to have friends on the Council of
the Revolution.

With the seizure of power by the army the actual substance
of the Egyptian people seems at last to have broken through

the social surface that overlay it. The old upper class of the state of the khedives and the kingdom was largely alien—Turkish, Balkan, Levantine. The dynasty, too, was alien; it had only an imperfect knowledge of Arabic, the language of the people. For some generations the real Egyptian element has worked its way up in greater numbers to important positions in politics, in trade and industry, and in intellectual life. From that element came Saad Zaghlul and Mustafa en-Nahas, the two Wafd leaders; Mohammed Abduh, the great reformer and theologian of Islam; and some of the leaders in trade and industry. But at first these were isolated cases, though their numbers grew as time passed.

The army, perhaps with the exception of the highest ranks, has always been an embodiment of the pure Eyptian race, recruited from the fellaheen. The urban element, largely alien, is hardly represented in it. One need only compare the heads of the Council of the Revolution with any ordinary upper-class people of Cairo, such as are still to be met in the upper ranks of the civil service and in business. At every step one meets among the officers figures that would look well among those of the ancient Egyptian frescoes of Thebes or among the statues of the age of the Pharaohs. The racial characteristics have been preserved for thousands of years in the villages of the Nile valley. Most of the officers come from the countryside, from the villages. Naguib's family, a typical officer's family, came from a village in the Delta. Gamal Abd-en-Nassir's home is in remote Upper Egypt. These people may not have actually come from among the fellaheen, but rather from the provincial middle classes, but they have at all events been in close contact with the daily life of the fellah. The emergence of the Egyptian element is something quite new. The Nile valley has been ruled since the end of the age of the Pharaohs by aliens—Persians, Greeks, and Romans, Arab caliphs and Turkish mercenaries, and finally by Europeans. The foreign element remained in the big cities, in Cairo and Alexandria. The country districts remained passive for two thousand years. Now, ostentatiously, the regime in Egypt is autochthonous. The rooting of the revolution in the villages is a hopeful factor, though also a good deal of an unknown quantity. Time will show what it is able to do for the forming of the "Egyptian nation."

Under Kings Fuad and Farouk the court, the landowners, and a new commercial and industrial element in the great cities formed a closely interwoven upper class. This numerically insignificant group controlled the bulk of the means of production both in agriculture and in the young industries. The political parties were the creatures of this upper class. The rapidly growing lower middle class, clerks and officials, professional men and traders, and the small class of the better-situated fellaheen, had very little to say in regard to the activities of those parties; still less had the great mass of peasants and workmen, who cast their votes reluctantly and impotently under the broad cloak of the Wafd or under the religious radicalism of the Moslem Brotherhood. The July Revolution gave freer play to the oppressed elements. An immense process of ideological fermentation has been started. Its ideas range from a new Caliphate to a Workers' and Peasants' Republic.

It is natural to draw comparisons with the revolution of the Young Turks and the work of Mustafa Kemal Ataturk. Many aspects of the outward events suggest an Egyptian repetition of what happened in Turkey a generation ago. Thoughtful Egyptians believe that events have shown that in Egypt the pendulum will not swing to ideological extremes. They do not expect either a pronounced laicism as in Turkey or the Islamic theocracy favoured by the Moslem Brotherhood. Naguib and Ataturk are two very different personalities, though it is arguable that both have had similar tasks to fulfil in the development of their peoples. The settlement between a liberal, laicist nationalism and Islam may hold dangers for Egypt. But it may just as well free the way for some new compromise. In time there may come some solution of the ideological confusion in which the whole Arab world finds itself today, a solution that may give it inward strength and stability. But that will take a good deal of time and call for a great deal of patience.

If the "Army Movement" is to have success and endure, it must follow the removal of the *ancien régime* by giving effect to the demands of Egyptian nationalism in foreign affairs, by procuring for Egypt, as Naguib put it in a mass demonstration in Cairo, "her place in the sun." Ataturk, too, would have been unable to complete the work of the Turkish renascence without freedom from foreign control.

Mukhtar, an Egyptian sculptor, has erected in Cairo a monument to the *Egyptian Awakening*. The monument shows a fellah girl with her hand on a rising Sphinx. To look at it is to be reminded that Cairo has been built under African skies. Eternal Egypt, old as the Pyramids and still with almost uncanny vitality and creativeness, speaks from Mukhtar's work. One realizes that it presents a spirit of Egyptian nationalism that remembers the Pharaohs and is protected by the sand ramparts of the deserts that closely shut in the Nile valley. It is the outward expression of a proud *noli me tangere* such as is to be found in all peoples of ancient civilization. Yet Islam and the Arab invasion long ago rejected any return to the self-complacency of the age of the Pharaohs. Egypt belongs irrevocably to the Arab-Islamic civilization; indeed, in more than one respect it is its centre. As soon as the Egyptians had recovered greater freedom of movement in foreign affairs—as happened after the Anglo-Egyptian Treaty of 1936—they turned their eyes to the Arab East. The long aloofness from Egypt's eastern Arab neighbours gradually gave place to a new approach. The young King Farouk was filled with the idea of Egypt's Arab-Islamic mission. There were fanciful plans for a new caliphate, which could not be realized, but Egypt's Arab orientation remained a lasting choice in foreign policy. Even the Wafd, to which no sort of Islamic clericalism can be attributed, adopted that line of policy. Thus Egypt prepared to take Arab nationalism under the leadership of Cairo. This was bound to have far-reaching consequences. So soon as Egypt took an interest in Arab affairs, her populousness and her economic strength were bound to make her the leader of the Arab world. As Egypt is not on the fringe but in the middle of Arab-speaking humanity, a window was suddenly opened also on the Arab countries of north-west Africa, which until then had lived apart from the main current of Arab development. As soon as Cairo was able and willing to pursue an Arab policy, the Arab national movement, whose various centres had until then been only loosely associated, grew into a solid complex, the Nile valley exercising the function of a geographical link between the eastern and western regions of the Arab world.

Egypt's national demands are as old as the British occupation. The struggle over them reaches back well over half a century into the past. There is really only one demand, in two parts: evacuation, and unity of the Nile valley. Mustafa Kamil proclaimed it as early as 1896: "When we demand the evacuation of our country by the British troops, we are demanding not only the liberation of Egypt itself, but the liberation of the whole Nile valley, because only one government can possess the Nile." Suez and Sudan are the slogans of the Egyptian nationalists. But while the Suez Canal is a world highway on the periphery of Egypt, the Sudan lies along a vital artery of the country, for whose twenty million inhabitants the water of the Nile is the arbiter of life and death.

It is true that the phrase "unity of the Nile valley" is not free from ambiguity. The geographical Nile valley embraces about a tenth of the whole African continent, and extends from the East African lakes to the Mediterranean. Five sevenths of the water carried by the river to its lower reaches come from the Abyssinian highlands, and it is from there that the fruitful Nile sediment is brought; two sevenths come from the lake region of East Africa. Before the introduction of the modern technique of water conservancy, nature controlled the river. Political problems of distribution of its water could scarcely arise then. It was the great dams of the last century that made the question of control of the distribution of the water acute. Theoretically the entire control of the Nile should extend to every region of its basin—to Kenya, Uganda, and parts of the Belgian Congo and Abyssinia. The Sudan cannot exercise full control, because, like Egypt, it is only a consumer, not a provider of the water of the river. So far-reaching a "unity of the Nile valley," tempting as it may be to modern regional planners, is beyond the range of any present-day political discussion. The problem is confined to the danger of competition between the two great consumers of the water, the twenty million Egyptians and the eight million Sudanese. Already Egypt has a surplus agrarian population of some millions. Her population is increasing by some hundreds of thousands every year. The Egyptians have therefore to extract the very utmost from the narrow strip of cultivable land on either bank of the Nile, and for that purpose they need much the largest part of the available Nile water. But the population of the Sudan is also rapidly increasing, and unlike its northern neighbour the Sudan still has large areas of cultivable land lying fallow, which could be made fruitful if there were more water. Egypt would be doomed to starvation if the Nile water was drained away by the Sudan. Thus the demand for a permanent union of the two countries of the lower Nile valley is a matter of life and death for overpopulated Egypt. What matters is the permanent character rather than the outward form of the unity sought.

After Kitchener's Anglo-Egyptian army had wrested the Sudan from the Mahdists, the country had come under a so-called Anglo-Egyptian condominium. In point of fact the Egyptian participation in the condominium grew more and more into a mere formality. The British and Egyptian views on the future of the Sudan were irreconcilable. The Wafd Government of Nahas Pasha denounced the condominium agreements in October 1951 and proclaimed Farouk "King of Egypt and the Sudan"; in doing so, it thought it could simply return to the conditions before the rising of the Mahdi and the British occupation. The claim to a continuing Egyptian sovereignty over the Sudan was based on the fact that in and after 1820 the ruling house had conquered the Sudan by arms and had established the overlordship of Egypt, or alternatively of the Ottoman Sultan. In 1841 the Sultan of Constantinople had confirmed the Egyptian Viceroy as "Governor of Nubia, Sennar, Kordofan, and Darfur." The regions mentioned roughly make up the present-day Anglo-Egyptian Sudan. Egypt was thus able to put forward weighty arguments based on history and international law. In the meantime, however, the Sudan has become something quite different from what it was at the time of its conqueror, Mohammed Ali, and of the khedives of the past. When the Nahas government offered the concession of a very limited self-government, the Sudanese were no longer ready to accept it. The rigid form of "unity of the Nile valley" offered by Nahas proved unrealistic and, indeed, brought its advocates the repute of antiquated imperialism.

The Sudanese claim to independence was rejected with determination in Cairo as a "British invention." By this attitude, however, the Egyptians robbed themselves of influence on further developments in the Sudan, while their action had done nothing to change the course of events. General Naguib himself wants the unity of the Nile valley; no Egyptian statesman could dream of giving way on that point. Naguib, however, clearly recognized the weakness of the Sudan policy of his predecessors. His origin and his career made him much more familiar with the Sudan than were the average politicians of the *ancien régime,* who frequently behaved to their southern neighbours with a good deal of arrogance. Naguib, on the contrary, agreed in principle from the first to the right of the "southern Nile valley" to complete self-determination. That, and no longer sovereignty and the royal title, was the point of departure of the conversations between Egyptians and Sudanese. The two parties found a common platform in the aspiration to "freedom of the Nile valley." Naguib's formula: "First freedom, then unity," paved the way for an understanding even with those of the Sudanese who in the past had been hostile to Egypt. It was a notable departure from the negative attitude of the *ancien régime.* It was possible to infer from it that the new Egypt was preparing to play a constructive part in the emancipation of the African peoples. In February 1953 Great Britain and Egypt came to agreement over the Sudan. Both of them formally confirmed in this agreement the Sudan's right of self-determination.

Half a century of British colonial rule has radically changed the structure of the Sudan. The foundations of a state and a constitution have been laid, and it is undeniable that there have come into existence at least the rudiments of a Sudanese nation and a Sudanese desire for self-determination. Egyptian nationalism has brought up a younger brother in the Sudan, the nationalism of the modern Sudanese elite. Sudanese cotton competes with Egyptian cotton both for Nile water and for foreign markets. Not only the British but a considerable number of Sudanese have earned very considerable sums from this cotton. In the towns the young educated Sudanese have formed a taste for the institutions of self-government; the British gradually brought it into existence, without much consideration for the Egyptian partner in the former condominium.

Khartoum, the capital of the Sudan, has its Parliament and its political parties. Sudanese politics, however, are still conducted largely under the influence of two great Moslem brotherhoods, which date back to the puritan wave of the nineteenth century. One of these brotherhoods follows the son of the Mahdi, Abdur-Rahman el-Mahdi. The other, which is older, is led by Ali el-Mirghani, whose father was an irreconcilable opponent of the revolutionary Mahdists. The Mahdiya is particularly strongly represented among the cattle-breeding tribes of the western Sudan. These tribes also provided the formidable warriors of the Mahdi. It is said that the Mahdiya has behind it something like one fifth of the Sudanese population. The supporters of Abdur-Rahman el-Mahdi have always been resolutely opposed to the Egyptian claim to sovereignty. The Brotherhood came into being, indeed, as a result of resistance to the rule of the Egyptian khedives of the nineteenth century. Ali el-Mirghani, on the other hand, is more inclined to support Cairo, if only because the Mahdi's son is his bitter enemy. The Mirghaniya (also known as Khatmiya) has its following mainly in the north and east of the Sudan, where association with Upper Egypt and blood relationship with Egyptians are particularly close. In addition to this regional distribution of the two great religious groups, there is the circumstance that several stages of civilization cut across one another on the soil of the Sudan. To begin with, Islam has reached the limit of its spread into the interior of Africa before the gates of the southern Sudan; the two million Negroes of the south—a quarter of the total population—are uninfluenced by Mohammedan doctrine. Secondly, within the Moslem Sudan the degree of Arabization varies: it falls away gradually from the north-east to the south-west. Thirdly, the hostility between nomads and the settled townsmen and peasants is more marked in the Sudan than elsewhere. The main strength of the Mahdiya seems to lie in the nomad African section of the Sudanese Moslems, while the Mirghaniya maintains predominance among the Arabized townsmen and peasants.

The Sudan is a heterogeneous country, many times the size of the great European states. Its far-flung regions have been brought together by alien hands and have not yet grown into an organic whole. These characteristics must be borne in mind if we are to understand the attitude of the Sudanese to the question of the unity of the Nile valley. The Sudanese divided into two camps in the matter of the answer. In one were the parties friendly to Egypt, in the other the partisans of the complete independence of the Sudan. The independence movement was concentrated at first almost entirely in the Umma ("People's") Party, in whose ranks were the followers of Abdur Rahman el-Mahdi. But not all the advocates of independence were also supporters of the Mahdi and his ambitions, and other groups made their appearance alongside the Umma. Thus were formed the Sudan Party, which advocates joining the British Commonwealth, and the so-called Republican Socialist Party. Both of these seemed to be seeking support from the non-Islamic Negroes of the south, where there is some apprehension of a hegemony of the Islamic-Arab north. The supporters of union with Egypt—perhaps in the form of dominion status—had originally collected in the Ashiqqa (Blood Brothers') Party. They, too, suffered from divisions, mainly resulting from personal rivalries, until General Naguib's persuasiveness induced the disunited groups friendly to Egypt to join together again. Behind the parties favouring union is the strong influence of the Mirghaniya. The dividing lines between parties are still fluid. The Sudan is to have a period of autonomy in home affairs, during which the various groups will be able to measure their strength and to determine the ultimate relations with Egypt. Whatever these may become, in future the Sudanese will have an influential voice in Nile valley questions. Their self-awareness has been roused, and a new national feeling has ripened, in which Arab, African, and Islamic components mingle.

There are compelling reasons for permanent good-neighbourliness between Egyptians and Sudanese. The Nile valley has an unusual geographical key-position. It is no exaggeration to say that in the world-wide realm of the British Empire the Nile valley was of importance second only to that of India. The effect of that position both on the Near and Middle East and on the African continent places a heavy responsibility on the peoples by the Nile. The Egyptian nation and its younger brother the Sudanese people have thus an important mission and a great opportunity. This demands political and social stability. The present task in the Nile valley is the creation and maintenance of that condition.

AWAKENING IN THE MAGHRIB

MUCH time passed before the spark of the Arab awakening sprang over to western North Africa. Nature favoured the isolation of the Maghrib from the heart of the Arab world and from the centre of Islam. Although the west and the east of the Arab world appear on the map as a compact continental mass, the Libyan Desert has always had the effect of a partition between the two halves. In the Maghrib, too, the intercourse between its various territories was always slight and intermittent. The Sherifian realm of Morocco continued to live in unconcern under the glass bell of the Islamic Middle Ages. The nominal overlordship of the Osmanli sultans over Algeria, Tunisia, and Libya made little change in their state of seclusion. It had the lasting result that in the provinces of the Maghrib a motley class of Osmanli *condottieri*, Moslems from Turkey and the Balkans, held sway. From these *condottieri* came the corsair deys of Algiers, the beys of Tunis, and the dynasty of the Karamanli, which for a period ruled autocratically in Tripolitania. It is true that Islam always preserved its full authority in the Maghrib. North Africa was always a fruitful soil for the faith, and the seed of puritanism that was sown in Arabia in the eighteenth century was multiplied later in the stern desert solitude of North Africa. The French annexation of the Atlas region produced hardly any repercussion in the Arab East. Conversely, the Arab renascence in the great towns of the East at first had no perceptible influence over the Maghrib. The case of Libya was rather different. There the Osmanli had re-established effective rule in the course of the nineteenth century and had tightened their hold over the country. The Tripolitan War, which resulted from the Italian landing in 1911, assumed the character of a demonstration of solidarity between Turks and Arabs under the ægis of Islam. Among the officers of the Sultan's army at that time were Enver Pasha and Mustafa Kemal (later Ataturk), and the Egyptian Major Aziz el-Masri. The events of the Tripolitan War were no more than an episode; they did not provide any strong impulse toward a national movement in the Maghrib.

In north-west Africa nationalism made its appearance several decades later than in the Arab East. This does not apply to Tunisia; this case was again an exception to the general rule. Not until the 1930's did a first strong current of nationalism flow through the Atlas countries. This time there is some slight evidence of connexion with the political emancipation of the Arab East. The Second World War then produced a great leap forward of the nationalism of the Arabs of the Maghrib. It is true that the difference in the conditions in the various countries outweighed the elements in common. For a hundred years Algeria has been very closely united with France. Only in the last generation did the protectorate of Morocco feel the influence of Europe at all deeply. Tunisia's relations with Europe and in particular with France have much resemblance to the case of modern Egypt.

One element is common to all the countries of the Maghrib, giving a special character to the Arab nationalism of that region: the peculiar nature of Romance colonization. The Latin colonial powers, unlike the British, have not confined themselves to administering and governing the conquered Arab-Islamic countries: they have sent large numbers of settlers into their territory, so that today about 1,800,000 Europeans, mostly Latins, have become permanently settled in North Africa. These European colonists form a privileged class in town and country. Here, therefore, the independence movement of the Arab nationalists has had to reckon with the claims of the European minority, and this has made agreement between the nationalists and the colonial power considerably more difficult than in the Arab East.

The Tunisians form the advance guard of the national movement in the Maghrib. In Tunisia the aspiration to greater independence was strongly in evidence when the rest of the Maghrib was profoundly apathetic. One result of this advanced position is that the Tunisian nationalists have today the best organization and the most widespread popular influence in North Africa. In some respects, indeed, they are actually ahead of the peoples of the Arab East. Even before the French occupation, Tunis was in relatively active intercommunication with southern Europe. Its upper class kept up its relations with Constantinople. The Tunisians therefore had two means of familiarization with the stock of ideas of nationalism. Thus it was possible for the Young Turks to set the example for the small group of "Young Tunisians," whose activities were contemporary with the first revolutions and national risings in the Ottoman Empire, in Persia, and in Egypt.

After the First World War a Tunisian delegation represented its aspirations in Paris. The similarity with the origin of the Egyptian Wafd is striking. The Tunisians were trying to secure recognition for the principle of the sovereignty of the Tunisian people. The demand for a Tunisian Parliament and for universal franchise headed the nationalist program, and the movement gave itself the name of Destour (Constitutional) Party. A modern constitution was to set limits to the sovereignty of the beys. In Tunis, however, the ruler and the Destour movement were not so sharply opposed as the court and the Wafd in Egypt. Nasir Bey, who was ruling in the first days of the Destour Party, was definitely friendly to the movement for a constitution. One of his sons, Munsef Bey, renewed during the Second World War his father's agreement with the nationalists. He is said to have stated that if necessary he would be the first president of a Tunisian republic. In 1945 the French deposed this pro-Destour Bey. France regarded the Destour's demand for a constitution as in conflict with the protectorate treaty. In that treaty the protecting power guaranteed the unrestricted sovereignty of the bey. It thus regarded itself as formally committed to the maintenance of the absolute monarchy.

At first the Destour Party embraced only a small group

of intellectuals and wealthy bourgeois. Not till later did it become a mass movement. The change was the work of the younger nationalists, who in 1934 parted from the Conservatives and formed the Neo-Destour Party. Thus Tunis was ahead of the events that took place a good deal later in many other Arab countries. The driving force behind the Neo-Destour was a lawyer named Habib Burgiba, a man of entirely French and Western intellectual character. The men of the Neo-Destour are virtually the Kemalists of the Maghrib. Their ideal is Westernization, the national state, and, though they have no desire for an acute breach with Islamic tradition in general, a laicist democracy. The party has several hundred local groups, and its active members are estimated at twenty thousand. They are to be found in all classes of the population. The organization of the Neo-Destour includes women and also, an unusual feature in the parties of the Arab world, the peasants. The strongest support of Tunisian nationalism, however, is the Tunisian Trade Union Federation. This body, which is independent of the French trade-union organization, has taken up an attitude of strong opposition to Communism and has adhered to the International Trade Union Federation. Thus the Tunisian nationalists have been able to win over the masses of workers and peasants and largely to escape the influence of Communism. Nowhere in the Moslem world has the co-operation between nationalists and trade-unionists assumed such proportions as in Tunis. The Tunisian Trade Union Federation thus considers itself called upon to play a leading part if nationalism is to be reconciled with the social demands of the masses of the Islamic Orient.

Not yet twenty years have passed since the first appearance of Arab national movements in Morocco and Algeria. The rising of the Berber prince Abdul Kerim in the mountains of the Riff in 1921 cannot be described as nationalistic; it was merely a tribal revolt unconnected with nation-alistic ideas. Morocco has first to struggle for the bases of a Moroccan nation. The Arabs and Berbers that face each other in the Sherifian realm are of roughly equal strength. Often no clear division between these two sections of the population is possible. Both Arabs and Berbers are Moslems, but the Berbers show the utmost unwillingness to accept the dominance of the Arab towns and the Shari'a Consitution. It is significant that the impulse to Moroccan nationalism came actually from a decree of the French protectorate au-thorities, aimed at strengthening the Berbers against the growth of the power of Arab-Islamic law. This so-called Berber Decree of 1930 hit the Arabs at their most sensitive spot; because it was suspected that there lay behind it the intention to interefere with the Arab-Islamic character of the country.

Morocco is able at all events to look back on the histor-ical tradition of a Sherifian realm; Algeria was never a separate state. Today it is constitutionally a part of metro-politan France. In this central member of the Atlas countries the political consciousness of the settled Arabs was aroused by the struggle for the civil rights of the Moslems. A grow-ing number of Arabs were showing themselves to be sus-ceptible of assimilation to French culture; but any readiness for this reached its limit when Westernization and the ac-quisition of French rights of citizenship were bound up with the abandonment of institutions that to a Moslem form essential and indispensable elements of Islam. Islamic feeling is too strong for Moslems to be willingly absorbed into an alien way of life.

Since the Second World War the Independence Party (Hizb el-Istiqlal) has been in the foreground of Moroccan nationalism. The Istiqlal has its strength in the Arab towns; it is emphatically Islamic; its leader is the son of a mufti,

Allal el-Fasi. In writing of Moroccan nationalism, mention of the young Sultan Sidi Mohammed ben Yussuf (deposed by the French in the summer of 1953) must not be omitted.

In Algeria the social tensions have been closely associated with nationalism. Even before the war the Arab propertied and educated class had a rival in a radical Moslem party of a proletarian type. The Algerian People's Party—it changed its name later—owes its popular appeal to a man of proletarian origin. El-Mesali Hadj, son of a bootmaker of Tlemcen, had had considerable experience of the Marxist parties of France before he worked up in his own country into the program of an Islamic Socialism what he had learned and heard in Europe.

The founding of the Arab League in the spring of 1945 raised a good many hopes in the Maghrib. Some of the Arab leaders in the Maghrib turned at once to this League of Arab states. The Tunisian Habib Burgiba, the Emir of the Senussi, and the representatives of Moroccan nationalism wished to see the North Africans associated with the work of the League. Their desire could not at first be acceded to in Cairo; but it was in any case the first important sign that the Maghrib was emerging from its isolation and once more seeking association with the rest of the Islamic world. A further step in this direction followed when, under a resolution of the United Nations, the Arab state of Libya was created under the rule of the Senussi. The creation of independent Libya not only made a wide breach in the colonial dependence of the Maghrib, but also extended the zone of Arab independence to the very gates of the Atlas countries.

Many political émigrés from the Maghrib have collected in Cairo. The Egyptian capital became a headquarters of the political efforts of the Arabs of north-west Africa. The differences, however, in the development of nationlism in the Maghrib made it difficult to find a common platform. Efforts were made to bring into existence a united front of the national parties from Tunis to Morocco, but they were not particularly effective. Relations with the Arab League were not free from friction. Habib Burgiba, the leader of much the strongest Arab party in the Maghrib, found himself frequently in conflict with the views of leading circles of the League, because he could not agree with the negative character of the policy pursued in Cairo.

The Maghrib is the last great Arabic-speaking region in which colonial rule is still maintained. What aims do the Arab nationalists of the Atlas countries pursue? Tunisia, Algeria, and Morocco are in very different situations, in regard both to their status under international law and to the degree of maturity of their national movements. We must therefore confine ourselves to discovering some general principles: indications of these are furnished by the pact under which the Liberation Committee for the Maghrib was founded in Cairo in January 1948. All the important nationalist parties of the three countries were represented in the drafting of that statement of a program. The statement contained a declaration and a demand. The signatories clearly stated that they were in favour of the unalterable attachment of the Maghrib to the Islamic and Arab civilization, and also in favour of collaboration with the Arab League. This was a clear rejection of the assimilation pursued by the colonial authorities and a refusal to allow the Maghrib to be regarded as an extension or appendage of Western Europe. The desire is to make a fresh treaty settlement of relations with the colonial powers—that is to say, France, and also her neighbour, the Spanish protecting power in Morocco—on the basis of independence. The overwhelming majority of the leaders of Maghrib nationalism, together with the Bey of Tunis and the Sultan of Morocco, have declared their readiness to safeguard France's economic and strategic interests and to preserve friendship with France. So far only a few extremists have raised the cry of complete separation from France. The Maghrib is bound up with the fate of the western Mediterranean basin, and it is closely interwoven with the French economy. Tunis and Morocco demand in the first place that the protectorate treaties, of which that with Morocco dates back to 1912, and that with Tunisia to the 1880's, shall be replaced by alliances on the basis of equality of rights. The Arabs of Tunisia and Morocco— Algeria is a special case—find it difficult to understand why their countries, which in many respects are more highly developed, should have a lower status than, for instance, Libya or the Sudan.

Thus, in so far as France does not hold rigidly to the old protectorate treaties, there should be room for the play of a French-Arab understanding in the Maghrib. It might not be so difficult if it were not for the awkward question of the European colonists. The future position of those colonists forms the worst stumbling-block in the relations between France and the Maghrib. The Arabs claim that the colonists should adapt themselves to the future independent Maghrib statehoods. The colonists see in any change in existing conditions a threat to their privileges, and use their means of influence in Paris to prevent it. How will it be possible to find a peaceful reconciliation of the interests of the great majority, the indigenous Moslems, with those of the small minority of immigrant Europeans? Here the independence effort of the Maghrib touches a dangerous explosive material, as is shown by the experiences in South Africa, Kenya, Malaya, or even Palestine. In this way the future of the Maghrib might hold very serious conflicts.

THE ARAB LEAGUE

ON March 22, 1945, seven independent Arab states signed the pact of the Arab League. "Unity and independence" had from the first been the double aim of the Arab national movement. The two are inseparable in the mind of the Arab nationalist. Developments at first took another course when, after the First World War, Arabia was split up into a number of states. But the farther the national idea spread among their peoples, the stronger became the Arabs' effort for unity. Arab nationalism never accepted the fact of partition. It was inevitable that within the separate Arab countries special interests, of dynastic, economic, or other nature, should develop and gain strength, interests with which the public movement for unity would have to reckon. Regional particularisms and dynastic jealousies set a brake on the pressure of public opinion; naturally, however, princes and governments could not escape from the appeal for Arab unity, nor did they want to. But no less naturally they wanted to see Arab agreement in a form that promised as much play as possible to their own particular desires. So long as the Arab states still had to struggle for independence, there could be no room for a policy of Arab union. With the progress of emancipation the path to Arab union, which had been blocked in 1918, was gradually cleared for fresh efforts.

The first step to a grouping of Arab states happened to be made where the Arabs had first entered world history, in the Hejaz. In the spring of 1934 King Ibn Sa'ud and the Imam of Yemen had gone to war with each other, and the peace treaty between them was drawn up in a town in the Hejaz. The event gained added importance from the fact that the treaty for the first time officially struck the note of Arab solidarity. Its preamble declared that henceforth there would be "eternal Islamic-Arab brotherhood" between the two kings and between their states. It added that the bonds of Islamic brotherhood and Arab race formed "a single nation" in the two countries.

Two years later King Ibn Sa'ud took a further step in the same direction by concluding a "Treaty of Arab Brotherhood and Alliance" with his neighbour Iraq. Yemen declared its adhesion to this league, and it was expressly declared that it was open to any independent Arab state that so desired to join the league. At the time of the signature of the treaty of alliance by the three states there was no Arab state in Asia Minor that fulfilled the condition of independence. There was no thought at that time of Egypt's joining.

The league of the three Arab kings may be regarded as a precursor of the Arab League, though its immediate effect was slight and it amounted to little more than a gesture of goodwill. Meanwhile the struggle for the Arab character of Palestine, which flamed up furiously in the mid 1930's, had lent new force to the idea of Arab unity and strongly impressed it on public opinion; and it is worth noting as an important innovation that at the Palestine Conference in London in 1939 there were not only delegates from the Palestine Arabs but representatives, for the first time, of the Arab states. This was an international recognition of the existence of interests common to all Arabs.

In 1943 Nuri es-Said, the Prime Minister of Iraq, who was a veteran of the Arab rising and a loyal servitor of the Hashimis, put forward a plan for Arab unity. Nuri Pasha's Arab league was to be confined to the countries of the Fertile Crescent. It was to be a union of Iraq with a Greater Syria as yet nonexistent. Foreign policy, defence, and certain economic questions were to be entrusted to a permanent federal council. The Jewish national home was to be given autonomy within Greater Syria. Nuri Pasha's proposals thus aimed at a federal state. A close association of that sort could only have a prospect of success within the limits of the Fertile Crescent. The entry of Egypt burst the bounds of the Nuri plan. In Cairo the Wafd was in power. Its leader, Mustafa en-Nahas, robbed the Iraqi of the initiative in Arab collaboration. The states of the Arabian peninsula which Nuri es-Said's draft had left out of account were brought in. A general conference of Arab governments met in Alexandria and brought the long negotiations to a conclusion. Its outcome, the so-called Alexandria Protocol, of the autumn of 1944, provided the basis on which six months later the Pact of the Arab League was concluded.

The Arab League came ultimately into operation as a federation of states. Until 1953 the membership was confined to the seven founder states: Egypt, Jordan, the Lebanon, Syria, Iraq, Saudi Arabia, and Yemen. The Kingdom of Libya joined the League as its eighth member in the spring of 1953. Outside the League remained only north-west Africa and the small principalities by the Persian Gulf. Since the League has to serve the interests of the whole Arab world, an annex to the statutes brings questions affecting non-member Arab countries within the League's field of activity. As with all federations, the statutes of the League strictly preserve the sovereignty of the individual states. The preamble itself is emphatic about "respect for the sovereignty of the member states." The principal organ of the League is the League Council. Each member has one vote, irrespective of its area or population, the Lebanon or Yemen counting equally with Egypt. All resolutions of the Council, with a few unimportant exceptions, require unanimity, so that each member state has a right of veto. The League has no authority to set limits to the sovereignty of any member by means of a majority resolution.

The Alexandria Protocol itself tried to secure greater

elasticity. It aimed at giving stronger expression to the idea that the League was no more than a stage in Arab unity and the opportunity for further steps should be preserved. Among other things, the protocol had aimed at preparing the way for a common foreign policy of its members. It contains, for instance, a provision that no Arab state shall in any case pursue a foreign policy that might be detrimental to the League or one of its members. It seems that various Arab governments energetically opposed these tendencies of the protocol. In their final form the statutes gave stronger expression to the principle of the inviolability of the sovereignty of the individual state. This was a clear victory for the advocates of federalism, and under their influence the League became in essence an instrument for the maintenance of the *status quo* in the Arab world. One concession was made to the advocates of revision of frontiers within the Arab world. Article 9 of the statutes gives members desirous of closer union the right to enter into agreements for that purpose. Thus the door remained open in theory for "Greater Syria," a union of the Fertile Crescent, or whatever other projects may emerge. In practice the distribution of power within the League makes the applicability of Article 9 more or less illusory.

The League bears the stamp of much the most powerful of its members, Egypt. Nothing else could be expected: Egypt has a much larger population than all the other six members put together, and economically it is far ahead of its partners. The headquarters of the League are in Cairo, the Egyptian capital, and Egyptian diplomats have from the first held the important post of Secretary General. Egypt's interest seemed to be best served by the maintenance of the existing balance between the Arab states. The formation of a united Arab state embracing the Fertile Crescent would have entirely upset that balance. Even apart from the jealousy between King Farouk and the Hashimis, that would have been felt in Cairo to be irreconcilable with Egyptian interests. Egypt was thus the natural leader of the advocates of federalism within the Arab League. She was joined by King Ibn Sa'ud and usually also by the Lebanon Republic. Against them the advocates of union were represented by the two Hashimi kingdoms, Iraq and Jordan. Thus in the League Council the votes of Syria and Yemen carried the day. Obviously such unstable equilibrium would be bound to be easily upset by any changes in relative power between the member states—and therefore between the two coalitions. Thus the union of the portions of Palestine that remained Arab with Transjordan to form the new "Hashimi Kingdom of Jordan" met with violent opposition from the federalist coalition led by Egypt, and might almost have been followed by the breaking-up of the League. Similar difficulties are bound up with the admittance of new members; for the question arises at once of the side on which the new member's vote will be found. The question first became acute when Libya became an independent Arab state, and therefore a claimant to the eighth place in the League. The Sudan, too, as Abdur-Rahman el-Mahdi has already made clear, might before long be claiming membership in the League.

The two coalitions within the League remained little altered until the revolutionizing events that began with the first Syrian *coup d'état* of March 1949 and then, in and after the summer of 1951, made a rapid succession of outward changes in the Arab states. The Hashimi Abdullah and King Farouk, two of the most persistent combatants on the Arabian chessboard, withdrew, and the great families of Damascus lost influence. These three had especially thrown the weight of their special interests into the controversy between federalists and unionists. The fronts within Arabia became more fluid, and the movement for Arab union, liberated from some of its fetters, made new progress.

During the Palestine war the Arab League did not gain what many Arabs may have expected of it. It also showed itself to be unable to secure a common attitude of its member states in great issues in world politics, such as the conflict in Korea. Hard things have consequently been said about the League, but its existing circumstances must be borne in mind. No more can properly be asked of the Arab League than is compatible with its Constitution. All federations of similar structure are set narrow and rigid limits by the principle of the unrestricted sovereignty of their members. To give only one example, the Germanic Confederation of 1815 suffered from that weakness from its birth. Like the present-day Arab League, it felt the continual difficulty of carrying public opinion with it that is bound to be felt by a union effected without regard to dynastic and other special interests. The disagreement between the advocates of a wider and a narrower German solution also finds its counterpart in the Arab world of today. The federalists are thinking of a great Arab League embracing as many as possible of the Arabic-speaking countries, which is scarcely conceivable except in a loose federation. The unionists want to begin with a small Arab federal state in the Fertile Crescent.

In order to amplify and strengthen the Arab League a "Treaty of Collective Security and Economic Co-operation" was signed in the summer of 1950. The making of this treaty was connected with Farouk's wish to frustrate certain plans of federation of the Hashimis. In consequence of this the Hashimi states adhered to the Treaty only two years later. So long as the armies of the Arab states are weak and poorly equipped, and the particular interests of the signatories have first consideration, the Arab pact of collective security has at most but a modest practical value. Now that the question of the regional defence of the Middle East has been raised, however, the Arab governments have shown an effort to recommend the pact of 1950 as the proper instrument of regional security and to put life into it.

It does not seem justifiable to draw from the League's failures conclusions as to the strength or weakness of the Arab peoples' effort toward unity. The League is the achievement of princes and a few leading notables. The part they played gives little idea of what politically minded persons among the Arab peoples think about Arab union. In the path of Arab nationalism the League of 1945 is not likely to be the last milestone. The Arab awakening—from the Tigris to the Atlas—has its place among the greatest of the revolutionary processes that are rocking our century. In spite of all inadequacies, in spite of all the disappointments and the frustrated hopes due to indecision and indiscipline, Arab nationalism is entitled to recognition for its stimulation of a genuine intellectual and political renascence. Its work is not yet completed, the last word has not yet been spoken about the new Arab world, because the Arab peoples and states are still in the midst of a transition.

CHAPTER SIX

The Persians: Incubus of Foreign Interference

THE BAZAAR AND THE MULLAHS

THE intermediate position to the burdens of which the world of Islam is exposed makes its appearance abruptly, without softening gradations, in Persia. In Persia the means of escape from pressure alike from the ocean and from the massive block of the Eurasian continent are of the frailest. Since Russians and Anglo-Saxons have faced each other threateningly and with suspicion, the territory between Turkistan, the Caucasus, and the Persian Gulf has been one of the weakest parts of the girdle separating the two great groups of powers. Thus the main trends of modern international policy have relentlessly dictated developments in Persia. Any gains to be had from successfully playing off the powers against one another are more than counterbalanced by the instability produced within the country in its weakness by the changing policy of the Great Powers. The soul of Persia is proud but very sensitive, and it feels deeply wounded by a destiny that leaves the country almost entirely helpless between the pressure and counter-pressure of the mighty. Something of the bitterness of a martyrdom seems to have been laid in the cradle of Persian nationalism. Essential features of the Shi'i faith of the Persians are found again in the special character of the Persian nationalist movement. Shi'i Persia has always paid supreme honour—indeed, fanatical veneration—to the martyr's crown.

Persia began to suffer from the British-Russian hostility in the first half of the nineteenth century. The offensive came from Russia; Great Britain found herself driven into the defensive against her adversary in Central Asia. The Russians were from the first in the more favourable geographical position. The richest and most important provinces of Persia are much more closely within Russian than British reach, and so, too, is the capital, Teheran, itself. The natural routes for Persian trade went across territories in which Russia's power was firmly established, while the Persian Gulf, where Britain was dominant, at first played only a secondary part in the Persian economy. The realm of the Kajar (Qajar) shahs lay helpless between the Russian hammer and the British anvil.

The rulers of the Persia of that day came from the Turkish Kajar (or Qajar) tribe. The Kajar line (1779–1925) brought little good fortune to the Persians, and the Persian nationalists have little that is good to say of that period. Persia then, however, made her first efforts to come into contact with Europe. Nasir ed-Din, Shah from 1848 to 1896, the most outstanding member of the Kajar dynasty, took a step unprecedented in Persian history, making extensive journeys abroad to see for himself what could be learned from Europe. He also sent young Persians of good family to study in France. As a rule the Kajar court preferred to listen to the Russians rather than the British, because it was soon found that the Russian czars were very ready to lend their protection to the autocracy of the Persian shahs. A so-called Cossack Brigade, formed on the Russian model and officered by Russians, remained for decades the strongest instrument of power on Persian soil. It was at all times a valuable protection for the reaction.

In 1890 the Shah, who was always in financial difficulties, wanted to sell to a British company for fifty years the monopoly of the production, sale, and export of tobacco. The affair was only one element in the general hunt for concessions which later was euphemistically called "peaceful penetration." The tobacco concession led to the first considerable popular movement against foreign influence and also against the Shah's autocratic methods. Shi'i priests called for a boycott of tobacco, and in the end the Shah was compelled to refrain from giving the concession.

The fight against the tobacco concession gives a first glimpse of the peculiar character of Persian popular movements, which was later to show itself again and again. The Shi'i priesthood, and also—in another way—the bazaar, represent the will of the people and the public opposition to the ruler and the government. To make clear the part played in Persia by the Shi'i mullahs, we need to realize the dogmatic attitude of the Shi'a to politics. The Shi'is, as already mentioned, are uncompromising legitimists. The only legitimate ruling line, in their view, is a line that can be traced back to Ali, the son-in-law of the Prophet, and the imams. As the last of the recognized imams, however, has been living for many centuries in "seclusion," there can be no legitimate power on earth until the reappearance of that Imam. Shah and government are merely the deputies for the Imam in his seclusion. Only the Safavid shahs were considered to have a degree of legitimacy, because their ancestry was traced back to one of the imams. Neither the Kajars nor the present Pahlavi dynasty possess any similar evidence of legitimacy. The accredited organs of the "Imam in seclusion," the only source of legitimacy, are not the wielders of secular authority, but the exalted scribes of the Shi'a, the *muzhtahids.* While the name "mullah" is used for the priesthood as a whole, and especially its lower ranks, the Arabic word *muzhtahid* denotes a man who is authorized and in a position to seek and pronounce a judgment of his own on questions of canon law, which in Islam, of course, always includes civil law. In Shi'i Persia, therefore, the position of the clergy differs substantially from their position in the countries of Sunni Islam. The *muzhtahids,* under the strict Shi'i conception, have the authority of organs of supervision of government activities. They exercise this function, however, not with the collective responsibility of a "Church," but as individuals. Obviously this Shi'i conception of the illegitimacy of all authorities, though it may express the individualistic tendency of the Persian, may easily open the way to anarchistic activities and revolutionary propaganda.

The "bazaar" in Oriental towns is simply the business quarter, definitely separated from the residential districts. Used figuratively, the word refers to the trading and industrial community, all those who in a pre-capitalist country make up its "economy." Everywhere in the Orient where the degree of industrialization and the association with world trade are still slight, the bazaar represents a factor of considerable influence and weight in public life. When the bazaar closes its doors and brings all business to a stop, the effect is virtually that of a general strike. Thus the mullahs and the bazaar are able to bring strong pressure on the government, and in Persia they have done so several times with effect. Although activities of these two groups

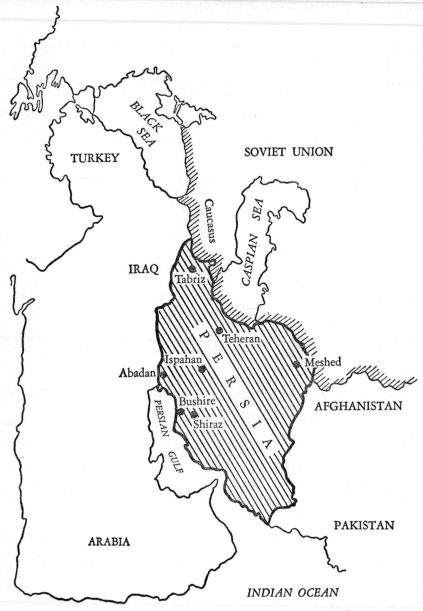

5: PERSIA'S INTERMEDIATE SITUATION

in public life are not primarily a consequence of European influences, they have increasingly been associated with the political efforts of the growing Europeanized class. In the various revolutionary outbreaks the mullahs and the bazaar have been in the forefront as important influences working on the masses. On the other hand, owing to the marked individualism of the Persian character, there has never developed any firmly organized national movement. An undercurrent of loosely connected nationalistic movements would spread through the country, disintegrating when the force of the current was exhausted. In Persia there is no counterpart of the Egyptian Wafd or of Kemal Ataturk's party organization or the Moslem League of Pakistan.

The call for a constitution to set limits to the Shah's despotism was first heard in the winter of 1905. It had just been seen how even the mighty Czar of Russia had had to make concessions to the movement for a constitution. Once more the instrument chosen by the Persians for wringing similar concessions from the weak but tyrannical Shah Muzaffar ed-Din was a typically Persian institution, the so-called *bast.* The nature of the *bast* is soon explained. Anyone who wants to lend special emphasis to particular demands takes refuge in a sanctuary affording absolute protection from any state intervention, and remains there until his demand is complied with. The *bast* is not a weapon to be resorted to lightly, especially when it is united with a closing of the bazaar. In some respects it recalls the civil-disobedience campaigns that Gandhi organized in India.

In December 1905 the sacred city of Qum, south of Teheran, was chosen as the scene of a great *bast.* The Shah promised a constitution; but it required another *bast,* this time in the British Legation, to make him keep his promise. Shortly before his death Shah Muzaffar ed-Din signed the Constitution, which, with a few amendments, is still in force.

That was in December 1906. The Majlis, the Persian Parliament, started its career.

The hopeful initiatives for overcoming the stagnation in the country fell all too soon between the millstones of world politics. The Anglo-Russian partition agreement of August 31, 1907 directed a heavy blow against the friends of the Constitution. The whole of northern Persia, the region politically and economically of crucial importance, was brought within the Russian sphere of influence. This implied a free hand for the Shah's autocratic propensities, and after the agreement of 1907 the British could no longer think of giving support to the Liberal reform movement. Indeed, the Ministers of the two powers issued a joint declaration that Russia and Britain could not tolerate further disturbance of the Shah by the reformers. What followed was an unbroken succession of disturbances that lasted till 1921. A *coup d'état* by Shah Mohammed Ali was followed by open revolution. The Liberal nationlists, whose stronghold was the province of Azerbaijan, and the south-west Persian tribe of the Bakhtiari, marched against Teheran and wrested the capital from the Shah's troops. In 1909, after the victory of the revolution, the Parliament deposed the Shah, and Ahmed, a minor, the last of the Kajars, ascended the Peacock Throne. Russian troops, however, had meanwhile occupied Azerbaijan, and did not evacuate it until twelve years later. Persia sank, especially after the First World War, into the chaotic state of an arena for the rivalry of foreign powers. What would have come of the first protest of the Persian national movement if the Persians had been left to themselves is an idle question. The British-Russian agreement at Persia's expense robbed that movement of success. But the work of the revolution of 1905–9 was not entirely destroyed. In those years Persia made the first steps from the fabulous realm of the Silver Lion to the national state. She had kept pace with the beginning of national movements among the other great peoples of Islam. As early as the first decade of the twentieth century the chain reaction of political upheavals revealed the interdependence of the Islamic Orient. The work of the Young Turks in Constantinople, the movement associated with the name of Mustafa Kamil in Egypt, the nationalist leagues in Damascus, the movement of the Young Tunisians, the founding of the Indian Moslem League, and finally the struggle for the Persian Constitution, all came in the same period. All were efforts to copy Europe. It is true that the enthusiasm for the political ideas and institutions that had been observed and studied in Europe could not alter the fact that the "nations" on which it was proposed to fit the raiment of a constitutional state existed as yet only in the minds of a very small section.

RIZA SHAH'S ARMED NEUTRALITY

THE Persian people is not easy to rule, even when it is spared foreign interference. It needed the coming of extraordinary events, together with the presence of a man of unusual qualities, to bring Persia for twenty years under a stable though harsh regime. Riza Khan came of a family in the Caspian province of Mazanderan. He appears to have been of purely Persian origin, and to have grown up in a circle with a certain military tradition. Riza thus became an officer in the Cossack Brigade. His abilities brought him to the command of the brigade, a rank till then reserved for Russian officers. The state of Persia at that time seemed hopeless. The central government in Teheran was but a shadow, with no real power. Riza Khan possessed in his troops the only effective instrument with which Persian policy could still be pursued, and all who then knew him bear witness that he was a convinced

Persian nationalist. He found a political ally, Ziya ed-Din Tabatabai, a young politician thirty years of age, the son of a *muzhtahid* of Shiraz, in southern Persia. In his youth Ziya ed-Din had witnessed the struggles for the Constitution. Nationalism and the desire for reforms, at the time when Persia was at the nadir of her modern history, seem to have driven him to action. On February 21, 1921 Riza Khan, at the head of his troops, carried out a *coup d'état* in Teheran, and Ziya ed-Din formed the new government. Similar combinations between officers and reformist politicians frequently occurred in the young states of the Moslem world. Riza Khan and Ziya ed-Din held together only for a hundred days. Ziya failed to achieve his aims, fell out with his military partner, and in the end had to leave the country. Riza Khan then moved resolutely toward unrestricted autocracy. It is not known whether he had serious ideas of creating a Persian republic. He sought the advice of the Shi'i clergy, and they thought that at that time the idea tasted too strongly of Europeanization. Riza Khan took the only possible alternative, perhaps not unwillingly. He deposed the last of the Kajars and had himself proclaimed Shah of Persia.

Riza Shah tried to protect Persia from the crippling influence of the British-Russian rivalry. Armed neutrality best accorded with his strong nature. Circumstances aided him in his course. During the twenty years of his reign Persia remained more or less aloof from the interests of the Great Powers. The pressure of the Russian colossus on the long, open northern frontiers of the country has always been a nightmare to the Persians, and the fear of being drawn into the wake of the northern neighbour was always felt in Teheran. Riza's main anxiety, too, during his reign was the Russian attitude. For most of the time, however, the Shah benefited by the fortunate circumstance that the Soviet Union, fully occupied with its own tasks of internal construction, remained on the defensive in its relations with its neighbour countries. The temporary weakness of the Soviet Union gave Riza Shah a breathing-space. The government of the *coup d'état* of February 1921 found already in existence the completed draft of a Persian-Soviet treaty of friendship. One of its first official acts was the ratification of that treaty. The czarist concessions and privileges on Persian soil were abolished by a stroke of the pen. Article 6 of the treaty contained a most important clause, giving the Russians the right to march into the country "in the event of a third power intending to use Persian territory as a base of operations against the Soviet Union." During Riza Shah's reign the Soviet Union was mainly content with excluding the influence of any other power from the north Persian glacis. Teheran gave full attention to this.

The Shah took advantage of the situation not only to lock the door against the Russians (and their Communist agents): he went further and did his best to bow out the British. The experience of the nineteenth century had shown that a Persia concerned for her independence was much more likely to go half-way to meet the British policy of what is now called "containment" than to fall in with the historical aims of the Russians, and accordingly it was at first supposed that Britain stood behind Riza Khan. The Shah's acts soon told a different tale. Under his rule came the first climax in the struggle against the concession of the Anglo-Persian Oil Company. Various motives lay behind the Persian attitude in the long oil conflict. At the back of them was the dislike of the influence of any foreigners, particularly non-Moslems. That feeling is not peculiar to Persia, nor is it confined to the peoples of Islam. But the unhappy fate of modern Persia has developed that feeling into a sort of neurosis. On top of that has come the feeling of being the subject of economic exploitation by alien interests. The two feelings have combined in the emotionally inspired attitude of the mass of the people. The politically minded upper class has other and tangible objections. Inevitably the British oil company developed into a state within the state. Not only had it the south-western Persian oil province of Khuzistan entirely in its power, but its economic might provided it with unusual influence in the background of politics in Teheran. An undertaking of the magnitude of the Anglo-Persian could not but be simply crushing in its effect on the primitive economic structure of Persia. In the end the Persians came to the view (and this is an important element in the oil conflict) that Persia would have better justification and a stronger position in standing out against Russia if the British influence, in which the oil company had become the principal factor, were removed or at least reduced. The Persians saw in the existence of a powerful economic organization in the hands of one of the two Great Powers interested in the country one of the chief hindrances to Persian neutrality. Whether the Persian arguments were sound will not here be discussed. Sound or not, they determined the course of events in Persia.

Superficially the oil conflict is largely economic. It is concerned with participation in profits and with the technical management of an important branch of industry. But anyone who confines himself to the purely economic discussion of the oil question is in danger of overlooking the political nature of the conflict. Persian nationalism is concerned primarily for the independence of the country and is interested only in the second place in the economic side of the question. It is true that only the later phase of the oil conflict has brought clearly into the foreground the aspirations of political nationalism. In retrospect Riza Shah's first blow against the Anglo-Persian is seen to have been only a brief prelude. In November 1932 the Shah cancelled the company's concession, which dated from 1901. The conflict thus begun was settled after a few months, and in May 1933 a new concession for ninety years was ready, with a few substantial financial concessions to Persia and a narrower delimitation of the region covered by the concession.

Riza Shah was not a "neutralist" in the sense that the word has acquired today. In his view, Persia's effective power of resistance was the first condition of neutrality as he understood it. The Shah had had no personal acquaintance with Europe. He was not a "Westernizer" in the intellectual sense. What he wanted was the outward machinery rather than the inward essence of the Western state and Western society. This technical conception of the national state also dominated his work of reform. Riza's first effort was to increase the defensive strength of the country and the central power in the state. The Cossack Brigade was replaced by a modern army and police, and the insubordination of the tribal khans was brought ruthlessly to an end. Never before or after Riza Shah was the power of Teheran more firmly and resolutely exercised.

Next came economic modernization. The Shah intended that Persia should acquire industrial plants, railways, banks. Trading monopolies gave the state control over thirty to forty per cent of Persian foreign trade. The profits of the monopolies served to finance the program of industrial development. In this way a fresh resort to foreign financial aid, which might have shackled Persia's independence, was avoided. Even the construction of the Trans-Iranian Railway, nearly nine hundred miles long, from the Persian Gulf to the Caspian Sea, was financed from the country's own resources, out of the income from the sugar and tea monopoly. While the ruler's energy was thus quickly and thoroughly changing the face of Persia, the peasant villages, where the great mass of the Persian people live, were scarcely touched by the reforms.

"L'état, c'est moi," Riza Shah might have said with the same justification as Louis XIV. The absolute power of the ruler rigorously cut down the power of the landowning upper class. The state control of trade and industry did much to destroy the past influence of the trading community, and the confiscation of church property reduced the influence of the clergy, though the Shah had gone to work very cautiously in every reform that might be resisted by the mullahs. Riza Shah was a Persian nationalist, and it was part of his program of reforms to make all possible play with the ideas of Iranian traditionalism. The new national movement took its models from the remote Iranian past. "Iran" became the official name of the country. (After the war the use of the old name, "Persia," was also permitted again.) The language was required to take on Iranian elements imposed by the authorities, Turkish and Arabic words being got rid of as far as possible. When the Shah finally gave to the dynasty he had founded the name "Pahlavi," this, too, was an emphatic reminder that the Persians should think of the great days of their—pre-Islamic —past.

The epoch of the reforming Shah was brought to a premature end by foreign intervention. The same thing had happened to the constitutional movement before the First World War. Even Riza Shah's iron will could not hold Persia permanently away from the whirlpool of world politics. If the Shah had seriously thought that Persia could continue indefinitely in armed neutrality between the Great Powers, the last years of his reign must have brought him bitter disillusionment. When the Anglo-Russian Alliance was formed during the Second World War, the situation of 1907 recurred, and the second partition of Persia became visible on the horizon. Riza Shah wanted to resist the pressure from the powers; but in so far as the Persian army went into action at all, in a few days it was completely eliminated. On September 16,

1941, after the entry of foreign troops, the Shah abdicated in favour of his son Mohammed Riza. In 1944, at the age of sixty-six, he died in exile in South Africa.

GHAVAM ES-SALTANEH:
A BAD DEAL FOR THE SOVIET

Two highly gifted *grands seigneurs* of the same generation as the exiled Shah dominated the Persian scene after the Second World War. Both belonged to the landowning aristocracy; both studied at European universities. During Persia's Liberal revolution they were at the age at which a man finally forms his outlook on the world. Both of them detested Riza Shah's autocratic methods, and both consequently felt themselves to be "victims of dictatorship." Except for these superficials, the two men differed radically in nature. Ahmed Ghavam (Qavam) es-Saltaneh was a diplomat of the old Oriental school. He was a master of the technique of politics in the old Oriental style; but he lacked understanding of what was preparing under the surface. Mohammed Mossadegh (Mussadeq), on the other hand, gave the impression of monomaniacal character. And so, on the road to the single aim that he pursued, he showed himself to have a masterly knowledge of the soul of the masses, and found his way instinctively in the labyrinth that in the Orient is called public opinion. Mossadegh did not tame the tiger, he rode it, or at all events tried to.

Riza Shah's reforms rested entirely on the powerful shoulders of that one person. During the two decades of his regime they were a one-man enterprise, and no attempt was made at any time to turn over the work to a party or other permanent organization. That may not have been deliberate on Riza's part; the Shah may have been convinced that in view of Persian individualism any such course would have had little chance of success if entered on. After that dictatorial ruler's abdication the figures and the methods of old came back, as though those two decades had been a dream. Only later was it recognized that the work of the reforming Shah had not ended without leaving a vestige of influence on the Persian community. The Persians have sometimes been described as the French of the East, and it has been said of Mossadegh that he was a rather milder Robespierre. In any case—to keep within the picture—the distance between Louis XIV and Robespierre was three generations: only a decade separated Riza Shah and the triumph of Mossadegh.

At the end of the war the Persians' first concern was to induce the occupation forces to withdraw, and to reunite the country. The press was again talking of a return to a policy of absolute neutrality. The British-Russian-Persian treaty of alliance of January 1942 laid down that the foreign troops had to leave Persian soil at latest six months after the end of the war. Calculated from the day of the Japanese capitulation, that period expired on March 2, 1946. British forces evacuated their zone in the south by the due date; but the Soviet Union, judging from its delay, seemed determined to secure pledges in Persia before the Red Army went back over the frontier. The Soviet occupation zone embraced five provinces, virtually the same region that in the partition of 1907 had been assigned as the Russian sphere of influence, except that Teheran, the capital, was excluded from the wartime zone of occupation. The Soviet had shut off its zone politically and economically from the rest of the country, so that the Teheran Government had little to say with regard to that zone. But the Russians had made no serious effort at any sovietization of their zone.

Inevitably we enter on the precarious soil of speculation as soon as we venture to pass judgment on the Soviet Orient policy. This reservation should therefore preface what here follows. If the Russians were in search of pledges in Persia, they could exert pressure in two ways. They could make use of separatist tendencies in the northern provinces and could artificially stimulate those tendencies. They could also create, in the form of a party or organization ready to serve them, an instrument of direct influence in Teheran. Without giving preference to either of these alternatives, the Soviet tried both. Success in playing the separatist card offered a sure but limited gain; a strong pro-Soviet party throughout Persia promised influence, though of a less direct character, right down to the Persian Gulf. In so far as the "revolutionary ripeness" of the country was attained, such a party seemed also the obvious bridge to a "People's Democracy." It would not be easy to make combined propaganda for separatism and for the idea of a Communist mass party, especially as the Persian nationalists' deep dislike of the Russians had to be reckoned with.

The beginnings of a Persian Communist Party are to be found shortly after the Bolshevik Revolution, in the oil city of Baku—on Russian soil. Its supporters were recruited from the many Persian nationals settled in the southern provinces of the Russian realm, and principally from Persian workers in the oil industry. A certain Jafar Pishevari soon worked his way to the head of that as yet insignificant party. He was born in the Persian province of Azerbaijan, but had lived for many years in Baku. Under the pseudonym of Sultan-Zadeh this man fulfilled important functions in the Comintern and also in the Near East section of the Foreign Commissariat in Moscow. The field of operations of the Persian Communists was confined almost exclusively to the northern provinces; the membership did not exceed a few thousands.

The old guard of Persian Communism, trained in Moscow, are now in a decidedly problematic relationship with another movement, the Tudeh ("Mass") Party. The Tudeh seems to have been a typical reflection of the western European Popular Front mentality. A Persian medical student at the University of Berlin, Dr. Arani, gathered together on his return home a group of Left-wing intellectuals. Riza Shah had the whole club thrown into prison in 1937, and there Arani died. After Riza Shah's abdication the others were released. They then founded the Tudeh Party. The first program of the party contained a conglomeration of Liberal and Marxist ideas, but nothing that could have been interpreted as Communism. Members of the Persian aristocracy lent their names in support of the party. Notably the Kajar clan, relatives of the dynasty dethroned by Riza Shah, were represented in surprising numbers. To that clan belonged the old Sulaiman Muhsen Iskandari, who for a time was honorary president of the Tudeh. Another Kajar must be regarded as at least a fellow traveller—Muzaffar Firuz, whose friendship to Russia may not have been entirely disinterested. In addition to a resentment of Riza Shah's "dictatorship," which was understandable in the Kajars, reminiscences of the Liberal revolution of 1906–9 found expression in the early period of the Tudeh. Whether the Soviet occupation authorities kept closely in touch with the Tudeh at the very outset, or even took an active part in the founding of the party, remains to be discovered. In any case, the Tudeh very soon appeared unmistakably as a fellow-travelling party in regard to Soviet foreign policy. In the course of time it also acquired in its organization substantial characteristics of the so-called "new-style parties," but it does not seem to have been assimilated to the other Communist parties. In the Tudeh the Soviet found an instrument that assured it in Persia opportunities of influence offered in no other Moslem country outside the Soviet frontiers.

Exactly one day after the Japanese capitulation—that is,

immediately after the six months allowed for evacuation had begun under the obligation entered into by the occupying powers in Persia—the Russians made the first move in what today looks like a carefully schemed manœuvre. Jafar Pishevari came forward in Russian Azerbaijan with a new "Democratic Party." To the unsophisticated the name might recall memories of the strong tradition of the Democrats of 1906 precisely in Azerbaijan. Actually the name sheltered no other than the old Persian Communist Party. Pishevari's "Democrats" demanded the autonomy of the Persian province of Azerbaijan, more consideration for the Turkish language, spoken by the majority in that province, and stronger representation of Azerbaijan in the Persian Parliament. Within the province the Tudeh organization was amalgamated with the new party. In December 1945 Pishevari took a further step. A so-called National Assembly in the provincial capital, Tabriz, proclaimed the "Autonomous Republic of Azerbaijan." Pishevari himself assumed the office of Prime Minister. The other key positions were entrusted to reliable men of the old guard of the Persian Communists. The Moscow-trained Salam-Ullah Dyavid became head of the secret police, organized on the Soviet model; an Armenian, Danishian, who could not speak a word of Persian, commanded the new "People's Army." To complete the picture, it was not forgotten to bring the Kurdish element into activity. A Kurdish "People's Republic" sprang up in the frontier district next to Turkey and Iraq.

The Persian army and police were prevented by the Soviet occupation authorities from taking any action against the separatist rebels. The Soviet Union now had in its hands a means of pressure upon the Teheran Government. Moscow would be making an attractive offer to the Persians if it gave its assent to the restoration of the unity of the country. So far everything seemed well calculated. Only, two things had not been thought of: that Teheran might be even more cunning than Moscow, and that the Americans would stand resolutely behind Persia.

On January 26, 1946, Ghavam es-Saltaneh took over the Persian Government. This septuagenarian landowner from Mazanderan, a province in the Soviet occupation zone, was generally supposed at the time to be friendly to Russia. He had shown interest in the Tudeh Party, and, after all, he would have to bear in mind that his properties lay under the eyes of the Red Army. The Russians were therefore not displeased to see him take over the government. Ghavam first showed his goodwill by arresting some pro-British persons, and then set out for Moscow, where he remained for three weeks. Stalin himself placed the Russian terms in front of his Persian guest—autonomy for Persian Azerbaijan, oil rights in northern Persia, and the retention of Soviet troops in certain parts of the country. The price was too high. Ghavam's Moscow conversations ended without result, which after all is not unusual in an Oriental trading deal. And, sure enough, a few weeks later the Russo-Persian deal was completed. Ghavam and the Russian Ambassador in Teheran agreed that the Soviet troops should entirely evacuate Persia within six weeks, that the Persian Parliament would ratify the agreement for a mixed Soviet-Persian oil company by October of that year, and that relations with the "Democrats" of Persian Azerbaijan must be an internal Persian affair. On May 9, 1946 the last Red Army men marched out of Persia. Russia's marionettes in Tabriz lost the protecting bayonets. It can hardly be said definitely whether Ghavam had merely been guided by the circumstances of the moment or had been playing a subtle game from the first. It makes no difference to the ultimate outcome. At first the head of the Persian Government had given the Russians every reason for satisfaction. He had taken the side of the autonomists of Tabriz and had himself admitted some Tudeh politicians to his Cabinet. Persia now had a Popular Front government of the type usual at the time in western Europe, and had complied with the Russian wishes. The influence of the Soviet Union in Persia had seemed firmly established. If the Russo-Persian honeymoon had ended all too soon, Ghavam could protest with some credibility that it had not been his fault.

Counteraction began in the south, where, as it happened, the British counted a good deal and the Russians not at all. The khans of the Kashgai tribe in the south-west Persian province of Fars rebelled against Teheran's Popular Front policy; other regions in southern Persia came to their support. These people's wishes could not be ignored in the capital, and Ghavam therefore decided to get rid of his Tudeh ministers. The glory of the Popular Front was quickly extinguished. All the more energetically did the Russian Ambassador press for the ratification of the oil agreement. That, however, required first the election of a new Parliament, and in Persia parliamentary elections always take endless time. Unfortunately, Ghavam told the Russians, it was impossible to have free elections so long as the arbitrary regime of Pishevari and his people continued in (Persian) Azerbaijan. For all that, it was a critical moment when the Teheran Government sent contingents of the Persian army into the "autonomous" province. The Soviet frontier was only a few miles away. But the Soviet troops did not stir, and the Communist rule in the province collapsed like a card castle. Jafar Pishevari sought refuge in the Soviet Union, where he was reported later to have died from a motoring accident.

The elections in Persia could now take their course, and at last, in July 1947, the new Parliament assembled. Ghavam laid the Russian oil concession before it for ratification, as provided in the agreement. Although the debate proceeded under strong pressure from the Russian Embassy, the members rejected the Prime Minister's bill almost unanimously. Instead of it they passed a bill strictly prohibiting all oil concessions to foreigners, even in the form of participations. Thus, after two years' vicissitudes, the Russians went away entirely empty-handed. They had neither the Popular Front in Teheran nor their tool in Azerbaijan nor the oil concession. All that remained to them for later times was the Tudeh Party, whose true strength seems to have been very doubtful even in Soviet eyes.

Bearing in mind the Russians' position in Persia at the beginning of 1946, it is really astonishing how entirely the situation changed in eighteen months in favour of Persia. Ghavam's diplomacy had extricated the country from the Russian toils. It is true that we must not be misled by this into overestimating the diplomatic resources of a weak country like Persia. All Ghavam's subtlety would have been helpless without the good fortune of the tension between the Anglo-Saxons and Russia, thanks to which the British and Americans had placed the trumps in the hand of the sly fox in Teheran. The Russians' first move was connected with the proceedings of the United Nations, to which Persia had appealed for aid before Ghavam came into office. The formation of the Popular Front Cabinet in Teheran had brought a British reaction, for it would not be easy to deny a British hand in the tribal revolt in southern Persia. And the Persian opposition to the Russian oil concession found its strongest support in American diplomacy. Confidence had probably been increased in Teheran by the fact that a few months earlier the Truman Doctrine had insisted on the American interest in the countries south of the Soviet frontier. The British, on the other hand, significantly held back in the oil question. The Foreign Office officially announced that it had no objection in principle to the granting of the oil concession to the Russians. The British seemed, on the other hand, to consider firm resistance necessary to the extension of Russian influence throughout the territory of the Persian state. Hence the strong reaction to the participation of the Tudeh Party in the government. In regard to Soviet influence in the northern half of the country, however, Great Britain had been very cautious in view of her own interest in southern Persia. If the Soviet Union was excluded from the north, there was always the danger of similar Persian proceedings against the British interests in the south. Actually the resolution of the Persian Parliament refusing the concession to the Russians also demanded a revision of the attitude to the British oil company.

MOHAMMED MOSSADEGH: A BLOW AGAINST GREAT BRITAIN

THE Persian Constitution furnished the Parliament, the Majlis, with unusually wide powers. Riza Shah, without formally abrogating the Constitution, had confined the activity of the members of Parliament to simple applause. After the abdication of the Iron Shah the Majlis resumed its rights more jealously than ever. The framers of the Constitution of 1906 had paid no great attention to the profound differences between Persia and the West and had given free play to their enthusiasm for the formalities of parliamentary democracy, with the practical result that a small clique was placed in permanent possession of the power of the state. The Majlis is an exclusive club of one hundred and thirty-six politicians, most of whom live on the yield of landed property or of wholesale trade. Two thirds of the members give as their profession "landowner." Outsiders have never made their way into this club in more than insignificant numbers. There are no genuine parties, and, at most, temporary coalitions of a few members, which call themselves parties. The members of the Majlis have always been far above any sort of group discipline, and so the picture of the Persian Parliament is reminiscent in many respects of the Parliament of the old Kingdom of Poland. Such excessive individualism is dangerous for peoples in an exposed situation.

In 1949 Shah Mohammed Riza carried through a reform of the Constitution. A Senate was formed, half of its members being nominated by the ruler; the Shah was also empowered to dissolve Parliament. But in its composition the Senate differed little from the Majlis, and the reform of the Constitution made no real change in the power of the landowning oligarchy in its parliamentary disguise.

Mohammed Mossadegh had been known as a striking, sometimes a little bizarre, figure in the Majlis since the end of the Riza Shah period. His family are among the largest landowners in the country. Mossadegh studied law in Paris and Fribourg, at about the same time when his contemporary and later opponent Ghavam was attending an English university. Mossadegh's mother was a Kajar, a circumstance not likely to diminish the repugnance he felt for Riza Shah's regime. Under that regime he had been banished to a remote place in eastern Persia. After Riza's fall, Mossadegh entered the Majlis and became an opposition leader. Between 1941 and 1951 Mossadegh, already well into his sixties, carried on a permanent feud against the various governments that succeeded one another. He knew how to make himself the centre of public attention. On one occasion he successfully organized a *bast* in the Shah's palace, as a protest against the government's conduct of the parliamentary elections. As a rule he had the support of about twenty members of the Majlis. His influence in Parliament was greater, however, than that figure would suggest, and it was still greater with the mass of the people, because of his uncompromising pursuit of his idea of liberating Persia from "oil enslavement."

Mossadegh first came into public notice when Sergei Ivanovich Kavtaradze, the Soviet Deputy Commissar for Foreign Affairs, appeared in Teheran in the autumn of 1944. Kavtaradze tried to secure a Russian oil concession in the five northern provinces of Persia. Mossadegh felt himself called upon to be the driving force of the resistance to this proposal. He brought forward a bill laying down categorically that any minister who entered into negotiations for an oil concession to a foreign power, or conferred such a concession, without the prior consent of the Majlis, should be severely punished. The Majlis passed the bill, and a furious Kavtaradze had to depart with nothing achieved.

Before long it was the turn of the Anglo-Iranian Oil Company. Negotiations for a revision of the existing concession were begun in 1949, with the approval of the Majlis. They led to the so-called Supplementary Agreement, which was to revise the treaty of 1932 in Persia's favour in some important points. The Shah and the government wanted the acceptance of the agreement, among other things because it provided an increased revenue from the concession, and with this it was hoped to finance a seven-year plan of reforms. In June 1950 the Shah called to the head of the government a man whom he personally trusted, General Ali Razmara, the young Chief of Staff. It was expected that the new man would proceed with the strong arm that seemed to be needed for a reform of Persian political and economic life. The Shah may have hoped that this reform might bring economic aid from America; if so, then in spite of the strong representations made to Washington by the American Ambassador, the Shah was disappointed. The Ali Razmara Government found itself empty-handed.

The Majlis sharply criticized the supplementary agreement with the Anglo-Iranian Oil Company. As there was no prospect of its ratification, the Finance Minister finally abrogated the 1932 treaty. That was at the end of December 1950. Meanwhile the oil question had become the centre of widespread national interest. Among the public a movement for the nationalization of Persian oil was visibly gaining ground. The movement, as usually happens in Persia in such cases, found expression in a vague but violent undercurrent of public opinion. Its advanced troops were formed by Mohammed Mossadegh's "National Front"; Mossadegh had meanwhile become chairman of the oil committee of the Majlis. To his supporters the oil nationalization was equivalent to the acquisition of national independence. After the successful repulse of the Russians, the British were to disappear. Only then, thought Mossadegh's friends, would Persia be able to pursue a policy of absolute neutrality.

With the nationalists were co-operating the Shi'i puritans. Since Riza's fall the clergy had recovered much of their influence. The Shi'i mullahs had again become a political force to be reckoned with. Most of them are equally against the West and Communism. What Mossadegh meant to nationalism, the mullah Abul Kasim el-Kashani became for the masses who were accustomed to following the guidance of the Shi'i mullahs. Kashani's career and personality show considerable resemblance to those of the ex-Mufti of Jerusalem. Kashani grew up in Iraq, in the town of en-Nedjef, where there is one of the greatest shrines of the Shi'a. In the First World War he fought on the side of the Turks against the British, just like the later Mufti of Jerusalem. Kashani found himself again facing the British in the Iraqi rising of 1920, in which the Shi'i tribes of the middle Euphrates played an important part. Finally the British insisted on the mullah's expulsion from Iraq. He went to Persia, but Riza Shah had no use for the zealot's services in the country, and Kashani resumed his wanderings. When the Shah himself had to go into exile, the mullah at once returned to Persia. He got himself elected to the Majlis, but he sought his field of operations in the background of Persian politics.

The mullah Kashani's power at first reinforced that of the nationalists, and it is difficult to say which of the two had the greater influence on events. Leading Shi'i jurists, when consulted by the mullah's followers, declared that the nationalization of oil was a demand in accordance with one of the principles of Islam. We may mention one of these *fetwas* (legal memoranda) on the oil question to give an insight into the line of thought. It is based, like all such *fetwas,* on a saying of the Prophet. A Moslem, it said, had set free a number of slaves, who were his only property, so that on his death the family were left without means. When the Prophet heard of this, he condemned that Moslem's action outright. From this precedent the *fetwa* concluded that it was certainly contrary to their religious duty if the oil, which after all ought to help to provide the means of existence for the Persian people, were given into the possession of foreign powers. Under these circumstances any objections to the nationalization of the oil were irreconcilable with the principles of Islam.

The chorus of the nationalists and the Shi'i puritans was joined, to the discomfort of both parties, by a third, the Tudeh Party. This quasi-Communist mass organization found itself in something of a dilemma. Its Soviet masters would be bound to say to themselves that the nationalization of the oil in British possession would destroy the last hopes of a Russian concession in northern Persia. If they considered the matter from the point of view of the traditional policy of the partition of Persia into spheres of interest, it would follow logically that Russians and British should not do anything to interfere with each other's interests in their zones of influence. From that point of view the British had taken up a reserved attitude in 1947 in the Russo-Persian oil dispute. On the other hand, the Soviet Union could not discredit its allied Tudeh Party in the eyes of the masses, because Marxism-Leninism requires Communists everywhere to come forward as the "advanced guard" of the national movements of liberation. Thus the Tudeh must carry on the struggle against the "imperialist oil companies."

Although the party had officially been declared illegal in 1949, it still had plenty of opportunity of pulling the strings of the agitation. Moreover, the prohibition had done little serious harm to the organization of the Tudeh. In some quarters the influence and strength of the party are immensely exaggerated; in others they are contemptuously dismissed. Serious reports from Persia assumed that under fairly conducted elections it might have secured fifteen to twenty per cent of the seats in the Majlis. The number of registered members of the party might be inconsiderable, but that disadvantage might be largely set off by the fact that the Tudeh was the only party deserving the name in Persia. In the course of the oil conflict it was found several times that the Tudeh leaders had learned something about the conduct of revolutionary tactics. The undesired comradeship of the Tudeh brought the nationalists a good deal of embarrassment. Neither Mossadegh nor the friends of Kashani wanted to pave the way for Communism, and after long experience the Persian nationalists fear nothing more than the intervention of their Russian neighbour.

Things began to move in March 1951. The Prime Minister, Ali Razmara, speaking in the oil committee of the Majlis, definitely opposed the nationalization of the oil industry. But the ground had already slipped away beneath the feet of the general's government. On March 7 Ali Razmara was assassinated as he entered a mosque. The assassin belonged to the Shi'i militant organization Fedayan-i-Islam ("Martyrs of Islam"). This secret society requires blind obedience from its members, and its leader was in the habit of issuing orders as he thought fit. Nevertheless, the connexion between this terrorist group and the preachings of the mullah Kashani is undeniable. Moreover, Kashani is reported to have expressed the opinion that individual assassination is the shortest path to liberation. In Shi'i ears such a statement does not seem the enormity it may seem here. And the history of the Shi'a is rich in acts of anarchistic terrorism. For the rest, the Fedayan-i-Islam represents just as heavy an incubus for the nationalists as do the activities of the Tudeh. It did not shrink either from blows at ministers of the National Front or from threats against the mullah Kashani himself. Around it spread the fearful shadow of the *Vehmgericht*. The murder of Ali Razmara set light to the powder cask. Next day the oil committee of the Majlis resolved to recommend the nationalization of oil throughout Persia. Both houses of Parliament called on the committee to examine the details of nationalization and draft a bill accordingly within two months. On April 27 Mohammed Mossadegh took over the government. On the 30th a new nationalization bill was introduced in the Majlis and the Senate and passed there and then; on May 1 it was signed by the Shah.

The course of the international conflict that now followed cannot be described in this section, which is concerned with the Persian nationalist movement. On October 3, 1951, the last three hundred British technicians left the soil of Persia, after the Anglo-Iranian Oil Company, in the activities of four decades, had made Persia one of the greatest oil-producers of the world.

As regards the foreign politics of the oil nationalization, Mossadegh had been trying to play the same game with Great

Britain which Ghavam es-Saltaneh had successfully played with the Soviet Union. The international tension between the two camps in world affairs seemed too violent and too permanent for any new partition of Persia between British and Russians to be expected. Relying on that, Mossadegh went to the uttermost limit. But the parallel with the elimination of Russian influence in 1946–7 was confined to the diplomatic field. Ghavam performed a diplomatic feat with no tangible effects on the internal order in Persia.

What the oil conflict has set in motion in Persia since the spring of 1951 is an internal revolution, the second the Persian people has experienced in this century. Purely economic arguments, however sound they may be in the eyes of Western diplomats and business men, miss the essential point of the events associated with the name of Mohammed Mossadegh. Mossadegh himself was from his origin anything but a social revolutionary. He was entirely fascinated by the idea of ending "oil enslavement." But the enthusiasm of the aged landowner supplied the channel for the irruption of new forces. Partly out of fear, and partly for the sake of the old device of diverting discontent by means of a foreign bogy, the old oligarchy controlling the Majlis joined him in agreeing to the nationalization of the oil industry. But the farther the avalanche fell, the more disturbed the Majlis visibly grew. Thus in the end there came in July 1952 the attempt to get away from Mossadegh's ideas and, by recalling Ghavam es-Saltaneh, to return to the paths of the old order. Then there were barricades in Teheran, and Mossadegh came back into power.

What was the nature of the wave that carried the man of the oil revolution? It is not easy to form a clear picture so close to the event in time. Nationalists and Shi'i puritans recruit their followers from much the same social elements

—the middle class, the intellectuals, and part of the urban proletariat, and finally, it should be added, the young generation that grew up under the reforming Shah. Persia had had twenty-seven governments in the ten years between Riza Shah's abdication and the outbreak of the oil revolution. If we compare the various lists of ministers, we find a small circle of eighty to a hundred politicians who took turns in the conduct of affairs. With Mossadegh's coming into power, new and unknown names appeared for the first time at the head of the ministries. They incorporated a sort of third element in Persian society, forcing its way up between the old landowning upper class and the peasant millions. But this second revolution in Persia had not the strength to achieve a genuine and lasting renascence of the country. The development took the form of a reckless gamble on the part of the "dreadful old man," who staged from his sickbed the drama of a Dictatorship of Irrationalism.

After the events of the summer of 1952 Mossadegh fell manifestly into dependence on the mob. His unrestrained pursuit of personal power alienated many who at first had been associated with him. The Senate was summarily abolished, the Majlis steadily robbed of influence. Finally, in his Jacobinist zeal, the Prime Minister did not shrink from attacking the last pillar of the existing order that seemed to stand in the way of his ambitions. He tried to cut down the prerogatives of the Shah. The attempt was his undoing. His opponents devised effective slogans that turned the masses against him. The landowners and the great merchants were aghast at the economic tendencies that seemed to underlie the Mossadegh regime. A large part of the army remained loyal to the Shah. Kashani and the majority of the Shi'i mullahs turned against the Prime Minister, sensing danger to Islamic tradition. Those who belonged to the Persia of the past talked secretly of counterrevolution. They felt that the shadow of the Persian Robespierre looked ominously like that of a Kerensky.

The trial of strength came in August 1953, when Mossadegh stretched the bow of his autocracy to breaking-point. Even then the old man might perhaps have held his own if he had taken advantage of the offer of the Tudeh Party to give him its support. But he was descended from the Persian aristocracy, and he would not go as far as that: the vision of a "people's democracy" seemed to frighten him. In a few hours the troops of General Fazlullah Zahedi, loyal to the Shah, had the support of the fickle masses of the capital, and were masters of the situation. Under the protection of the army, the old Persia had secured a breathing-space.

The oil conflict has cost Persia 200,000,000 dollars, according to the estimate published by the Zahedi Government of the fall in value of the oil shares since the enactment of the nationalization laws. Mossadegh entirely miscalculated the reaction of the world market when he thought he would be able to overcome the British oil blockade. The gap left by the loss of production of Persian oil was filled in a relatively short time by the increased production of the Arabian oilfields; the loss of the Abadan refinery was gradually made good by new construction. It ought, in any case, to have become clear that without an understanding with the great Anglo-American oil companies which now control the world market, Persian oil was condemned to remain unsalable. There was little to be gained from interesting outsiders in Persian oil. The loss to the Persian economy could only have been made good, if at all, by an intensification of trade with the Soviet Union, and that would have been impossible except at a political price which even the Mossadegh regime was not prepared to pay. The Zahedi government seems to wish to pursue the path of an understanding in the oil conflict. Harsh reality is showing the deep-seated desire for Persian freedom of movement in world politics to be quite unrealistic. In the course of modern Persian history it has proved again and again that Persia cannot go over entirely to either of her powerful neighbours without seriously disturbing the balance between the Great Powers. Thus Persia's destiny seems to be caught in a vicious circle.

Mossadegh's fall must be regarded as a success for the West and a defeat for the Soviet Union. Whether it will lead to a stabilization of conditions is as yet an open question. Up to now the marked individualism of the Persian people has always interfered with the country's political stability. It now seems as if the rule of Riza Shah was a reluctantly endured exception. One thing, it is true, remains unaltered: Persia's intermediate situation. Even after the British have evacuated the last great position of foreign influence on Persian soil, the Persians cannot withdraw into an undisturbed idyll in face of the world-wide implications of the disagreements between the Soviet Union and the Anglo-Saxons.

CHAPTER SEVEN

The Indian Moslems: The Road to Pakistan

SHAPING A NEW NATION

IN THE chronicle of Indian Islam the ninety years between the deposition of the last of the Great Moguls and the birth of the state of Pakistan may come to look like an interregnum. It is true that long before their end the Great Moguls in Delhi had been exercising no more than a fictitious rule, but even the fiction still provided the Moslems with support and a tradition. When even that fell away, the Moslems, who had been the lords of India until their place was taken by the British, were at first as if orphaned. After the great rising of 1857, the "Indian Mutiny," they had to admit that the Hindus had supplanted them in economic and administrative affairs. For a time the British were inclined to give preference to the Hindu element, because they regarded the Moslems as mainly responsible for the Mutiny. The Hindus also realized, as a rule, better and more quickly how great were the opportunities offered by the great advance of trade,

industry, and banking in the shadow of the *Pax Britannica*.
A Hindu bourgeoisie sprang up, and the first beginnings of
Indian national feeling made their appearance. It gained con-
creteness in the founding of the Indian National Congress,
which assembled for the first time in Bombay in 1885. The
"Congress," whose founders included some English Liberals, aimed at looking beyond the deep differences between
the two great religious communities, and basing its program
and its labours on the unity of India within the boundaries
set by British rule. It recognized only one all-Indian nation.
The course of the most recent history of the Indian subcontinent has not supported that contention.

The Indian Moslems entered the epoch of modern nationalism with divided feelings, and when the political ability and the strength of will of Mohammed Ali Jinnah finally
united the Moslems behind the demand for a sovereign
state of their own, a long and excited division of opinion
within Indian Islam came to its end. Controversy had centred
on the crucial question whether the Moslems should join
in an all-Indian national movement or work for their own
nationality and statehood. Many Moslems had been active
members of the Congress Party, and the advocates among
the Moslems of an all-Indian state were never entirely si-
lenced, even after the creation of Pakistan. But it could not
but be clear to every Moslem that the conception of an "all-
Indian nation" implied the predominance of the Hindus;
there were roughly three times as many Hindus as Moslems.
In addition to this, at the beginning of the twentieth century
the second generation of the Congress movement insisted
much more strongly and emphatically on the Hindu spirit
and the Hindu past of India than the founders of the movement had done. The more sharply the contours of Indian
nationalism stood out in the Congress Party, the more widespread grew the anxiety among the Moslems lest, failing

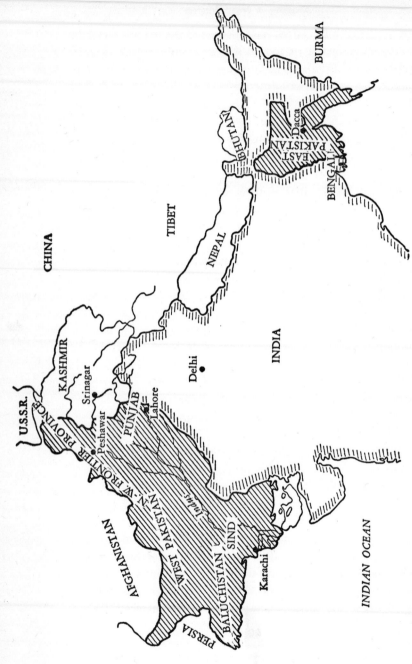

6: PAKISTAN

timely precautions, Islam should be submerged in a Hindu sea. As the prospect of Indian self-government drew nearer, anxieties and hesitations naturally grew still more acute. The clearing up of internal differences in Indian Islam during the nineteenth century had strengthened the Moslems' position. Sayyid Ahmed Khan, one of the great reformers of Indian Islam, would have nothing to do with Moslem participation in the Congress movement. He warned the Moslems that they would be in subjection to the Hindu majority, and he was one of the first to describe the Indian Moslems as themselves a nation. Ahmed Khan died in 1898. Thus the thesis of the "Moslem nation" was put forward quite early. The anxiety about the continuance of their own way of life led to the formation of the greatest nation of Islam. It is a nation lacking a compact territory, a common language, and common origin. The fact that in spite of this the Indian Moslems pursued to the end the path to Pakistan shows how much resolution and mutual loyalty the members of the Islamic community can bring to bear today, as soon as they feel that they are in peril.

In 1906, members of the landowning Moslem aristocracy, the Aga Khan among them, determined to form an organization to safeguard the political rights of the Indian Moslems. The Moslem League was thus at first, like the Congress twenty years earlier, an affair of notables, landowners, and princes. The Moslem upper class represented in it bore for the most part the stamp of English education, and it was widely felt that the Moslem League would best serve the interests of Indian Moslems in association with the British. At that time Lord Curzon was Viceroy in New Delhi, and with his broad outlook he saw clearly the connexion between the Islamic world and the security of India. Lord Curzon accordingly made no secret of his desire for the friendship of the Indian Moslems. To that end he carried through the partition of the province of Bengal. The Hindus were indignant; the Moslems were glad to see a substantial reduction of the influence of the Hindus in that province, commercially and industrially the most important in British India. The partition was later revoked; but the dispute over the fate of Bengal, where forty per cent of the Indian Moslems live, contributed greatly to the growth of political consciousness among large numbers of the Moslems.

It is true that it was a long time before the Moslems thought of demanding a state of their own. There was a period at first during which Moslems and Hindus joined in a common platform, demanding self-government and independence from British overlordship. At that time the majority of the Moslem politicians were still ready to agree to Indian union in some form. In 1918 League and Congress agreed at Lucknow on the main features of an all-Indian constitution, though with strong guarantees for the rights of the Moslem community. The various provisions of the Lucknow Pact might be summed up by saying that the Moslem League agreed at that time to the uniting of the Indian subcontinent in a single state, but not to the fusion of the various populations in the mould of an "all-Indian nation." The guarantees provided for the Moslems in the Lucknow Pact might be taken as meaning simply that the Indian state visualized by the originators of the pact was to have the character of a federation of two peoples. The Lucknow Constitution therefore took care to assure the continuance of the existing equilibrium between Moslems and Hindus in the fundamental law of the state.

The Lucknow Pact was the climax of the collaboration between Congress and the Moslem League. At that time the League could not by any means contend that it represented a majority of the Moslems. In general the Moslems were still at the outset of their political development, with the Hindus a decade or two ahead of them on the same road. The "all-Indian nationalism" represented by Congress is, roughly speaking, twenty years older than "Moslem nationalism." It is a striking fact that this same lapse of time, twenty years, separates the Lucknow Pact from the spread of the idea of a separate Moslem state. Indian Moslem students at Oxford were the first to bring forward in debate the program-defining name "Pakistan." *Pak* means "pure," and Pakistan thus means "the land of the pure." At the same time the word contains, according to the inventors of the name, the initials of the various Moslem countries of India.

Pakistan was to become a Moslem state entirely separated from Hindu India. The Pakistan idea in this form was a product of the study, and at first it secured no widespread attention. The difficulties seemed immense—indeed, practically insuperable. It is true that it was possible to point to compact regions in the north-west and in Bengal whose Moslem character was obvious and indisputable, but as a general rule the Moslem and Hindu regions of India were interlocked in much the same way as Catholic and Protestant Germany. Large minorities would inevitably remain on either side, however the frontiers were drawn. The opponents of the Pakistan plan seemed to have overwhelming arguments on their side. But the opponents did not reckon with the personality of Mohammed Ali Jinnah, under whose leadership the Moslem League grew into a mass movement.

Moslem nationalism thus entered the stage of maturity. Mohammed Ali Jinnah brought the Pakistan idea out of academic discussion into the political struggle. In Lahore in 1940 he succeeded in getting adopted as the program of the Moslem League the demand that the regions with Moslem majorities should form an independent state. The Indian Moslems, Jinnah declared, were not a minority but a nation, with a right to a state of its own. It is true that he had first somehow to collect the political forces for the building of Pakistan. As lately as in 1937 the provincial elections had shown that the Moslem League could not yet claim to be the undisputed spokesman of Indian Islam. The League gained less than a quarter of the seats reserved to Moslems. The Congress Party was thus able to contend with some justification that the League was no more than a dissentient group. Had not many more Moslems voted for the Congress platform than for that of the Moslem League? Moreover, apart from the Congress Moslems, there were a number of Moslem parties and organizations openly opposed to the program of an independent Moslem state on Indian soil.

Before ten years had passed, the situation had been entirely reversed. The League drew the Indian Moslems to itself like a magnet as the day of Indian independence, and with it the prospect of an all-Indian state, approached. Well based or ill, the fear of "Hindu imperialism" was too great to fail to have its effect on the Moslem community. In 1946, new elections took place both for the provincial parliaments and for the central government. This time the League gained nine tenths of the Moslem votes; the only part of India in which it suffered a clear defeat was the North-West Frontier Province. The fronts were now clearly and cleanly defined. On one side was the Moslem part of the population of India gathered behind the Moslem League, whose banners bore the demand for "Pakistan." On the other side the Congress Party held fast to the all-Indian state. It could speak now, however, only for the Hindus and an insignificant fragment of the Indian Moslems. The British pursued the plan of the all-Indian state until the final phase of the new political order. Jinnah made the utmost use of his diplomatic abilities to gain recognition for Pakistan and to help it to victory. In February 1947 Clement Attlee, then Prime Minister, informed the Commons that Great Britain would withdraw from India at latest in June 1948. Lord Mountbatten went to New Delhi as the last in the proud succession of viceroys. There he was very quickly convinced that there was no escape from the partition of the British heritage. The Congress Party, too, gave way before the strength of Moslem nationalism and its leader, Jinnah. On August 15, 1947 the green flag of the new Indian Moslem state was hoisted in Karachi.

The partition was purchased with heavy sacrifices in men and money. There began enormous migrations of Moslems and Hindus across the newly defined frontiers. The atmosphere of the autumn of 1947 approached the heat of civil war. Hardest hit was the Punjab, where once more a struggle over the destiny of the Indian subcontinent came to a climax. Between ten and fifteen million people are said then to have lost their homes. But even after all the migrations to and fro, nothing like a clean segregation of the two Indian nations was attained. Pakistan still had a not inconsiderable Hindu minority. Within the frontiers of the "Indian Union" remained about as many Moslems as the combined populations of Turkey and Persia.

Under such circumstances it is not surprising that there have been many doubts of the wisdom of the partition of India. Some have blamed Jinnah's intransigence, some the British, some the failures of Congress politicians. There may be substance in all three criticisms. But are they not superficial? Was not the partition the outcome of the elemental clash of two worlds on Indian soil, a clash that was bound to come as soon as the British hold relaxed? Islam in India, as everywhere else, has retained the characteristics with which it entered the country: it has not allowed itself to be absorbed into the population of the great quasi-continent. To understand the events of the partition, it is necessary to keep in mind that background. The farther we go from the events of 1946–7, the clearer and the more compelling becomes the recognition of the vitality of Moslem nationalism. Pakistan's first lustrum has not justified the pessimists whose voices were heard by the cradle of the new state.

THE HEIRS OF MOHAMMED ALI JINNAH

A PORTRAIT of Pakistan will show clearly many of the features familiar in the other young states of the Moslems. Here as there landowners and army leaders, eagerly reformist effendis and Islamic puritans, are the chief figures on the political stage. The only differences are in their relative strength in the various states, in the degree of social differentiation, and, last but not least, in the political temperament of the peoples. To judge by the first five years of the new Indian Moslem state, the Pakistanis are a nation with strong nerves, persistent in their conservatism. That does not mean that they are incapable of passionate outbreaks. It is in any case a sign of firmness of purpose that Pakistan has overcome the loss of its two leading statesmen without serious trouble. Mohammed Ali Jinnah, the Qaid-i-Azam ("supreme leader") of the new Moslem nation, died only a year after his state and people had entered on the difficult and unfamiliar tasks of independence. Soon afterwards the country suffered a second blow. In 1951 Jinnah's closest collaborator, Liaqat Ali Khan, then in the prime of life and active service to his country, was shot dead by an assassin.

Jinnah's name was so closely bound up with the birth of Pakistan that to many people he was a symbol of the state itself. His popularity was astonishing, for Jinnah had none of the characteristics of a tribune of the people. His keen, cool intelligence won its greatest triumphs on the floor of parliaments and in diplomacy. Jinnah fulfilled among the Moslems a similar function to that of Gandhi among the Hindus. But one has only to compare these two eminent men of modern India to realize how differently Moslems and Hindus approach the things of this world. Jinnah was absorbed by this life; he was too entirely concerned with this life to have been able to acquire the methods and mentality of a Gandhi. Jinnah was a wealthy man of aristocratic type and spotless elegance, a man far removed from any sort of speculative philosophy. His father was a rich dealer in hides, who had gone from Karachi to Bombay, where Mohammed Ali Jinnah was born in 1876. The family was not of the Sunnite persuasion of the great majority of the Indian Moslems, but belonged to the sect of the Khojahs. This is one of the countless offshoots of the Shi'a. It is something like a caste, in so far as one can only become a Khojah by birth. Most but not all of the Khojahs are followers of the Aga Khan. Jinnah was a believing Moslem, but by no means a fanatic, or he would hardly have married a Parsee lady. He became an uncompromising militant for the Moslem state comparatively late in life. As a young and successful lawyer he first joined the Congress Party, and he was nearly forty years old when he found his political home in the Moslem League. In 1916 the later creator of Pakistan was taking a prominent part in the drafting of the Lucknow Pact, but even during that honeymoon of Hindu-Moslem collaboration he would not move an inch from the thoroughly effective guarantees demanded for the Moslem community. Thus there was already a sort of prelude in Jinnah's life to his step to Pakistan. In the 1930s the influence of this Bombay lawyer in the Moslem League was unchallenged, and soon he was the Qaid-i-Azam of the Indian Moslems on their road to independent statehood. Jinnah showed the utmost single-mindedness and determination. Shortly before the partition the suggestion was made that the two Indian dominions should have a common governor general. Jinnah countered the idea by demanding that he should be the first governor general of Pakistan. Partition was not to be evaded by a last-minute compromise.

When Jinnah died, the stability of his creation did him all honour. The gap could be filled at once from the inner circle of the leadership of the Moslem League. The League had been a good preparatory school for leadership in the business of state, and now that the Moslems had to build their state it became evident how much the educative work of the reformers of Indian Islam had achieved. Liaqat Ali Khan, Pakistan's first Prime Minister, Nazim-ud-Din, Jinnah's successor as Governor General, the Foreign Minister Mohammed Zaferullah Khan, and Ghulam Mohammed, the third Governor General, are all alumni of the Indian Moslem University of Aligarh. One of the most famous English universities was the usual concluding stage of their education. All of these men except the last are sons of the Moslem aristocracy. Liaqat Ali Khan came from a Persian family that had migrated to India during the time of the Moguls; his family is said to trace its descent from the pre-Islamic kings of Persia. Nazim-ud-Din comes from a princely family of Bengalese Moslems. The worldly wisdom of the heirs of Mogul rule, coupled with a dose of Anglo-Saxon political thought—such is the impression conveyed by the group who have controlled Pakistan in the critical years of its early development. The leaders of the Moslem League who today hold sway in Karachi still include the earlier generation. They exercised firm and able control of the launching of the ship of state. But the Indian Moslem nation will not be ruled for all time by men from Oxford and Cambridge. What will be the ideas of their successors, who no longer have any association with the British-Indian past, but have entered the broad and turbid current of modern Islam?

The Moslem League is today Pakistan's only organized party of any importance. Such parties outside the League as have made their appearance are as yet no effective opposition. Pakistan thus has in practice something of the character of a one-party state, but that is a transitory condition, a sign of youth in political life. The Moslems are going cautiously to work in building their state. The work on their Constitution had not been completed in 1952, and at times the Constituent Assembly is doing the work of a central parliament. In the first years energies were fully taken up with gaining a firm footing.

It certainly implies no disparagement of the political sense of the Pakistanis that during the period of state-building internal political issues have been confined within the bounds of the Moslem League. The League has the wide scope of a national "movement," without a social and economic program. Like all such movements—the Wafd, for instance—the Moslem League cuts across all sections of the population. The cement of Moslem nationalism unites conservative landowners and social reformers of more or less radical origin, clericals and laicists. Most of the politicians of the school of Jinnah represent the middle course in home and foreign politics. On the right of them is a wing with an expressly Islamic orientation. (It should be said that the term "right," borrowed from Western political usage, is a convenient comparison that should not be taken too literally.) Pakistan's "Islamic Right wing" has much in common with the puritans of the Egyptian Moslem Brotherhood, the followers of the Persian mullah Kashani, and similar groups to be found today in every Islamic country.

On the opposite wing are the social reformers, the "Left," so to speak, of the Moslem League. They, too, have their parallels in the other parts of the Moslem world. Between Left and Right, Jinnah's successors have endeavoured to follow a course that may smooth away differences. There have not yet been general elections, as in the neighbouring Indian Union. They are not expected for some years to come. The outlines of political life in Pakistan have, therefore, still to be clearly defined.

Pakistan is a country of peasants. Nine tenths of the population gain their living on the land. The industrial regions of the former British India are almost entirely in the Indian Republic. This has its disadvantages, but there is one advantage: in normal times Pakistan, unlike India, is on the whole independent of food imports. The country produces a number of important argicultural raw materials, such as jute, cotton, and tea, whose export greatly assists the balance of payments and the finances of the state. Pakistan being a country of peasants, land distribution is naturally the principal internal problem. Different conditions of agrarian land-ownership in the various provinces show their different historical development, but on the whole large estates still predominate. Land reform thus impresses the observer as one of the great controversial issues in the country. Politics are also influenced by the rivalry between the various provinces of the new state. For Pakistan is a federal state of five provinces, each of which is very conscious of its individuality.

In its territorial situation Pakistan is one of the strangest states there have ever been. To begin with, it is divided into two portions separated by a flight of eight to nine hours, or a journey by sea lasting a fortnight. Moreover, the portions thus separated lie, so to speak, in two different worlds. West Pakistan comprises the middle and lower Indus valley. It is a river oasis—about the same size as Egypt—and bears the plain marks of the Islamic intercontinent. The people of West Pakistan are mainly wheat-eaters; population and food supply fairly correspond. East Pakistan, on the contrary, is unmistakably a portion of monsoon Asia. It is an overpopulated rice country, and its rapidly growing population requires correspondingly increasing food imports. East Pakistan has one seventh of the area of the state, but more than half of the population; the density of population is eight times as great as in West Pakistan. West and East Pakistan, moreover, are divided not only by these social differences, but in language. The eastern part of the state speaks Bengali; the western maily speaks Urdu, which is the official language of the state.

East Pakistan's jute and tea exports bring in important quantities of foreign exchange. Politically and socially, however, it is a cause of some anxiety. East Pakistan is a part of the former British-Indian province of Bengal; it has two thirds of the population of that former province, but the trade and industry of Bengal, together with the capital, Calcutta, have fallen to India. While the Moslems of the Indus valley have lived in continual contact with the great Moslem block of the Middle East, the Bengalese Moslems are mainly descendants of converted Hindus of the lower castes. Frequently a Hindu is the landlord and a Moslem the tenant farmer. Thus in East Pakistan the conflict between Hindu and Moslem has a special social note, and this does not make it easier to live with the Hindu minority, which runs into millions.

Pakistan achieved consolidation fairly quickly. But more water will have to flow down the Indus before the country's several sections have become firmly united. If all that was needed was to create a firm, indissoluble bond between the two widely separated halves of the state, that in itself would be a task such as has rarely faced a newly formed nation. But West Pakistan has its own internal tensions still to resolve. Four provinces have found themselves suddenly united: the Punjab, Sind, Baluchistan, and the North-West Frontier Province. Pakistan's capital, Karachi, following the examples of Washington and Canberra, has been made a federal territory. The Punjab (so named from its five rivers), fertile and cultivated, was partitioned in 1947, like Bengal, between India and Pakistan. It suffered in consequence from serious social upheavals—one more reason for political instability. The Punjabis feel themselves to be the rightful masters of the new state. Their province is far the most populous in West Pakistan. The heart of Moslem rule in India has always been in the Punjab, and Lahore, the capital, is reputed the cultural centre of Indian Islam. It is thus not without reason that many people regard political tendencies in the Punjab as important indications in regard to Pakistan as a whole. It was also in Lahore that at the beginning of 1951 the political conspiracy to overthrow the regime, formed on the familiar model by a combination of military officers and Left-wing intellectuals, had its headquarters.

Next to the Punjab lives the Afghan Pathan of the North-West Frontier Province. The two populations have never been able to endure each other, the settled inhabitants of the rich plains of the Indus and the warlike, hardened type of the sterile mountain country. There will be more to say about the Pathans. Punjabis, Pathans, and the peoples of Sind and Baluchistan, all have their particularisms. Over against them the federal capital, Karachi, represents the unifying element of the great Moslem nation, whose population is exceeded in size only by Chinese, Indians, Americans, and Russians. Here is first formed the new type of Pakistani. That type will be the true heir of Mohammed Ali Jinnah.

The Pakistani has the pioneering urge to a new Islamic order. His national future is bound up with that. The Constituent Assembly has prefaced its work with a few general principles. Among them is the principle that the state must be ruled "in consonance with the laws of Islam." Those who have laid down that principle are not religious fanatics, and there is no ground for any suggestion that Pakistan is aiming at an Islamic theocracy. The country's leaders are in search of a middle way between the radical laicists and the iconoclastic puritans. Equality among human beings, said Liaqat Ali Khan once as Prime Minister, is one of the best things that Islam has to offer the world. "We believe that a society resting on the Islamic principles of liberty, equality, and social justice is the best alternative to either capitalism or Communism." That was an ambitious statement. It has in it the nucleus of an "Islamic democracy" and an "Islamic socialism," which have no intention of being merely borrowed assets. Pakistan represents a great effort to enable the Moslem community to give an answer to the questions of the twentieth century without undermining the Islamic way of life. Much will depend on the success of the experiment, both for the Moslems and for the peace of the world.

THE CITADEL OF ASIA

THE north-west is the weather side of the Indian subcontinent. In the wide spaces of Central Asia the storms have brewed which in past ages have swept over India—with the single exception of the European invasions from the sea. The peoples of India have been able to put up a successful resistance to the pressure from Central Asia only when the gateway in the north-west was well guarded. A natural rampart, difficult to surmount, is formed by the high range of the Hindu Kush between the western Himalaya and the Afghan city of Herat. Behind the Hindu Kush a second, less formidable range also hinders access to the Indus valley. In spite of its immense natural irregularities and obstacles to communication, the region bounded by the Hindu Kush, the river Indus, the ocean, and the eastern frontier of Persia is a strategic unit. It looks down on Turkistan, Persia, the Persian Gulf with its coastal oilfields, and the great India of the Hindus. It is the citadel of Asia. About fifty million

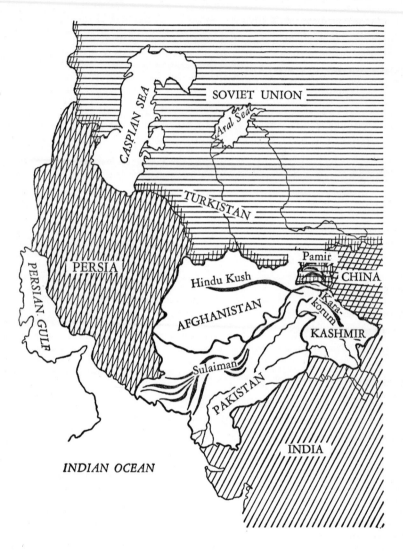

7: THE CITADEL OF ASIA

people inhabit this fortress, people of Indian, Iranian, or Turkish race, almost all Moslems. They are spread over West Pakistan, Kashmir, and Afghanistan. For a hundred years the British watched over the internal stability and external security of this Asian citadel. Since their withdrawal the grip that held together the artificial strategic and political creation of the Indian north-west frontier has lost its efficacy. Old conflicts between the peoples of the citadel have revived, and new ones have been added to them. So long as they are not settled, the fortress between the Hindu Kush and the Indus has lost some of its value to the security of Asia.

The British first came into the north-west of India at the beginning of the nineteenth century. They found two states between the Land of the Five Rivers—the Punjab—and the Hindu Kush: the realms of the Afghans and the Sikhs. Present-day Afghanistan is a creation of the Durrani tribe, and indeed the work of only two great clans of that tribe. The Afghan state had been in existence exactly two hundred years when the British left India in 1947. Its founder, Ahmad Shah, came from the family of the Sadozai; a second great clan of the Durrani tribe, the Barakzai, provided the governors of some provinces. For a time the realm of the Afghans extended throughout the north-west of India, embracing almost all the territory now included in Afghanistan itself, Pakistan, and Kashmir. After the sudden fall of the Sadozai, the branch of the Barakzai living in Kabul gave to the country the forceful emirs of the nineteenth century. Meanwhile there had been events that had thrown back the Afghan dominion far from the Indus. The first was the strengthening of the power of the Sikhs in the Land of the Five Rivers.

The Sikhs first enter history as a militant religious order. The origins of the Sikh religion are to be found in the reaction between Islam and Hinduism in the time of the Moguls. In spite of this relationship with Islam, the Sikhs soon became mortal enemies of the Moslems. At the climax of its political power the militant Order of the Sikhs dominated the whole of the Punjab, parts of Kashmir, and what afterwards became the North-West Frontier Province. The British, after two difficult wars, ended the rule of the Sikhs. But they did not succeed in finally overthrowing the Afghan state and so reaching the natural frontier of the Indian territory at the Hindu Kush. The mountain race of the Afghans was too hard a nut to crack. The frontier of British India was therefore drawn half-way between the Indus and the Hindu Kush, along the passes over the ranges leading from the north-east to the south-west. The British sought the security of this high mountain rampart against Turkistan by indirect methods. They created the vassal state of Kashmir on the upper Indus, from where the passes of the Karakoram form the trade route to Chinese Turkistan. And though they were unable or unwilling to reduce Afghanistan to the same dependence, they took care that that guardian of the Hindu Kush should at all events form a buffer against the steamroller from the north.

The state of Kashmir was an artificial construction first put together in 1846, when the British were faced with the task of bringing order into the heritage of the Sikh rulers. It was a mosaic of various isolated mountain regions with no recognizable interconnexion. The fertile and populous Kashmir valley, in the north-western Himalaya, gave its name to the state as a whole. The British conferred on a Hindu family of Dogra Rajputs the dignity of Maharajah of Kashmir. The Maharajah entered into the same treaty relation to the British-Indian Crown as the many other principalities of India. Kashmir played the part of an advanced frontier post over against Eastern Turkistan and Tibet.

Kashmir's neighbours were borderlands of the weak Chinese Empire. There was no likelihood of any threat to India from across the lonely mountain passes of the Karakoram. Different was the case with the Hindu Kush state of Afghanistan, whose northern neighbours were the Russians. The viceroys in Delhi were undecided whether or not to extend their direct control as far as the Hindu Kush. They had to content themselves with subjecting the foreign policy of the Emir of Afghanistan to the control of Delhi, leaving him his own master in all else. From the Treaty of Gandamak (1879), which laid this down in detail, is usually dated the part played by Afghanistan as a buffer state between the British soldiers in India and the Russian armies in Turkistan. The tedious drawing of frontiers carefully avoided any direct contact between the two Great Powers. Even on the inaccessible Pamirs, the "roof of the world," British and Russians placed a long, narrow peak of Afghan territory between them. The Emir found this unprofitable increase of territory most troublesome, and the British had to recompense him for the cost of administration of the "gooseneck." Thanks to this device, India and the Russian Empire have no common frontier.

Behind the Afghan buffer state, a chance emergency solution rather than a product of strategic requirements, lay the famous north-west frontier of India, with the Khyber Pass and the forts of the British-Indian army. The rulers of Afghanistan wrangled tenaciously with the British over the drawing of the frontier line. When in 1893 the "Durand Line" was finally drawn (Sir Mortimer Durand was the British negotiator), the Afghan Emir made no secret of his dissatisfaction at the removal of millions of tribal relatives from his influence. The period of the "buffer state" came to an end after the First World War, and British-Indian control of the foreign policy of Kabul was dropped. It was not forgotten, however, to append to the treaty that made an end of the protective relationship an annex that once more mentioned the recognized interest of Kabul in the Afghan tribes beyond the Durand Line.

The task of the British-Indian army along the north-west frontier of the Indian subcontinent has fallen mainly on the shoulders of Pakistan. The Pakistanis were not ill-prepared by nature for this task, for three fifths of the British-Indian army were always recruited from the part of India which today forms West Pakistan. But if it was confidently expected at first that the Moslem state would work in close collaboration with its Indian neighbour on the safeguarding of the subcontinent as in the past, any hope of that vanished in the course of the partition. As feeling grew heated in the two new states, it became impossible to discuss the idea of a common defense policy. Suddenly it was realized that the British withdrawal had dislocated the carefully planned organization in the North-West Frontier Province for the security of India. The question at once arose what should take the place in Kashmir of the former bond with the British Crown. At the same time Afghanistan announced its reawakened interest in the destiny of the North-West Frontier Province. The view was expressed in Kabul that the British-Afghan treaties had been rendered null and void by the British withdrawal from India, and that Pakistan could not be automatically regarded as the legal successor of the British on the north-west frontier. The relations between the peoples of the Asian citadel were anything but friendly.

Seventy-five to eighty per cent of the four million inhabitants of the state of Kashmir are Moslems. Only in the south-eastern part of the state are the Hindus in the majority. The people of the authentic Kashmir—that is to say, the inhabitants of the Kashmir valley—have provided some of the famous names of Indian history. Mohammed Ikbal, the national poet of the Indian Moslems, was a Kashmiri. The Hindus, too, are indebted to that picturesque mountain country for a national leader; Pandit Nehru's descent is traced back to an aristocratic Hindu family of the Kashmir valley. Bonds of sentiment such as these on both sides help to explain some of the undercurrents of the Kashmir dispute.

The Kashmir Moslems and their Hindu prince did not get on together. But the tension was due more to the autocratic bearing of the Maharajah than to the difference of faith. The Moslem League has few followers in Kashmir. Most of the Kashmir Moslems followed the leadership of the Sheikh Abdullah, who was a personal friend of Nehru and was largely in agreement with the ideas of the Indian Congress Party. Sheikh Abdullah organized a party of his own, the "National Conference," with Moslem and Hindu support. He was more or less in sympathy with the views of the Left wing of the Congress Party, and this brought him into sharp conflict with the Maharajah. The ruler proved the stronger, and Sheikh Abdullah was thrown into prison. Such was the state of affairs in Kashmir when the British left India, and the mountain state had to decide whether to go over to Pakistan or India.

Pakistan counted on being joined by Kashmir. The Moslem majority in Kashmir seemed to justify that expectation, but there were also other reasons for it. The value set by Pakistan on the mountain country on its northern flank is reminiscent of the relations of the Egyptians with the Sudan. Kashmir controls the upper Indus and, still more important, the region of the sources of some of its great tributaries. The agriculture of the Punjab and of the lower Indus valley depends on irrigation, and this depends in turn on the water supply from the mountains of Kashmir. There was further anxiety about the defence of Pakistan, which might become an unendurable burden if the Indian Republic gained possession of the strategic key-positions of Kashmir. Finally, the geography of the overland routes seemed to demand that the state of Kashmir should join Pakistan.

Immediately after the partition the disturbances extended to Kashmir, and disorders quickly followed. The Moslems in the mountains of western Kashmir revolted. The news spread rapidly in the adjoining regions of Pakistan. The tribes of the North-West Frontier Province (now Pakistani) had always been of an adventurous nature; they seized the opportunity to start a "holy war" against the extension of Hindu rule to Kashmir. A government of "Free Kashmir" (Azad Kashmir) was proclaimed in the region of the revolt. The parts of Kashmir lying farther to the north-west joined the new Moslem state of Pakistan on their own initiative. The state of Kashmir, an artificial creation, was breaking up. The Hindu Maharajah had resigned himself to joining Pakistan, but his entourage induced him to change his mind; he fled for asylum to India. He formally declared his country's adhesion to the Indian Union and appealed for Indian troops to come to the defence of his country from "Moslem invasion." But the Maharajah now had to assure himself of support from public opinion in Kashmir. He remembered Sheikh Abdullah, whom he knew to be congenial to his new protector, Nehru. Sheikh Abdullah, released from imprisonment, at once took the reins of government in Kashmir into his hands.

Throughout 1948 Pakistan and India carried on an undeclared war on the soil of Kashmir, until in January 1949, through the mediation of the United Nations, an armistice was concluded. The demarcation line virtually partitioned Kashmir between the armies of Pakistan and India. In the west, Azad Kashmir controlled about one third of the territory of the state, with a quarter of the population; India— or Sheikh Abdullah—had possession of the much more important and much larger eastern part, with the Kashmir valley.

Sheikh Abdullah had his own views as to the future of Kashmir. He remained loyal to his association with India and his friendship with Congress politicians; but he had no intention of letting Kashmir become simply a part of the Indian Union. Elections were proclaimed for a Constituent Assembly; they yielded, as everyone knew they would, a one-hundred-per-cent majority for the friends of Sheikh Abdullah. As time went on, it became more and more evident that Abdullah was aiming at an autonomous Republic of Kashmir as a state of the Indian Union. In the summer of 1952 he went to New Delhi to negotiate with Pandit Nehru and the Indian Government. The result came very close to his aspirations. If the agreement is carried out, Kashmir will become a republic within the Republic of India. The rule of the Dogra maharajahs, begun a hundred years ago, is over. A characteristic Kashmir nationality is being developed by Sheikh Abdullah. The partition of Kashmir by the armistice line is accepted as an accomplished fact, while the effort is being made in the United Nations to find a solution for the conflict between Pakistan and India.

At first the Moslem League—and therefore the Pakistan program—had had little success among the Moslems of the North-West Frontier Province. There the part of Sheikh Abdullah was played by two Moslem supporters of Congress, Abdul Ghaffar Khan and his brother Khan Sahib. Abdul Ghaffar Khan, like Sheikh Abdullah, wanted union with India. His party, the Red Shirts of the Khuda-i-Khidmetgar ("Servants of God"), were clearly dominant in the province until 1947. Then, however, the adherents of Pakistan gained the lead; had they not done so, the embryo state would have suffered disaster. A plebiscite was held in the province in the summer of 1947, and yielded a majority for joining Pakistan. In the partition of the subcontinent, therefore, the North-West Frontier Province went to the Moslem state, and when provincial elections were held, in December 1951, the Moslem League was able to register a clear victory.

A dangerous explosive material has accumulated in the citadel of Asia. It is the smouldering unrest among the war-like Afghan mountain tribes. The Sulaiman mountains, in the corner between the Hindu Kush and the Indus, are the homes of the Afghans. The number of Afghans is not closely known; estimates vary between eight and twelve millions. They speak the Pukhtu language, a branch of Iranian. The people are known by a name derived from that of their language: Pukhtun or Pakhtun (Pathan). The frontier line drawn by Sir Mortimer Durand between British India and Afghanistan cut through the territory inhabited by the Afghans or Pathans. Less than half of them were left in the state of Afghanistan; the majority of them live in the North-West Frontier Province. The British took only part of that province under their direct administration. The region, difficult to control, of the tribal groups—Waziris, Afridis, Mahsuds, and others—was treated as a sort of protectorate, in which the British-Indian army did its best to maintain peace and order. The control of the tribal region always immobilized strong military forces, and the Pathan tribes were a source of continual anxiety both for the British-Indian army and for the rulers in Kabul.

It is impossible to speak of an "Afghan national consciousness" among the Pathan tribes; what they do show is a defiant, undisciplined will to freedom and a traditional lust for loot. The rulers in Kabul have always kept a watchful eye on all that goes on in the tribal region, and in addition to this the present Afghan royal family has its connexions in north-west India dating from the time of the great Afghan Empire of a century and a half ago. The Durand Line was agreed on with the British, and Kabul is no longer ready to recognize it with Pakistan; and though there is no actual propaganda for the union of the Pathan "irredenta" outside that line with the Afghan "mother country," the demand is made that the Pathan tribes shall be given independence. In the summer of 1949 the Afghan National Assembly ostentatiously denounced all agreements entered into with the former British Indian Government concerning the tribal region. Since then the demand for a tribal state of "Pathanistan" has been heard in the mountain country east of the Indus. Pakistan has no intention of meeting the wishes of Afghanistan. It insists on the Durand Line as the internationally authorized frontier between the two Moslem states of the north-west region. It has established its authority in the tribal region much better and more quickly than many people expected. And, finally, the Pakistanis point out that they have expended more on the pacification and economic development of the North-West Province than the whole expenditure of the Afghan state. Economic difficulties were always one of the main causes of unrest in the mountain country of the Pathans, so that gradual economic improvement is the best way to achieve lasting peace and order there.

CHAPTER EIGHT

The Turks: Anatolian Stability

YOUNG TURKS' HIGH-FLOWN PLANS

A FEW miles from the Anatolian shore of the Bosporus is the village of Polonesköy ("the Poles' village"). Foreigners in the capital, Istanbul, who do not feel inclined to do without the pork that is tabooed by Moslems appreciate the village as a source of pork products. The inhabitants of Polonesköy preserved until quite recently the language and customs of their mother country. Some generations ago the Ottoman Sultan granted asylum in this village to Polish refugees from czarist rule. Not a few fighters for national freedom came to Turkey from eastern Europe and also from Italy during the nineteenth century. The year 1848 especially brought a flood of émigrés, especially from Poland, Hungary, and Italy. As a result, much of the essence of the national movements in Europe came to the knowledge of the Sultan's subjects. It found ready acceptance, especially because the new contacts of the Ottoman intelligentsia with western Europe were beginning to work in the same direction.

One Sunday in July 1865, five respected citizens of Constantinople made a memorable excursion into the refreshing coolness of the heights by the Bosporus. Obviously they meant to have a serious political discussion, for one of them had taken the trouble to get hold of the statutes of the Italian Carbonari and of a Polish secret organization of a similar character. The five men resolved to copy the example of the conspirators of the Italian *risorgimento,* and so began the secret society of the "Young Osmanli" (Yeni Osmanlilar), aiming at the introduction of a constitution. The Young Osmanli lasted only a few years, because the Sultan's police soon got wind of their existence and proceeded against the members. Later, however, that first Turkish secret society found imitators.

The sultans well knew the internal weaknesses of their conglomerate empire. In the Sultan's palace it was realized that the edifice of the empire, old and behind the times as it was, could no longer resist the assault of a new age. The instrument of government must therefore be reformed, and Sultan Mahmud II was the first resolutely to face the task. The Janizaries, who had become thoroughly insubordinate troops, were harshly brought to heel and disbanded. In their place Mahmud created the basis of the modern Ottoman army. His second concern was the training of a modern civil service. Mahmud II was one of those constitutional reformers who unconsciously prepared the way for nationalism. The heritage that the reforming Ottoman sultans left to the Turkish nation was primarily a corps of officers and officials educated in Europe. From this class the leaders of the future Turkish nationalism were mainly drawn. The commercial middle class of the Ottoman Empire was less suited to that role, because it was mainly of alien, non-

Turkish origin. When, however, the last rulers of the house
of Osman went in search of foreign medicines for the weakness of their empire, they failed to avert the destiny of the
"Sick Man by the Bosporus." Such reforms as they conceded
were in any case no more than patchwork and were brought
to an early end by the autocratic regime of Abdul Hamid,
whose state was already in the grip of the disintegrating
forces of nationalism.

The cradle of the Turkish national movement was in the
Balkans. When the European powers turned their gaze to
the south-east and began to consider a partition of Macedonia,
then still under Ottoman rule, the officers of the Turkish
army in the Balkans considered that the time had come for a
change in Constantinople; they attributed to the hated despotism of Sultan Abdul Hamid the main responsibility for
the decay of the empire. At that time the garrison city of
Salonika was a veritable nest of conspirators; there the "Committee for Union and Progress" (Ittihad ve Terakki Cemi-
yeti) had its principal fulcrum on Ottoman soil. Founded
in Geneva at the beginning of the 1890's, that committee was
much the most important association of the Turkish liberals.
It was a secret political organization, formed on the model
of the Freemasons and the Carbonari. The men of that committee became better known under the name of "Young
Turks."

All preparations had been completed when in July 1908
Major Niazi led his troops in sign of revolt into the mountains of Macedonia. In a few weeks the Young Turks' Revolution had defeated the Sultan. Abdul Hamid was forced to
restore the Constitution of 1876, from the shackles of which
he had long freed himself. The Sultan made another attempt
at a counterrevolution. Supported by the influence of the
Moslem clergy, he incited the masses of the capital against
the "Westernizers." But even this manœuvre was no longer

of any avail to the wily Abdul Hamid. The Young Turks led the Macedonian army corps against the capital and compelled the Sultan to abdicate. The Ottoman Empire assumed the character of a constitutional monarchy. But Mehmet V, the new ruler, was no more than a decorative figurehead, and from 1909 to 1918 the Committee for Union and Progress, the party of the victorious revolution, held almost dictatorial power. The decade of the Young Turks was marked by almost continuous wars—the war with Italy, the Balkan Wars, and finally the First World War. In those storms the Ottoman Empire went down, and the Turkish nation was born.

The inner circle of the Young Turk Party was formed by the triumvirate of Enver, Talaat, and Jemal. Of these three men, Enver Pasha did most to impress the Young Turk movement on the memory of later generations. There are those who say that his family were of Bosnian origin; but he is generally regarded as an Albanian, and the Albanians are proud to count him among the many capable politicians and strategists whom that small Balkan people has given to the Near East. Enver chose the military profession. He gained some of his training in the Persian Guards, and later served as Turkish military attaché in Berlin. After the Young Turk Revolution, Enver became Minister of War in Constantinople, and there influenced all important decisions on the policy of the empire. A contemporary wrote of Enver that he was energetic and ambitious, but lacked the sense of what was attainable. Brilliant and of great personal courage, he was the strong man of the Young Turks, but his plans were altogether too high-flown.

Like Enver, the two other triumvirs were Balkan Moslems. Talaat Bey, a former official in the Ottoman postal administration, was a Pomak (that is, a Moslem of Bulgar nationality); Jemal Pasha was a native of the island of Lesbos and

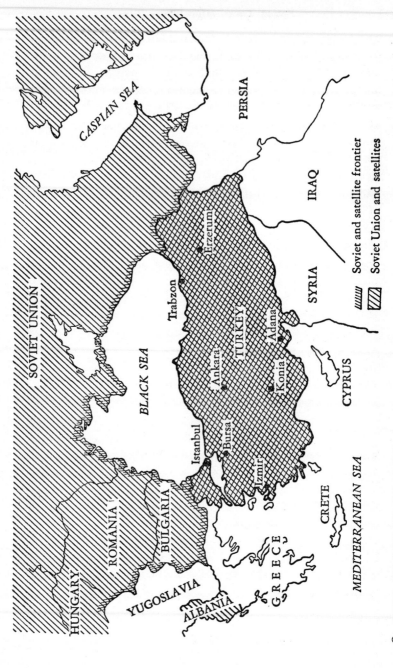

8: THE TURKISH BRIDGE

half Greek. Jemal became commander-in-chief in Syria in the First World War, and in that capacity took severe measures against the Arab nationalists of Damascus. In general the influence of the Balkan element among the Young Turks was very considerable. This may be attributable to the Salonika days, and also to the circumstance that the mixed Moslem-Jewish sect of the Dönmeh, characteristic of that port, were relatively strongly represented in the Committee for Union and Progress. Whether Dönmeh or men of the Balkans or Anatolians, they all regarded themselves as "Turks." Macedonia, as a frontier country of Islam—and also of Turkish rule—was a particularly good centre for the heightening of national consciousness.

The philosopher of Turkish nationalism was supplied by another frontier country, south-eastern Anatolia. The work and life of Ziya Bey, who later adopted the old Turkish name of Gökalp, cover the whole long period from the weak beginning of a Turkish national feeling to the Republic of Ankara. He was born in the town of Diyarbekir, in the Turkish-Kurdish-Arab frontier territory. There his father held the responsible post of keeper of archives. In addition to the customary Islamic curriculum, the young Ziya gained acquaintance with liberal ideas from Europe; for in remote Diyarbekir were living some politicians banished from the capital. After the revolution of 1908 Ziya Bey, who meanwhile had made a name as a writer, was elected to the central committee of the Young Turk Party. He was a convinced supporter of the movement throughout its advance right up to the Kemalist national state; when he died, in 1924, he was a member of the Great National Assembly. Although Ziya Gökalp was never in Europe, he had learned much from the West, though he would not have been ready to throw every tradition recklessly into the melting-pot of "Westernization." "We belong to the Turkish nation, to the

Moslem community, and to European civilization"— Ziya Gökalp aimed at establishing the intellectual basis of Turkish nationalism on that principle. The effects of his influence on the generation that created and developed the new Turkey will long endure. Ministers, members of Parliament, and journalists of the Kemalist Republic listened to the lectures of Professor Ziya Gökalp at the University of Istanbul. The history of the modern Islamic nations can show perhaps only one parallel to the influence of Ziya Gökalp, that of the Indian Moslem poet Mohammed Ikbal in his country. As Ikbal aroused enthusiasm for the new Moslem state of Pakistan, so Ziya Gökalp's ideas prepared the way for the national Republic of the Turks. Both were good Moslems; each was the poet and prophet of a coming nation.

Modern nationalism, whether Greek, Turkish, or Arab, was an explosive among the many peoples of the Ottoman Empire. Naturally the sultans of the nineteenth century regarded with suspicion the rise of a Turkish national consciousness. The police were set to hunt down those who dared to speak of a "Turkish" nation and a "Turkish" mother country. A remedy was sought in Constantinople—not only by the sultans but also by the liberals among their advisers— in the artificial production of a "sense of Ottoman citizenship" without regard to religion or race. The Constitution of 1876 was framed in the spirit of such an "Ottomanism," and at first the Young Turks appealed to a sense of "Ottoman" statehood. But the "Ottomanism" of the Young Turks did not long resist the impact of realities. It may be that the men of "Union and Progress" thought they could unite incompatibles, the empire and the nation. At bottom, however, they were Turkish nationalists, and that decided the issue. The Ottomanism of the reform period was buried for ever when the 1911 program of the Young Turk Party emphatically rejected any form of national autonomy such as the fathers of the Constitution had originally had in mind. But what banner should be unfurled to renew the prestige of Constantinople? Since, after the Balkan Wars, the Ottoman Empire was virtually confined to two Moslem peoples, the Turks and the Arabs, there were those who advocated the pursuit of an Islamic path. Others sought salvation in the Pan-Turkish idea. They were ready to dispense with the un-reliable Arab provinces and to work instead for the union of all Turkish peoples. The Islamic direction was likely to arouse British opposition; a Pan-Turkish policy would imply a struggle with the Russian Empire.

The Young Turk Government concluded an alliance with Germany and entered the First World War at the side of the Central Powers. On the day after the declaration of war the Young Turk Party executive issued an explanatory state-ment, in the course of which it said: "Our people's national idea requires us to destroy the Muscovite enemy so as to se-cure a natural frontier uniting and embracing all men of our race." That was openly and unmistakably the program of a Greater Turkey. But in the same breath the statement pro-claimed an Islamic aim: "Our religious feeling requires us to liberate the Islamic world from the rule of infidels." It was soon discovered that each of these points went far be-yond the powers of the Ottoman Empire. The Young Turks were not of one mind as to the advisability of participation in the war, but in the end Enver Pasha's view prevailed, that the opportunity was at hand for inflicting a decisive de-feat on the hereditary enemy, Russia.

Enver's Islamic expectations were disappointed on the Arab fronts in Syria and Mesopotamia. The untamable will of the Young Turk dictator turned with all the more energy to the Caucasus and Turkistan. Did not the Russian Revolu-tions of 1917 seem to bring nearer the dissolution of the Russian Empire and so the liberation of its Turkish peoples?

Enver called for the formation of a Caucasian state and for self-determination for the Turkish peoples between the Volga and the southern frontier of Turkistan. The collapse of the Ottoman Empire in October 1918 brought Enver and his friends down from the clouds. There was an end of their ambitious plans, and the leaders of the Young Turk regime had virtually to flee from Constantinople. Enver began a peregrination that lasted years, to Berlin, Moscow, Batum, and the longed-for Turkistan. There the gallant man died in August 1922 in combat with the Bolsheviks. With all his mistakes and failings, he was of uncommon stature.

The Young Turks, and Enver in particular, did not escape from retrospective censure for imposing on the Turkish people an effort beyond its strength. But, true though that charge is, it should be remembered that the Young Turks could not simply throw overboard the heavy ballast represented by the Ottoman Empire in its last years. They had to carry it to the bitter end, for they were not only the pioneers of new ideas but also the heirs of the past. Thus the Young Turk movement incorporated a passing phase of Turkish nationalism. Only after the course of events had torn off the husk of the Ottoman Empire could the Turkish nationalists proceed unhindered to the pursuit of the attainable. They did so with the realism and the sturdiness characteristic of the Turkish people.

FIRST MIRACLE: REBIRTH IN ANATOLIA

THERE were early warnings against squandering the remnants of the power of the Ottoman Empire. It was admitted that the cultural affinity of the various Turkish peoples must be nurtured, and that in the field of ideas Turkish nationalism and the Pan-Turkish idea are inseparable; but opinion was divided as to the pursuit of the dangerous path of political Turanianism. The critics held that the Turkish nation must absolutely resist any temptation to adventure: any concern with the Turk beyond the frontier would be playing with explosives. The first thing was to assure the progress of the Ottoman Turkish nation. The advocates of caution were to be justified only too well. Toward the end of 1918 the independent existence of the Turkish people itself was at stake, and the chorus grew of those who gave the warning to attend to first things first. This limited objective was called "turkey nationalism"—that is to say, metropolitan nationalism. It was a natural reaction to the advocacy of big but premature ideas that might degenerate into adventurousness.

Mustafa Kemal, an officer of tested and recognized ability, had always been a wholehearted metropolitan nationalist. He was born in Salonika, the birthplace of the Young Turk Revolution. There are different versions of the origin of Kemal's family; this is not surprising in view of the shifting of populations in the Ottoman Empire. The family may have come from Anatolia, but it seems more likely, as the Albanians insist, that Kemal had Albanian blood in his veins. His grandfather had been an officer; his father was a civil servant and an outspoken advocate of liberal reform. Thus all the elements of the true type of the Young Turk were combined in the young officer Mustafa Kemal. At twenty-nine he was chief of staff of the army corps whose march on Constantinople forced Abdul Hamid to abdicate. Kemal soon found himself sharply opposed to the triumvirate at the head of the Committee for Union and Progress. He was on particularly bad terms with Enver Pasha. Kemal was distinguished from the first by a clear sense of what was attainable, and he regarded Enver's Pan-Turkish national state as entirely out of reach. He was sceptical of the war aims of the Young Turks. At that time he stood aloof from politics;

on many battlefields, however, he showed himself an eminent soldier. Then a sudden chance gave the impulse to his great achievement, and Kemal created the state of the Turkish nation.

After the armistice of 1918 the confusion in Anatolia provided difficult problems both for the Sultan's government and for the victor states. Mustafa Kemal Pasha was then living in retirement in the capital. He was regarded as an officer without political affiliations and, indeed, an opponent of the fallen Young Turk regime. He was therefore appointed Inspector General of the eastern provinces, and commissioned to proceed to eastern Anatolia and there to supervise the demobilization of the Turkish units. The general accepted the commission, and landed in Anatolia in the Black Sea port of Samsun on May 19, 1919. Bad news arrived from the capital; it became clear that the Allies, and particularly the British, intended to partition even the remnant of Turkey left after the amputation of its Arabian provinces. Lloyd George seemed to be entirely won over to the plan of a Greater Greece spanning the Ægean. What other explanation was possible when Greek troops were permitted to land in western Anatolia and to march from Smyrna (Izmir) into the interior? The Sultan's government was robbed of all freedom of movement, especially when Allied soldiers occupied Constantinople. In that desperate situation Kemal Pasha resolved on resistance on his own initiative. Instead of disarming the remaining units of the Turkish army which he found and sending them home, he proceeded with the mobilization of Anatolia, the Turkish nucleus territory, for which the sultans, and also many Young Turks of the capital, had at best but a depreciatory smile. And now, to the universal astonishment, it was discovered what strength was concealed in its peasant and warrior people, in spite of the long drain of war.

Kemal Pasha summoned a national congress, on his own

responsibility, in Erzerum; another soon followed it. On September 9, 1919 the general issued the program of the national revolution: "The entire Turkish territory within the frontiers established on October 30, 1918" (the date of the armistice) "between the Ottoman Government and the Allies and inhabited by a Turkish majority shall form a united, indissoluble whole." For the first time a movement had taken up the demand for the Turkish national state.

Constantinople declared the general a "rebel," and the British press spoke of "the bandit Kemal." At first no one took any more notice of the Anatolian revolt. The Sultan's government signed the dictated Treaty of Sèvres in August 1920. Kemal Pasha had no intention and no means of retreat. From then on there were two governments, the Sultan's Cabinet in the occupied capital, and the national government, which chose Ankara as its capital. Ankara was out in the wilderness, a place scarcely known to anyone who was not actually an archæologist or an impassioned tourist of the Orient. But it was precisely that wilderness, the vast, trackless space of Anatolia, that was Mustafa Kemal's best ally, because it provided him with what he needed most urgently of all, a breathing-space. In Ankara there was nothing to fear from the Soviet Government, or from the French, who might have made difficulties farther south. Both powers entered into agreements with Kemal Pasha's national government. With the rear thus covered, the general was able to take up the struggle with the Greek invaders, and there happened what few would have expected from the Anatolian effort: the Greeks were driven back to the Ægean. For a moment there was indecision in London whether or not to intervene. Lloyd George's battle-cry went unheard, and in the elections the man who had identified British Near East policy with the Greek expansionist adventure was brought down. In October 1922, after its occupation of Constantinople, the national government was undisputed master of the situation. The victor powers of the World War invited Kemal Pasha's envoys to fresh peace negotiations on the basis of a sovereign, unpartitioned Turkey.

The Turkish national state was a revolutionary innovation. It had no precursors in past history as had, for instance, Egypt or Persia. As recently as the beginning of the present century Anatolia was by no means a purely Turkish country. There were large, closely knit settlements of Greeks in the west and on the Black Sea coast, of Armenians in the east, and of Kurds in the south-east. The national, homogeneous Turkey, in which ninety per cent of the population are Turks, is the result of events that have happened since 1914, especially the Armenian deportations during the years of war and the exchange of populations with Greece. There remained only the Kurds. Although the Kurds have given some trouble to the new state, their gradual fusion with the Turkish nation does not now seem out of the question.

Mustafa Kemal Ataturk ("Father of the Turks") was granted a decade and a half after the conclusion of the fight for freedom, to complete as he wished the edifice he had invited the Turks to build. So far Ataturk is the only great political reformer in the Moslem world who has left behind him a national political doctrine independent of his person, a concrete ideal. He not only brought his country factories, railways, and other technical elements of a national state, but also—something of much more importance for sound further progress—gave his people in "Kemalism" a guiding line for its future course. Kemalism is the conscience of the Turkish national state. It presents, briefly, an interconnected system of principles, six in all. These principles have become elements of the Turkish Constitution. Anyone who infringes them or diverges from them dissociates himself from the Turkish state.

Kemalism, to begin with, is "republican." The Sultanate of the Osman line has been brought to an end, and Turkey has been declared a republic (Türkiye Cümhuriyeti). "Democracy" is a second principle of Kemalism. Ataturk raised the sovereignty of the people to the ruling principle of its constitutional existence. All power in the state issues from the popular representative body, the Great National Assembly, which appoints not only the government but the President. So long as Turkey remained a one-party state, that concentration of powers in Parliament meant "dictatorship in the name of the people."

While a further Kemalist principle declares the "revolutionary" spirit of a new regime, the two points "state control" and "laicism" have given modern Turkey its distinctive characteristics. "State control"—that is, of economic affairs—carries a suggestion of socialistic programs of nationalization, but that is not intended. The Kemalists have demanded positive state action not for the sake of any social ideology, but because they were following a definite aim in national policy which can only be understood in connexion with the nature and the development of the former Ottoman Empire. As the Turkish people had shown no particular inclination to industry and commerce, economic life had been mainly in the hands of its non-Turkish elements or of foreigners. If Kemalism intended to develop national Turkish control of trade and industry, as was demanded in theory by the idea of the national state, and in practice especially by the pressure of the world economic crisis, that course could only be organized through state activities. Accordingly the Turkish Republic proceeded in the 1930's to the deliberate adoption of state planning, and with good success. But the further Turkish trade and industry developed, the more weighty became the arguments for relaxing strict forms of state control. Such at least was the view of later critics of economic policy.

Ataturk's laicist reform is the central element of the "Westernization" of the Turkish nation. This principle was of special concern to the creator of the state, and has found application in a number of laws, from the prohibition of the fez to the recitation of the Koran in the Turkish language. Laicism has already been referred to at length. The energy with which this reform was carried out was probably due to a reaction from the waste of effort entailed by the Islamic schemes of Abdul Hamid and especially of Enver Pasha. Any repetition of such policies was to be prevented once for all, and in the view of the Kemalists only a radical cure promised lasting success.

The foundation of Kemalism is the Turkish nation. Obviously, therefore, "nationalism" had to appear among the six Kemalist principles. State control of economic affairs, the separation of Islam and politics, republican democracy—all these things can only be understood if account is taken of the strictly nationalist background of modern Turkey. Ataturk always described his work as a definite break with the Young Turks and, of course, still more with the Ottoman sovereigns. This applies unquestionably to the political conception of Turkey; but it is no contradiction of the contention that the Kemalists themselves are rooted in the ideas of the earlier Turkish nationalism. Most of the men who distinguished themselves in the national revolution of 1919–22 came from the Young Turk movement. The political conception was narrowed from the unattainable "Turan" to the Turkish national state, but the Kemalists inherited the essence of Turkish nationalism from their predecessors. Ziya Gökalp will hardly have felt that there was any break in his intellectual work when he went from Constantinople to Ankara to give his support to the saviour—indeed, the creator—of the Turkish nation. In spite of its abrupt change of political course, there has been continuity in Turkish nationalism.

SECOND MIRACLE: TWO-PARTY DEMOCRACY

DURING the centuries of the struggle of the Ottoman Empire for existence, the Anatolian peasant bore the heaviest burden of warfare. This continued under the Young Turks. The armies of Enver Pasha suffered severely in the deserts of Arabia and by the shores of the Caspian Sea. Scarcely anything shows more eloquently the change that has come than the fact that Kemalist Turkey is today one of the very few countries that can look back on a whole generation of undisturbed peace. The annals of the Ottoman state can show no period of peace of such length. And yet the era of Kemalism includes the years of the greatest and most widespread world war.

Turkey remained unmoved by the menaces and the temptations to which it was exposed during the war. For Kemal Ataturk had made a dislike of adventures, a sober weighing of Turkish vital interests, the second nature of the national state he had inspired. When he died, the Lausanne statute in regard to the Straits had been revised in favour of Turkish sovereignty, and the incorporation of the Sanjak of Alexandretta (the Hatay) in Turkey had been enacted. This brought the national revolution to an end so far as relations with the outer world were concerned. Thereafter Turkey felt herself to be a state with its last requirements met in external relations. She had no further territory to seek beyond her borders, and therefore aligned herself with the anti-revisionist group of powers. When the Second World War came, the Turkish bridge between the Balkans, the Caucasus, and the Arab regions found itself in the centre of the strategic lines: Ataturk's successors kept strictly to the paths of prudence. Ankara's diplomacy succeeded again and again in neutralizing the pressure and counter-pressure of the belligerents, while the Turkish army, fully prepared, kept watch along the borders of the fortress of Anatolia. Anyone who studies Ataturk's conception of Turkish national policy can only come to the conclusion that the Turkish Republic confined itself during the Second World War to basing its political efforts in external affairs on the Kemalist principles. The lesson of caution learned through the collapse of 1918 was not forgotten. There was no lack of reproach for the Turkish policy of neutrality. But now that the passions of the war years have abated, it should be asked without heat what would have been the state of the peace in the Near East today if the caution of Kemalist Ankara had not brought Turkey safely through the dangers of disaster. That the modern Turks are not "neutralists" out of principle or weakness has been sufficiently shown in the post-war years.

Kemal Ataturk died in November 1938. He was succeeded by Ismet Inönü, the son of a military judge in Izmir. Ismet Inönü was little younger than Ataturk, and like him an army officer. He might be regarded as the second man in the Kemalist regime from the beginning of the national revolution; he was Prime Minister until the year before the death of Ataturk. Inönü was inevitably outshone by the brilliance of his great predecessor; but the events of the twelve years of his presidency offer no faint praise for Ismet Inönü's policy. The "old man" may have been a more obstinate and hardheaded master in Tsankaya, the presidential palace, but that in no way detracts from his achievement. A master of caution, sometimes to the point of lively suspicion, Inönü played an important part in keeping Turkey out of the war and unharmed by it. But perhaps the "old man's" greatest service was to pave the way for the great experiment of a balanced party democracy, even at the price of the loss of some personal power.

Most of the men round Ataturk were clear on one point: Kemalism must not be allowed to degenerate into dogmatic rigidity, but must be adapted to the development of the Turkish nation. Ataturk had made the Republican People's Party (Cümhuriyet Halk Parti) the executor of his reforms. During his life there was only that one party, and behind it the administration was carried on rigorously but with patriarchal benevolence by the dictatorship of the Kemalist bureaucracy. Kemal Ataturk himself made two attempts to form an opposition party. Both attempts were quickly broken off because signs seemed to appear that behind the façade of the opposition there were forces coming into action whose purpose might be merely to destroy his still incompletely safeguarded achievement. Not enough time had passed since the overthrow of the earlier regime; the time was not yet ripe for the next step.

It was in November 1945 that Ismet Inönü spoke in the Great National Assembly of the "democratization of public life" as the next objective. At that time there was nothing tangible in existence outside the People's Party. Five years later Ataturk's successor, who had taken over all the power of an authoritarian regime, was sitting on the front bench of the parliamentary opposition, as if Turkey had for years been observing the rules of Westminster. For mastery of the difficult task of staging genuine revolutions without tears, credit had been given in the past mainly to the British. The Turks seem also to be masters of it. It cannot have been easy for Inönü to decide to reduce the rigour of political life in the country, with a war of nerves being carried on against Turkey by her northern neighbour. Under such circumstances the risk was great enough, and the Turks might have gone more cautiously in their development of Kemalism if the Truman Doctrine of March 1947 and American military and economic aid had not offered protection. The sense of increased external security strengthened the cautious "old man's" position, and the arguments of objectors were weakened by the reminder of the existence of the American ally.

There was considerable resistance within the ruling People's Party to any change of the one-party system. It came mainly from the so-called Right wing of the party. Such men as Recep Peker and Sükrü Saracoglu took the view that there should be a minimum of interference with the patriarchal regime of the strong hand. There were signs, too, of a measure of radical Jacobinism when the old guard of Kemalism would not move from the position that the party of the revolution was the only authorized interpreter of the "will of the people." There was especially violent opposition when Inönü revealed his desire to separate the office of the president from the party leadership and to give it the function of an arbitrator above the parties. Until then the president had incorporated the unity of party and state. The Kemalists of the old school made a determined stand against the proposal: in their view it threatened to undermine the principle of the "sovereignty of the people." Thus there took place behind the scenes a bitter struggle in the People's Party, with varying fortunes, between the old guard and the liberals, many of whom belonged to the younger generation. Ismet Inönü tended generally to side with the moderate liberal element. His influence was brought to bear in securing the admission of the younger generation in the party to a share of responsibility.

The opposition took formal shape in January 1946 in the Democratic Party (Demokrat Parti). Its founders were all old and tried Kemalists; some of them had even been active in the Young Turk movement. Until 1945 they had still sat in the Great National Assembly as members of the People's Party; their only disagreement with the majority of that party lay in their conviction that the time had come to enter a new stage in the Kemalist revolution. Four members of the People's Party, Celal Bayar, Adnan Menderes, Fuat Köprülü, and Refik Koraltan, had left the party in protest against "all laws of dictatorial character," and these members became founders of the Demokrat Parti. Celal Bayar, a man of İnönü's age, took over the leadership of the opposition. He is the son of a village schoolmaster of western Anatolia. He entered the banking profession and worked for a time in the Bursa branch of the Deutsche Orient-Bank. His interest in politics and particularly in reform and nationalism was shown by his earlier membership of the Committee for Union and Progress. He was one of the first to respond to Kemal Ataturk's call for resistance in Anatolia. He became the economic expert of the Kemalist regime. Celal Bayar was regarded as the obvious successor to Ataturk and İnönü; otherwise he would hardly have replaced İnönü in 1937 as head of the government. A certain personal rivalry between these two paladins of Ataturk's seems to have continued from that time. Adnan Menderes was born, like Bayar, in the Ægean coastal region of Anatolia, and was educated in the American college of Izmir. He is a landowner and has always been mainly interested in agriculture. Professor Fuat Köprülü is descended from a famous family that played an important part in the great days of the Ottoman Empire; he had gained an international reputation by his researches into Turkish history. Köprülü was a pupil of Ziya Gökalp and had taken an active part in the discussion of the nature and aims of Turkish nationalism that marked the epoch of the Young Turks. The banker, the agriculturist, and the professor were the three men whose names were most closely associated with the further development of Kemalism.

In the summer of 1948 a third party, the National Party (Millet Parti), split away from the Democrats. It has been called a party of the discontented, because it offered decidedly sharper criticism than the Democrats of the existing conditions, and especially of President Inönü personally. Thus the National Party seemed often to come very close to the limit of what might give the Kemalists the disturbing impression of an opposition dangerous to the state. But even the leaders and founders of the Millet Parti, such as Marshal Fevzi Chakmak and the former Minister Hikmet Bayur, shared with their opponents a past in the ranks of the national revolution.

In one generation the Turks had stripped Kemalism of the more primitive forms of the past. In many respects the social structure of the Democratic Party reflects the social development of the country. Officers and civil servants were the executors of the Turkish *risorgimento,* and even the Kemalist People's Party shared with the Young Turks the social feature that the political leadership showed a preponderance of the military and bureaucratic types. In the Democratic Party, on the contrary, there was a clear preponderance of the trading and professional middle class and the prosperous farmers. Ataturk's reforms had promoted the formation and strengthening of the Turkish middle class. It was not purely by chance that theÆgean provinces and the commercial city of Istanbul offered good soil for the new party. Western Anatolia, naturally fertile and in contact with the Mediterranean, is economically one of the most advanced regions of the Republic. The prosperity of its cities and of the countryside also increased political awareness, and it was only natural that in general the farming and trading middle class demanded greater freedom. In particular, the desire was widespread for a more liberal interpretation of the two principles of laicism and state control. People were no longer ready to put up with authoritarian direction of religious life and of trade and industry, to which the old Kemalists had been accustomed. All these things combined to give impetus to opposition. For the first time in the history of the Turkish national movement the Democratic Party brought to its head men of "civilian" origin. Enver, Ataturk, Inönü, had all been army officers, but Celal Bayar came from the banking profession and from economic life.

In Ismet Inönü's time a breach had already been made with the tradition that the army held a special position in the political life of the country. The chief of staff was directly responsible to the President. The defence budget had to be formally approved by the Great National Assembly, but it had become almost customary law to approve it without any debate or questions. The chief of staff had for many years been Marshal Fevzi Chakmak, who had long been associated with Ataturk and was a soldier with conservative views. When the Marshal retired, in 1943, the relationship between the army and the civil powers was changed. The General Staff was placed under the Prime Minister, and later, in the summer of 1949, a civil Ministry of Defence was created. The change aroused no great interest, but it was obviously of deep significance for a nation in whose development the army has played an outstanding part.

When Ismet Inönü promised the democratization of public life, the Republic was approaching a change of generations. Gradually the ranks thinned among the older men who had themselves taken part in the revolution and still had a lively memory of the past. Their place was taken by younger men who had known only Kemalist Turkey, and who were therefore much more open-minded in regard to the questions of the day than the Kemalists of the old guard. In the post-war period the men of thirty-five to forty-five years of age were pressing forward to gain influence and power in political life. It cannot be said that the young men were to be found in any greater numbers among the Democrats in opposition than in the People's Party; but it was largely the younger men who joined in the demand for the ending of the single-party regime.

Many people were sceptical at first about the reality of the change. The dominant party had permitted the change, giving lip-service to democratization, but, after all, it was in possession of all the power of the state. The real test would be the way the elections were conducted. The first elections in which several parties could come forward took place in the summer of 1946. The Democratic Party had been in existence for barely six months, but though it was scarcely possible at that time to speak of free elections, it was able to secure 66 out of 465 seats in Parliament. Everything now depended on whether a new franchise law would be enacted before the next elections, due in 1950, and would guarantee a free consultation of the electorate. A first franchise bill entirely failed to satisfy the opposition. When the new elections drew near, an amended bill was debated for a full six months. In the end the People's Party agreed to the desired guarantees: the polling was to be supervised by the judicial authorities, there would be unrestricted freedom of assembly, and broadcasting was to be free to all parties. On February 25, 1950 the new franchise bill was passed in the Great National Assembly by 341 votes to 10. It may be that the government party made these concessions in the confident expectation of securing a majority in any case. It was generally assumed that the opposition would gain considerably, but there was no expectation of a landslide. The action of the men who then had the destinies of Turkey in their hands showed, however, that the Turks had not lost their readiness for evolution in political and social life.

On May 14, 1950 the Turkish people went to the polls. The participation in the voting reached the remarkably high average of 80 per cent. Of the votes cast, the Democratic Party received 55 per cent, and the Republican People's Party 40 per cent. Thanks to the system of the cumulative vote, the landslide had come. The Democratic Party gained 408 seats, the People's Party only 69. The National Party had to content itself with a single seat. Celal Bayar became the third President of the Kemalist Republic; Adnan Menderes became the Democrats' first Prime Minister. When the program of the new government was read to the Great National Assembly, the "Leader of the Opposition," Ismet Inönü, was loud in its praise. The Turkish nation had passed unscathed through the danger zone between two stages in its development.

In spite of the period of preparation under Ataturk and Inönü, it was running a great risk to call upon the masses of a people that for centuries had lived in subjection to authoritarian rule to become arbiters over their government. It made the feeling and the aspirations of the masses a power in the state. The great bulk of the Turkish people are Anatolian peasants: 80 per cent of the 21,000,000 Turks are peasants, and only ten per cent live in towns with more than 100,000 inhabitants. There are not yet even half a million people employed in industry. The three great cities, Istanbul, Ankara, and Izmir, elected only 62 of the 487 members of the present Parliament. All the rest of the members come from country constituencies or from the small towns bound up with the countryside, and have therefore to keep in close touch with Anatolia to satisfy their constituents. It is true that most of the urban and commercial population voted against the government party in 1950; but it was mainly the peasants who then put the Democratic Party into power.

We may fairly speak of a Turkish "economic miracle," connected to some extent with the change of political leadership in Ankara. Turkish agriculture as a whole had until then been stationary, but in very few years it passed through a phase of rapid, almost lightning expansion. Between 1948 and 1952 agricultural production increased some 40 per cent. No less striking is the growth in the real income of Turkish agriculture. Three or four years ago it stood at the pre-war level. In 1951 it was some 70 per cent and in 1952 nearly 90 per cent above pre-war. As the other branches of industry have not advanced to the same extent, there has been a notable shifting of the level of income in favour of agriculture. Although Turkey has always been a country of peasants, the total income from agriculture has not in the past exceeded 50 per cent of the national income; it has now advanced to between 60 and 65 per cent. Rural Anatolia has emerged from stagnation and neglect.

To speak of Anatolia as a granary is no longer merely to dream of the future. Up to the end of the 1920's Turkey was a grain-importing country. During the two following decades Turkey had either a grain deficit or a slight grain surplus, according to the very irregular agricultural yield. On the whole, Turkey was self-supporting in grain. Since 1952 the country has become one of the important grain-exporting countries. The extent of the change from deficit to surplus is shown still more plainly when account is taken of the fact that in the same two decades, from 1930 to 1952, the population of Turkey grew from 14,000,000 to 21,000,000 and the standard of living has slightly improved. In the last five years before the Second World War the grain yield averaged 6,500,000 tons; in 1950 it was 7,500,000, and in 1952 almost double pre-war: 12,000,000 tons. No less sensational has been the improvement in the Turkish cotton crop. One is reminded of the great time of the early overseas development when one learns that Turkish cotton has yielded private fortunes of two and three and even thirty million Turkish pounds. The peasants who combine grain and tobacco culture have also made good money. Needless to say, farmers who have made millions are exceptions to the general rule in present-day Turkey. Much more important is the fact that in Anatolia a farming middle class has come into existence and is growing in numbers as a political and social support of the young Turkish democracy.

In the elections of May 1950 the Democratic Party also profited by its advocacy of religious freedom. It believed that it owed to this some part of its success with the peasants. Under the pressure from their own ranks, in which there was a good deal of resistance to radical laicism, the Democrats accordingly made at first a number of concessions in the religious field. In point of fact, however, the dividing line between beneficent consideration for Islamic feeling and involuntary encouragement of intrigues against reform was soon obscured. Islamic associations similar to those in the rest of the Moslem world made their appearance. There was open invitation to battle against Kemalist "freemasonry and freethinking." In the end the government has once more taken up a clear attitude against this misuse of Islam for purposes inimical to the state. There is today no acute danger to the regime from the Islamic reaction. But it remains to be seen how Kemalism and Islam will ultimately come to terms.

As regards the present prospects of party politics in the Turkish democracy, the permanence of the Kemalist reforms seems assured in the fresh air of free elections. The ballot paper can at most effect a changing of the guard in Ankara, and not a change of regime. Government and opposition alike are keeping a close watch on all elements whose attitude to the democratic Kemalist regime is not entirely clear. Since May 1950 the Turkish Republic has been a genuine two-party democracy. No less notable than the victory of the Democrats was the fact that the two great parties monopolized the votes: even the violent polemics of the National Party had brought no result. As the relative voting showed, there was no very great difference between the voting strength of the Democrats and the Republicans. Nor are there differences of any great importance in the home and foreign policy of the two parties. To that extent, quite apart from the superficial detail of the party names, there is some justification for claiming a certain resemblance to the American system. The differences between the Democratic Party and the Republican People's Party are mainly differences of method. The Republicans, in accordance with their tradition, are a rigidly led party, with a certain measure of authoritarianism; decisions within the Democratic Party are more largely influenced by the rank and file. If "order" and "freedom" deserve to be called the two guarantees of political stability, it may be said that the Republicans are more concerned for "order" and the Democrats for "freedom."

Government and opposition take their stand on the common basis of Kemalism. But the according of considerable freedom in domestic politics was almost bound to bring grist to the mills of those who make no secret of their hostility to the Kemalist Republic. As for Communist infiltration, it finds no easy access to Turkey, because watchfulness in relation to their Soviet neighbour is, so to speak, bred in the bone of the Turks. The case of the Islamic puritans is rather different. Their movement, noticeable throughout the Islamic world, cannot be denied all access to Moslem

Turkey. Against all perils the Kemalists, whether Democrats or Republicans, put up a resolute and effective resistance. The two-party democracy had no intention of opening the door to enemies of the state. A survey of the Turkish national movement shows that the Turks are a nation of great steadiness. This, too, may serve as an indication of the future.

THE LEGEND OF THE "RED APPLE"

MODERN nationalism came to the Turkish-speaking peoples from two sources. Western and central Europe, especially France, were the school of the Young Turks in the Ottoman Empire. But even before the ideas of liberal Europe had gained access from those quarters, other Turkish peoples had long been in close contact with the Russians. The northern Turks by the Volga and in the Crimea came at an early date under the rule of the Russian czars—the Volga Turks as early as the sixteenth century, the Turks of the Crimea during the reign of Catherine II. At the beginning of the nineteenth century the same fate befel the Azeri Turks, who until then had belonged to the political and cultural realm of Persia, and finally the Turkish peoples of Central Asia were not spared by Russian expansion. Whatever ideas influenced the Russian people in the nineteenth century spread to the subjugated Turks, soonest and most strongly, of course, where there had already been close economic and spiritual intercourse. It is not surprising, therefore, that the Crimean and Volga Turks were the first to cultivate the seeds of national consciousness, even before the Turks of the Ottoman Empire. In a certain sense they may claim to be the pioneers of Turkish nationalism, if that conception is given a sufficiently wide definition. Among those two peoples an intelligentsia and a middle class of purely Turkish character had developed at a time when in the Ottoman Empire the sense of being a "Turk" had scarcely struck root.

A Crimean Turk, Ismail Gaspirali, who was born about the time of the Crimean War, aroused national consciousness among the Turks. Gaspirali, son of a civil servant, was a schoolmaster, and for a time he was Mayor of the Turkish town of Bahcesaray. He was an enthusiast for the overcoming of the barriers of the various Turkish dialects and for the establishment of a common Turkish written language. He devoted his newspaper *Tercüman* to that task. From the platform of the *Tercüman* the ideas of the Crimean Turkish intellectuals were spread far and wide among the educated Turks of the Russian Empire. Ismail Gaspirali was an eager advocate of "unity of the Turks in language, thought, and deed." Younger supporters like his brother-in-law Yusuf Akchura, a Volga Turk, and an Azerbaijan scholar, Ali Hüzeyinzade, followed him in the preaching of Turkish unity. In this case, too, the influence of the Russian ruler and neighbour was felt. While the Russians sought a spiritual home in Pan-Slavism, the Turks in Russia set their hopes on the union of the peoples of "Turanian" origin, and if Slav expansionism allied itself with the missionary zeal of the Orthodox Church, Turkish defence could have the support of Islam's power of resistance.

The Turks of Russia naturally looked for support to the Ottoman Empire. Russo-Turkish emigrants of all classes sought refuge under the Ottoman Sultan, so that, for example, there were a good many more Crimean Turks to be found within the Ottoman frontiers than in the Crimea itself. The universities of Constantinople gave their education to many of the Turks of Russia. Their presence also gave the Ottoman Turks a sense of Pan-Turkish community. In the struggle for nationality and religion along the line of contact between Slavs and Turks this sense had become more acute than by the Bosporus, where it took long for awareness of racial relationship and interest in the Turks beyond the frontiers of the empire to grow.

1   Osmanli (Turkey)
2   Idel-Ural (Volga Turks; Bashkirs)
3   Azeri Turks (Azerbaijan)
4   Turkistan
5   Crimean Turks (deported in 1946)

9: DISTRIBUTION OF THE MOSLEM TURKISH
   PEOPLES

Turkish nationalism made no difference between Crimean Turks and Ottomans, or Turks from the Volga or Baku or Bukhara. Turks from Russia—for instance, Ismail Gaspirali

—had taken their place in the executive of the Young Turk Party. They contributed to developments among the Young Turks in the direction of a Pan-Turkish movement. In this period Constantinople (Istanbul) was assigned a new role. In the course of more than two thousand years that city had been the goal and the symbol of the aspirations of many peoples, of their will to power and of their ideas. Among the Young Turks it also acquired the rank of a spiritual centre of the Turkish world.

"The land of the Turks is not Turkey, nor is it Turkistan: it is a wide, eternal country—Turan." In these high-flown words the young Ziya Gökalp—himself an Ottoman, not a Russo-Turk—expressed his enthusiasm for the idea of "Turanianism." A halo of romance surrounds the land of Turan, that newly discovered, mythical, primeval home of all the Turks. Maps do not show the name. Its first appearance, so far as is known, is in the sacred books of the ancient, pre-Islamic Persians. It is applied to the steppes of Central Asia, whose nomad population was a permanent nightmare for "Iran," the country of peasant civilization. In the age of modern nationalism a romantic conception of history shows "Turan" as a symbol of Turkish unity. Many peoples of the East have procured signposts for national aspirations from the world of myth, and the Turanists did the same. Ziya Gökalp drew from a Turkish myth the title for a volume of enthusiastic verses, *Kizil Elma (Red Apple)*. It appears that the origin of the legend of the "Red Apple" is to be found in Byzantium. The tradition is that a statue of Justinian showed that Byzantine Emperor with a golden apple in his hand, as the symbol of world rule. The Turks evidently took over the tradition for their own ends. Gökalp puts into the mouth of a mullah this interpretation of the "Red Apple": at present the "Red Apple" is only a land of fancy; it will not become reality until the Turks have found the way to their true national civilization. Thus the story is concerned with the hoped-for country of future Turkish greatness and unity. But Gökalp also brings in the Turkish past. When the Turkish peasant hears of the "red apple," he thinks of the old Turkish realms. As soon as the dreams of "Turan" were translated into concrete political aims, however, they suffered the same shipwreck as the missionary dreams of Pan-Slav writers. Ziya Gökalp later renounced the political Turanianism of his youth. But the sense of the essential unity of all Turks survived this excursion into political romanticism.

For a short time the Russian Revolution of 1917 opened the way to self-determination for the Turks of Russia. But united action by the various Turkish peoples of Russia soon proved impossible. The situation was different in each case, and views therefore diverged widely on whether to be content with simple autonomy or to aim at complete separation from the Russian realm. Only in the Crimea and in Caucasia were the conditions favourable to the formation of independent Turkish Moslem states. The Crimean Turks, the Turks of Azerbaijan, and the Moslem mountain peoples of the northern Caucasus proclaimed independent republics. For geographical and economic reasons that path could not be followed by the Turks of the Volga region (Tatars and Bashkirs), though those peoples had taken a leading part in the national movement of the Turks of Russia. The Tatars and Bashkirs decided on autonomy for their country, giving it the name "Idel-Ural" (Idel is the Turkish name of the Volga). The last of the regions inhabited by Turks, Turkistan, had the geographical advantages of the Crimea and the Caucasus, lying on the periphery of the Russian realm. But the opportunity of the years 1917–18 found the various Turkish peoples of the immense country divided and unprepared. Turkistan was only beginning to awake to a sense of Turkish nationality.

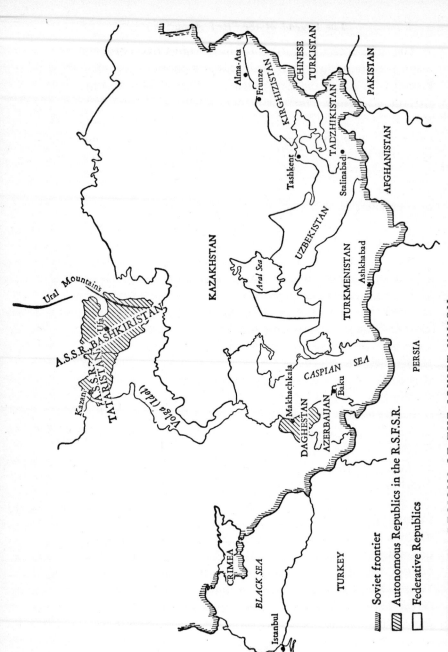

IO: THE MOSLEM REGIONS OF THE SOVIET UNION

The efforts of the Turks of Russia could have brought lasting success only if there had been an opportunity of association with one of the Great Powers. In 1918 there was little prospect of that. The collapse of Germany and of the Ottoman Empire created a vacuum behind the Russo-Turkish peoples. The British made some moves toward intervention in Caucasia and in Turkistan. In the so-called "Indian school" of British foreign policy there was discussion of the possibility of increasing the security of the Asian nerve-centre of the Empire by creating a girdle of independent Turkish states. But the idea was not seriously pursued: Great Britain at that time was too heavily committed in other quarters.

When the Moscow Government had secured some measure of stabilization, it was free to proceed with the reconquest of the great colonial empire that the czars had accumulated. Under the cover of the Bolshevik doctrine, the Russian people again extended their rule over Islamic regions. By 1925 the Moslem Turkish regions were subjugated once more. The self-determination of the Turks of Russia, so recently invoked, disappeared again. In its place the Soviet Union put the Communist version of "autonomy" in the form of a number of Turkish Soviet Republics, four in Turkistan (Uzbekistan, Turkmenistan, Kazakhstan, and Kirghizistan), and one in Caucasia (Azerbaijan), and finally in Turkistan the Soviet Republic of the Iranian Moslem Tadzhiks. These six regions have the rank of so-called federal Republics of the Soviet Union. A stage lower is the autonomy of the Tatars, Bashkirs, Crimean Turks, and a few Moslem peoples in the R.S.F.S.R. Under the outward form of "autonomy" the life of the Russo-Turks was subjected to Lenin's formula: "National in form, Communist in essence."

Very little news has reached the outer world about the fate of the sovietized Moslem peoples. Moscow has kept the regions with Turkish populations, especially in Central Asia, with quite special stringency out of the sight of unauthorized persons. Apart from carefully guided propaganda tours, they have no contact with the Moslems beyond the Soviet borders. Similarly the Soviet Union has taken the most rigorous measures against the slightest expression of any Turkish sense of unity. Beyond any doubt, three decades of Soviet rule have deeply affected the structure of the Turkish communities in Russia. There have been transfers of population on the largest scale. Whole Turkish peoples—for instance, the Crimean Turks—have been subjected to compulsory migration and have disappeared from the map. The migration of Slav populations, which already under the czars had invaded the regions settled by Turks, has been pushed farther in the wake of the Five-Year Plans and of wartime administration; already one quarter of the population of Turkistan seems today to consist of Slavs. The Slav steamroller represents a grave menace to the national existence of the Turkish peoples in the Soviet Union.

A generation is long enough for the thoroughgoing introduction of the social and economic revolution of Communism. The Communist order of society is therefore an accomplished fact in all the parts of the Moslem world that belong to the Soviet Union, and it will be wise to entertain no illusions as to the permanence of that social achievement. But does that necessarily mean that the forcible sovietization has broken the will of the Turks of Russia to maintain their national character?

It would be a contradiction of all past experience if the change of social constitution had brought the nationalism of the Russo-Turks to its end. There is no need to adduce the activities of the many Russo-Turkish émigrés in order to discover the cause of national resistance. Even for those who have no connexion with the "capitalist" outer world and can have no conception of any but a Communist order of society, the dominance of the Russian element in their own country is a heavy burden. In the Communist parties of the Turkish Soviet Republics, Russians and other non-Turkish elements carry a weight that in no way corresponds to the national composition of the population; as a rule, more than half of the party members and officials are Russians. The key positions of the Ministries of the Interior and the Police are all held by Russians. No Communist of Turkish-Moslem origin has yet been seen in the inner circle of the Soviet Government, though the Turks (and other smaller Moslem peoples) form ten to fifteen per cent of the population of the Soviet Union.

The annals of Soviet rule are rich in complaints of so-called nationalist deviations among the Communists in the Turkish peoples. At the Congress of Turcologists in Baku in 1926—the last occasion on which the Turks of Russia and those outside the Soviet frontier were able to meet—some Turkish scholars of the Volga brought forward a demand for the creation of a Turkish "language federation." "We Turks cannot isolate ourselves from one another"—that declaration could then be openly made, though Russian suspicion of any reference to Turkish unity was well known. A few years later a great political trial was concerned with the peril of a Turanian Communism. The chief defendant was a teacher named Mirsayyad Sultan Ali, a Volga Turk and a member of the Communist Party. He and his friends were charged with having tried to form a party of "Moslem peasants, workers, and intelligentsia," undeterred even by the colonial imperialism of the Russians. The charge-sheet even quoted a plan for a Turkish Communist state, extending from Idel-Ural to Turkistan. It might be objected that these stirrings of a Communism with an Islamic tinge took place at the outset of sovietization, and therefore are now only of historical interest. But almost a generation later the "nationalist deviations" have not ceased. The party organs of the Turkish Federative Republics of the Union had frequent reports of such cases, ending in due course with sentences of punishment and purges of the nationalist elements. The Turkish intelligentsia of Central Asia seems to have been specially affected. Russian Central Asia is a neighbour of China, and it is asserted that the formation of the Chinese Communist People's Republic produced a good deal of agitation and unrest in the Soviet Republics of Turkistan. A great Communist state had suddenly sprung up in their immediate neighbourhood, and the people of Soviet Turkistan evidently gained the impression that it was not a satellite but a partner of the Russians. Perhaps they inferred that there could be a Communism without Russian domination. No more than surmise is possible; but it is significant that in 1950 the party organ of the Soviet Republic of Uzbekistan said that there had been widespread nationalist movements in Turkistan, nourished by the hope that a great war might bring liberation to the country. The struggle between Russians and Turks is older and more elemental than what the Bolshevik theorists call "bourgeois nationalism." And the sovietization of the Turks of Russia has destroyed that movement only where it has proceeded to physical extermination. The power of the Russian state, however, is so great that every form of national resistance and nationalism among the scattered and numerically weak Turkish peoples must seem hopeless.

CHAPTER NINE

The Moslems' Oil

WEALTH BY THE PERSIAN GULF

DRAW a straight line on the map northward from the Persian Gulf through the Caspian Sea to the foot of the Urals and it will be found that that line, running almost along the fiftieth degree of longtitude, marks the geographical axis of the Islamic world. The discovery would have been of no particular significance if it were not that along that line, according to the present state of research, lie the greatest oil deposits in the world. There is naturally no connexion between the spread of Islam and the accumulation of oil deposits beneath the soil. It happens that the Moslem peoples have settled round a vast basin full of oil. It is a chance circumstance of which the world only became aware in the last half-century. The precious basin appears to be a double one. Its southern part embraces the shores of the Persian Gulf. It has convenient access to the world routes of oversea transport and trade, either through the Persian Gulf and the Indian Ocean or through the eastern Mediterranean. To this region belong the Arabian shores of the Persian Gulf and southern Persia. The northern oil basin is embedded in the Eurasian continental mass. Its situation and extent may conveniently be described with reference to the Caspian Sea, the greatest inland sea in the world. Round this sea are the oil deposits of the Caucasus, the Volga-Ural region, Turkistan, and northern Persia.

The oil deposits of the world are estimated at present at 10,000,000,000 to 11,000,000,000 tons, or about twenty times the extraction in 1951. They are distributed with extreme irregularity over the earth. Europe, India, China, and the greater part of Africa have little oil, and most of the deposits exist in two great regions, the Western Hemisphere and the centre of the Islamic intercontinent. In the statistics of oil extraction North and South America have for decades held the lead. The estimated deposits in the Western Hemisphere, however, take the second place. Rather more than half of the still unexploited oil is believed to lie in the countries of the Moslems, and forty-seven to forty-eight per cent in North and South America. The rest of the world has next to none. The lion's share is possessed by the southern part of the great Moslem double basin, for the oil deposits by the Persian Gulf are estimated at 4,000,000,000 to 4,500,000,000 tons, or two fifths of the world supply. The greatest good fortune seems likely to fall to the tiny Arabian principality of Kuwait, whose sandy soil promises to hold more oil than the vast Soviet Union. Not much smaller are the deposits in Saudi Arabia; then come southern Persia and Iraq. Even without Persia, the deposits in the Gulf region remain impressive and unequalled in the world. The Arabian countries by the Gulf have between them almost one third of the world supply. Thus the Arabs possess the greatest potential of the fuel indispensable in war and peace.

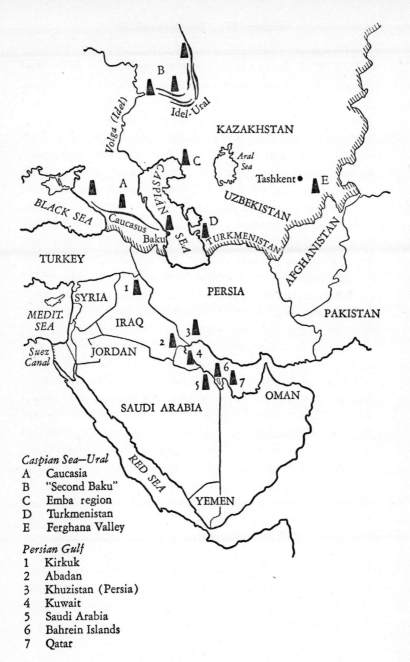

Caspian Sea—Ural
A   Caucasia
B   "Second Baku"
C   Emba region
D   Turkmenistan
E   Ferghana Valley

Persian Gulf
1   Kirkuk
2   Abadan
3   Khuzistan (Persia)
4   Kuwait
5   Saudi Arabia
6   Bahrein Islands
7   Qatar

II: THE MOSLEMS' OILFIELDS

The northern oil basin is to all appearance less richly endowed. With the exception of northern Persia, it lies within the frontiers of the Soviet Union. Its oil, virtually the whole of the Soviet oil, amounts according to Russian estimates to about 1,000,000,000 tons, or just a tenth of the world supply. Some non-Russian experts place the figure lower. Apart from the great oil basin by the Persian Gulf and the Caspian Sea there are further oil deposits in Moslem countries. The southeast Asian offshoots of the Moslem community (Indonesia and British North Borneo) have oil deposits of 180,000,-000 to 200,000,000 tons. The quantity is relatively small, but it forms the only important source of oil in the Far East. Egypt's oil is at present a remote and isolated outpost on the western border of the main oil zone. The picture here drawn of the distribution of supplies may be modified in a few points, for geological exploration in the world is still proceeding. But it may be anticipated that the Moslems will retain the leadership among the great oil-owners of the world.

In 1907, when the British and Russians agreed on the delimitation of zones of influence in Persia, the negotiators had no reason to take any notice of Persian oil. The British were mainly interested in the south-eastern provinces near the Indian frontier; Khuzistan, the later oil province in south-west Persia, played only a minor part. Not until the year following the conclusion of the treaty of partition were the first borings made in the mountains of Khuzistan, and a further five years passed before production had advanced to the stage at which Persian oil came into the world market. Oil from the Arabian countries did not enter world trade until the 1930's, after the pipeline from northern Iraq to the Levant coast had come into operation. Gradually the prospectors brought to light the immense wealth of the zone round the Persian Gulf. Oil deposits were found in the Bahrein Islands, in Kuwait, and in Saudi Arabia. Before the Second World War the extraction in the Middle East still remained within the modest limit of 16,000,000 tons a year, or six per cent of the world extraction. In comparison with the rapid increase in extraction soon to be shown by the statistics of Middle East oil, the pre-war output was no more than a small beginning. Persia alone then supplied three fifths of the total, and only Iraq and the Bahrein Islands also counted at all. The oil output of the Orient seemed likely to show a steady but gradual and limited increase, when suddenly, after the Second World War, the tempo of development showed an undreamed-of acceleration. The miracle of the oil of the Persian Gulf is, however, only of recent date. At the end of the war the extraction (27,000,000 tons) did not greatly exceed the pre-war figure. And the increase was almost entirely due to more intensive exploitation of the field in south-western Persia. Meanwhile the large-scale entry of Arabian oil into the world market was in preparation. Saudi Arabia, and a little later Kuwait, went over to mass production so quickly and so intensively that these two Arabian countries quickly came close to the output of the much older Persian fields. The extraction by the Persian Gulf rapidly mounted: in 1947 it was 40,000,000 tons, in 1949 it was already 74,000,000, and in 1951 the 100,000,000 mark was almost reached, and that though the British-Persian oil conflict fell in that year. Between 1938 and 1951 the world extraction more than doubled. In spite of that, Arabian and Persian oil increased its proportion of the whole from six to sixteen per cent and more.

The oil-producing lands of the Middle East themselves consumed little. Nor is it to be expected that they will ever require a substantial part of their extraction. Their markets are therefore remote from the fields by the Persian Gulf. The large consumers are in the countries of the Old World with little oil of their own, especially highly industrialized western Europe, and in the second place south-east Asia, Australia, and Africa. While the latter markets are conveniently and cheaply supplied from the Persian Gulf, that is not the case with the much more important European market. Either the long journey must be made by tanker round the Arabian peninsula and through the Suez Canal, with the heavy canal charges; or the oil must be pumped twelve hundred miles by pipeline to the eastern Mediterranean. For the oil brought from the sources in northern Iraq, only the second channel is available. The first pipeline was therefore laid from Kirkuk, in the mountains of Iraq, to Haifa and Tripoli (Lebanon). This first line was able to deal with 4,000,000 tons a year, and its opening in 1934 was a great event. Now that modest beginning has long been outdistanced by the adventurous achievement of the great Arabian pipelines. In December 1950 the Americans brought the Trans-Arabian pipeline into operation. Its eleven hundred miles unite the oilfields of Saudi Arabia with the port of Sidon (Saida) in Lebanon. The Iraq Oil Company greatly increased the capacity of its network by laying a new pipeline parallel to the pre-war one and a further huge conduit from Kirkuk to the Syrian port of Baniyas. The Iraq Oil Company suffered severely, however, from the Arab economic blockade of Israel. Haifa, one of the two terminal points of the old pipeline, is in Israel. The Iraq Government has therefore stopped using the pipeline to Haifa, and construction of the parallel line was ended shortly before reaching the Israeli frontier. These two pipelines would have added 6,000,000 to 7,000,000 tons a year. More than half of the annual production of oil (not including Persia) is thus denied the use of the pipelines, and a large part of the oil for Europe has to continue the long tanker voyage through the Red Sea and the Suez Canal.

When the question of refining the oil of the Middle East came up for consideration, there was a choice between refining it in the Middle East or in the consuming countries of western Europe. At first it was decided to do both. Six great refineries were started in the immediate neighbourhood of

12: WEALTH BY THE PERSIAN GULF

the Middle East oilfields—at Abadan in Persia (one of the greatest and best-equipped plants in the world), Bahrein, Ras Tannura (Saudi Arabia), Kuwait, Haifa, and Tripoli. These

six refineries together can deal, at full capacity, with 45,-
000,000 tons of crude oil a year. Two of them, however,
have been put out of action by the political developments of
recent years. Haifa, with a potential output of 4,000,000 tons,
has worked only to a fraction of capacity since the Palestine
war, and Abadan, with 26,000,000 tons' capacity, has virtually stopped all production since the British-Persian oil
dispute. Such refineries as are left in the Middle East can at
best deal with no more than one sixth or one seventh of the
crude oil extracted. Pipelines and refineries call for heavy
and risky capital investment. Plants are constructed and then
need political and military protection. The readiness to build
further transport and refining plants thus depends entirely on
what the foreign ministries and general staffs of the Great
Powers think of the security of the Persian Gulf region.

In spite of its rapid growth, the oil extraction by the Persian Gulf has not yet reached its peak. Already estimates of
future extraction are double the 1951 figures. The high oil
potential of the Persian Gulf region is shown by the fact that
the loss of the oil of south-west Persia was quickly made good.
The gap left by Persia was filled by her Arabian neighbours
without effort. Saudi Arabia and Kuwait are rapidly advancing toward a goal of 40,000,000 to 50,000,000 tons a year
each. Iraq holds out the prospect of increase in three years
up to an annual extraction of 30,000,000 tons. Apart from
these three great producers, there may be surprises in other
fields by the Persian Gulf. Before very long Arabian crude
oil will be available at the rate of 100,000,000 to 150,000,-
000 tons a year. The future of Persian oil is at present veiled
in obscurity; but it is fairly safe to set the potential extraction
in the oilfields of Persia formerly worked by the Anglo-
Iranian (formerly Anglo-Persian) Oil Company at about the
same as that of Saudi Arabia or Kuwait; that is to say, 40,-
000,000 to 50,000,000 tons a year. Indisputably the Per-

sian Gulf region is today the most important oil-producing region outside the United States.

The oil reserves of the Islamic world have been opened up by European and American capital. Up to the Second World War British capital was far ahead, controlling about four fifths of the oil extraction of the Orient. Much the most important producer was the Anglo-Iranian Oil Company, whose shares are mainly held by the British Government. While Persian oil was entirely under the control of that British company, the international consortium owning the Iraq Petroleum Company (I.P.C.) had acquired control of most of the oil of Arabia. The early history of the I.P.C. runs parallel to that of the political partitioning of the Arabian territory of the former Ottoman Empire. The Americans insisted, however, on being consulted in the oil question, and the ultimate composition of the I.P.C. was the result of a compromise between the interests of the British and French and the wishes of the Americans. The partners in the I.P.C.—five great oil companies—bound themselves under a special agreement of 1928 to take no separate action within the Arabian portions of the former Ottoman Empire, either by acquiring concessions or in the fields of refining or trading. The oil cartel of 1928 became known as the Red Line Agreement, because the region reserved to joint operation was marked on the map with a red line. Between the two World Wars the concessionaires pursued on the whole a policy of restricted exploitation, apparently in order to preserve the oilfields. Not until the Americans entered energetically into the Middle East oil industry did rapid development begin, after the Second World War.

Half of the capital invested in the Middle East oil industry has been invested since 1945. This in itself shows the change in the tempo of exploitation. American companies that were not bound by the Red Line Agreement had had oil concessions since the 1930's in some of the Arabian countries, including Saudi Arabia. In 1946 the two great American companies participating in the I.P.C. sought participation in these other concessions, in order to start full-scale exploitation of the oil of the Arabian peninsula. At first there were difficulties due to the obligations under the Arabian oil cartel. The French raised objections to the separate action of their American partners in the I.P.C., fearing that the development of Iraqi oil, one of France's main sources of supply, might be neglected. The matter was settled by a compromise under which, in return for the promise to make a rapid increase in the rate of extraction in Iraq, the restrictions under the Red Line Agreement should be waived. That finally cleared the way for the accelerated working of the oil deposits along the Gulf. The changes that have come since the war in the Middle East oil industry have brought the Americans to the front place. British and American capital had been roughly on a level until the nationalization of Persian oil robbed the British, at one stroke, of the main pillar of their enterprise. Since the Persian events the greatest oil-producer by the Persian Gulf has become the Arabian-American Oil Company (Aramco) in Saudi Arabia, closely followed by the (British-American) Kuwait Oil Company. In the autumn of 1952, American companies controlled about two thirds of the extraction of Arabian oil.

The relations between the foreign companies and the oil-owning states by the Persian Gulf are governed by a number of concession agreements. The earliest date from before 1914. The imposing oil power of the Anglo-Iranian was built upon the famous concession granted in 1901 by the Shah of Persia to a British subject, William Knox D'Arcy. The deposits in northern Mesopotamia were also the subject of a pre-war concession, granted by the Ottoman Sultan, of which the founders of the Iraq Petroleum Company claimed to be the legal heirs. The oil concessions still in force date from the inter-war years. Their detailed provisions vary from country to country, but they share certain general characteristics. They are valid for fifty to fifty-seven years, a long period. The region to be exploited under the concessions covers extensive portions and sometimes the whole of the territory of the state granting them. The concession companies enjoy a number of extraterritorial rights—for instance, exemption from taxes and other dues. Under the agreements the governments of the oil-producing countries have no influence over the commercial policy of the concessionaires. In particular, they have no means of influencing the decision as to the scale of development and exploitation of the oil deposits in their own country. Extracting, refining, and sale take place, independently of the country's balance of payments, exclusively on account of the concessionaires. The oil concession thus forms an enclave within the economy of the producing countries. Over against the rights of the concessionaires stands the duty of paying royalties. Apart from various payments, such as the wages of labour, which the concession companies must pay in the currency of the country, the oil appears in the balance of payments of the producing countries only in the form of royalties.

In Persia, Iraq, and Saudi Arabia the royalties averaged 1.5 to 1.6 dollars a ton at the end of the war. The rates were a good deal lower in Kuwait and Bahrein, between 0.6 and 0.7 dollars a ton. The total figure automatically grew, of course, with the rapid increase in extraction after 1945. But the financial clauses of the agreements came under increasing criticism from governments and public opinion in the Middle East. Instead of the fixed rates, which were very low in comparison with the rates in other oil countries, it was desired to secure a participation in the profits of the concession companies. A first step in this direction had been made in the revised Persian oil concession of 1933.

The post-war negotiations between the Persian Government and the Anglo-Iranian Oil Company produced no result, but at the end of 1950 a revision of the royalty system in Saudi Arabia came into force. In an agreement of December 1950 Aramco granted Saudi Arabia participation on a fifty-fifty basis. The total dues to the Saudi Arabian state were fixed at half the net profit after deduction of the American taxation; in addition to a fixed minimum rate, a duty is payable, the amount of which is calculated on the company's profit. In the course of 1951, partly under the influence of the events in Persia, Iraq and Kuwait secured new agreements on the basis of similar financial terms. This has established the general principle of the sharing of profits between government and concessionaire. The result of the revision of the financial clauses has been that today the royalties amount to more than double the earlier figures. From an average of $1.50 they have advanced to $3.72 to $5.20 a ton.

The concession agreements cannot be dissociated from the relations in general between the West and the Islamic countries. Although they have the outward form of private business agreements, the exceptionally strong position that the concession companies necessarily have in relation to the more or less weak national economy of the oil-yielding countries gives the agreements an eminently political character. They came into being at a time when the political order of the Middle East still showed strong colonial characteristics. The cry for the revision of the concession clauses must therefore be interpreted in a similar sense to the demand for the revision of political treaties that has become clamant in the Islamic world since the war. It is widely felt that a new formula suited to the changed conditions has been found in the idea of partnership. Aramco especially has tried to work in this direction. Although the political and social conditions, and not least the strength and intensity of nationalism, vary greatly in the different oil countries, the developments show an interconnexion that justifies regarding the Gulf oil problem as a whole. The case of Persia shows that for a satisfactory solution it is not enough to consider only the economic side of the question. The nationalization of the Persian oil industry has made a deep and radical breach in the *status quo* of the concessions. It is true that the new National Iranian Oil Company is at present a great unknown, but the Persian experiment is being attentively watched by the neighbouring countries, and it will not be without influence on the forms of partnership in the oil industry of the whole Gulf region.

GROWTH OF OIL ROYALTIES

in million dollars (at $2.80 to the pound sterling)

COUNTRY	1949	1950	1951	1952
Saudi Arabia	55	100	155	170
Kuwait	9	12	30	139
Iraq	10.5	10.5	38.5	110
Qatar	—	—	3.8	9
Bahrein	1.5	1.5	3.8	6.3
Persia	38	44.9	23.8	—
	114	168.9	254.9	434.3

SOURCES: *Middle East Journal,* Washington; *Commerce du Levant,* Beirut.

Growing figures of extraction, together with the increase of the royalties, are directing to the Persian Gulf region a stream of wealth, of dimensions that would not have been dreamed of only a little while ago. In the first years after the war the total amount of the royalties paid to the oil countries of the Middle East was sixty to seventy million dollars. By 1951 this figure had already been quadrupled, though in the meantime Persia, which had accounted for the greater part of the royalties, was no longer included. For 1952 the income of the Arabian oil states was estimated at four hundred or even five hundred million dollars. Even this is far from the ultimate limit. It is expected that the next decade will bring a further increase up to roughly 1,000,000,000 dollars a year. Such an increase of wealth has its light side, but it also brings anxieties and raises new questions. The royalties go mainly to only three Arabian countries with roughly eleven million inhabitants in all: Saudi Arabia, Kuwait, and Iraq. Thus the Sheikh of Kuwait, whose subjects are scarcely more numerous than the inhabitants of an average European capital, is receiving every year hundreds of millions of dollars, while the Arab countries of the Levant are receiving nothing beyond the dues they collect for the transit of the oil. It has therefore been suggested that the oil revenues should be diverted to a common Arabian pool. Out of this pool the economic and social development of the Arabian countries could be financed on a basis of equality and in accordance with relative urgency. Derricks, refineries, and pipelines have created an Arabian economic complex that extends beyond the frontiers of the individual states. Thus the oil industry is yielding a new impulse to cooperation and perhaps also to new forms of political union. The economic revolution produced by the advance of Arabian oil supplies new energy for the effort toward Arab unity. In addition to this, the new importance of the Persian Gulf as the principal oil region of the Old World is a reminder of the fact that this is a region with a number of unsettled political questions.

The Persian Gulf, said an Englishman once, is the hub of the Islamic world. He meant this in a geographical sense, because the Gulf is at the centre of the region inhabited by the peoples of Islam, between the Turkish Straits and the Indus, and also between Morocco and Moslem Indonesia. The border between Persians and Arabs is by the Gulf, and Pakistan, the new Indian Moslem state, watches over its entrance. Moreover, Iraq and the Persian Gulf form an important corridor for commerce and communication with India and the Far East. In the history of world trade this route has competed with the route via Suez and the Red Sea, and the Baghdad Railway, connected with the Gulf route, was a parallel with the Suez Canal in the politics of communications. Until the discovery of the oil resources, the expression "hub of the Islamic world" had only this geographical significance. The Gulf coasts are uninviting, poor in ports, and rendered almost unusable by parching heat. The three great states bordering on the Gulf, Persia, Iraq, and Saudi Arabia, are of a continental character and turn their backs on the sea. In spite of its central situation, therefore, the Persian Gulf was never able to form the hub of the Islamic world in a political or cultural sense; it would be more accurate to describe it as the back yard of the Islamic house. Modern world communications went past the Gulf, but did little to disturb its accustomed life. Oil brought the first change in the face of the Gulf region and in the existence of its inhabitants.

The British included the Persian Gulf at an early date in India's security zone. They regarded it as their duty to see that no foreign power should approach their Indian possessions from this side. As early as 1824 the British Indian Government appointed a Political Resident for the Persian Gulf. He established his headquarters first in the Persian port of Bushire, and later on the Bahrein Islands. The British

269

brought stability in place of the disturbed conditions they found by the Gulf. They recognized the various Arabian principalities, and concluded protectorate treaties with them. The treaties reserved the foreign relations of the Arab potentates to the British Resident. In this way Kuwait, the Bahrein Islands, Qatar, and the sheikhs of the Trucial Coast were brought under British protection—or rather British Indian; for it was the Foreign Minister of the Viceroy in Delhi who was responsible for policy by the Persian Gulf. The protectorate treaties were concluded toward the end of the nineteenth century, and therefore long before the first drop of oil was brought up on the coast of the Persian Gulf. The political status of the small Gulf principalities has remained to this day as laid down by the treaties of fifty to sixty years ago. International law calls Kuwait, the Bahrein Islands, and the territories of the other petty Arabian rulers "States with special treaty relations to Great Britain." The British Resident by the Persian Gulf still has his headquarters on the Bahrein Islands. But there have been many changes since that post was created for the security of India. With the British withdrawal from India, the main reason for which the British protectorate over the waters of the Gulf was established has ceased to exist. On the Persian side of the Gulf, British influence is considerably reduced if not ended. The Persian nationalists even claim the Bahrein Islands, on the ground that long ago the islands were subject to the shah of Persia. The British protégés by the Gulf, especially the Sheikh of Kuwait, have risen from inconsiderable desert potentates to exceedingly rich oil-owners, and with the oil American influence has grown powerful in this region. Iraq and Saudi Arabia belong to the Arab League. The picturesque little principalities do not. The political constitution of this region clearly no longer suits the new role of the oil gulf in world trade and in international politics.

THE ETERNAL FIRES OF BAKU

ONCE in the past the Islamic Orient was for a time supreme in the world's oil extraction. That was in the early years of petroleum, when that material was mainly used for lighting and its use as a source of energy was almost unknown. The first triumph of the oil of the Orient was achieved before the resources of Persia and Arabia had been discovered. The first derricks of the Orient were built, not by the Persian Gulf, but on the small peninsula of Apsheron, close to the town of Baku, a spur of land pushing out twenty-five miles into the Caspian Sea. Statistics show this oil as "Russian oil," because it comes from within the Russian realm. For all that, Russian Azerbaijan is a country inhabited by Moslem Turks, and the oil in the neighbourhood of its capital, Baku, is part of the oil of the Moslems. At the turn of the century Russia was extracting twelve million tons of petroleum annually, half of the world's output at that time; and almost all of it came from Baku.

A millennium and a half ago, when the Sassanid kings ruled over Persia, the sacred fires of the ancient Persians burned in the temples of Persian Azerbaijan. The name is supposed to be derived from the Persian word *azer* (fire), and it was long thought that the eternal fires of the temple of Baku were fed with petroleum. Research has thrown doubt on both these guesses, but the descriptions given by mediæval Arab geographers show that petroleum has long been familiar in Russian Azerbaijan. *Naphtha* is an ancient Iranian word. The beginnings of the modern oilfields of Baku date from 1860–70. The oil wealth of the Apsheron peninsula proved so great that the oilfields of the Baku region count among the most productive in the world. In the last eighty years the borings in the small district round Baku have brought 700,000,000 tons of oil to the surface.

In 1952 the Soviet Union came third among the oil-producing countries, after the United States and Venezuela. Much the richest and most important of the Soviet oilfields are in the three main regions settled by Russian Turks. The only other fields of importance are in the Ukraine, the northern Urals, and the island of Sakhalin. The great bulk of the Soviet oil extraction is in the Islamic region. The oil-fields outside that region supply at present only five to six per cent of the total Soviet output. Thus almost the whole of the 42,000,000 tons shown in the Soviet statistics for 1951 comes from the Islamic intercontinent. It does not follow that the Soviet Union is faced in its oil extraction with similar problems to those of the West in the oil region by the Persian Gulf. The Moslem Turkish regions of the Soviet realm are in every respect so firmly held in the political and economic grasp of Moscow that conflicts over the disposal of their oil or the methods of its exploitation are inconceivable. But though it might seem at first that in the distribution of the oil of the Orient the Russians have gone away empty, an analysis of the Soviet output in its regional and national aspects shows that Russia has assured herself of a very good share of the oil of the Moslems. There is not only the oil of Arabia and Persia: the Turks, too, live on oil-drenched soil. Nine tenths of the Soviet oil is Turkish.

Caucasia still contributes most to the Soviet oil supply. It is true that the star of the Baku oil is declining; signs of exhaustion are showing themselves. But Baku is still at the head of the Soviet oilfields. Before the war it was yielding over 20,000,000 tons a year. At that time Baku was the most important oil region anywhere in the Middle East, for its output exceeded that of the south-west Persian sources by fully twenty-five per cent. In 1938 Baku yielded three quarters of the Soviet output. Since then Baku has lost not only absolutely but relatively. At the end of the fourth Soviet Five-Year Plan the Baku yield of 17,000,000 tons was only forty-five per cent of the Soviet production. The oil regions on the northern slope of the Caucasus (Grozny, Maikop, and Daghestan) also show a fall in output, but this is due not only to exhaustion of the reserves but to severe war damage. Before the war Caucasian oil, taking all the regions together, supplied ninety per cent of the Soviet consumption; today it supplies no more than a good half. This does not mean that the Caucasus is losing its vital importance to the Soviet. Its output of 21,000,000 tons a year is indispensable to the Union, and also irreplaceable for a long time to come. An oil industry is not to be shifted at short notice. The development of Russia's oil industry was confined almost entirely to Baku and the Caucasus in the past hundred years. Transport and refining were centred on that region. The great bulk of the Soviet oil refineries are in the Caucasus. The Baku region has refineries with a total capacity of 18,000,000 tons a year. Here, by the Caspian Sea, are the most important refineries, apart from Abadan, in the Middle East. Add to this the oil industry of the northern Caucasus, and we find that four fifths of the Soviet oil-refining capacity is concentrated at the foot of the Caucasus. Since the Caucasian fields cannot any longer supply all the crude oil with which the refineries can cope, additional crude material has to be brought from other fields in the Soviet Union. Thus Baku and Caucasia remain the heart of the Soviet oil industry.

Azerbaijan is a borderland of the Soviet Union. To evade the dangers involved in Baku's strategic vulnerability, the Russians have taken care to develop a "second Baku" north of the Caspian Sea. It is connected with a series of oil deposits between the Volga and the Ural Mountains. This region, too, is largely Turkish soil, in the territory of the north Turkish Tatars and Bashkirs, to which the national movement of the Turks of Russia gave the name "Idel-Ural." One of the centres of the second Baku is the autonomous Soviet Republic of the Bashkirs; its capital is Ufa. In the 1930's the oil of "Idel-Ural" was more closely prospected and developed, at about the same time as the Arabian oil a few thousand miles farther south. Considerable as the development of these fields has been, it has been far from producing the sensational results achieved in the Arabian oil countries. Before the Second World War "Idel-Ural" produced only six per cent (1,600,000 tons) of the Soviet output. Since then the figure has grown to 10,000,000 to 12,000,000 tons a year, so that one third of the Soviet consumption can now be covered by supplies from the region between the Volga and the Urals. But this north Turkish oil region of the Soviet Union cannot compare with the wealth of Kuwait and Saudi Arabia.

The third Turkish country under Soviet rule, Turkistan, also makes its contribution to the Soviet oil supply. It has long been known that there are oil deposits at various points in the wide area of Turkistan. The fields have been developed on a large scale in the last fifteen years. Turkistan's oil output increased from 1,000,000 tons in 1938 to 3,600,000 in 1950. Here again the quantities are relatively modest. Three districts in Turkistan are engaged in oil extraction, all on much the same scale. In the Soviet Republic of Kazakhstan is the Emba region, on the north-east coast of the Caspian Sea. A second group of oilfields are found near the Caspian port of Krasnovodsk, in the Soviet Republic of Turkmenistan, and a third in the fertile Ferghana valley, in the Soviet Republic of Uzbekistan. But the oil worked under the Soviet regime among the Turkish peoples is entirely outdistanced by its richer rivals along the Persian Gulf.

Summing up the oil output of the Moslem peoples of the Middle East, we get the following results. Before the war, 65 per cent of the extraction belonged to the Soviet Union and only 35 per cent to the countries round the Persian Gulf. Thirteen years later the relationship had been reversed: 70 per cent of the oil extracted in the Islamic region belonged in 1951 to the countries of the Persian Gulf and only 30 per cent to the Turkish federal republics of the Soviet Union. The Soviet Five-Year Plan for 1950–5 provides for a further increase of production in the Turkish oil regions up to more than 60,000,000 tons. Even this makes no change in the relative importance of the Moslem Turkish oil districts to the Soviet. The Soviet Union remains dependent for ninety per cent of its oil on the output of the nearer and remoter neighbourhood of the Caspian Sea.

How much of the economic yield of Soviet oil goes to the oil-possessing peoples and territories cannot be ascertained. It is impossible, therefore, to make any comparison with the oil revenues of the Arabs. The Soviet oil industry is organized in the form of state trusts, whose management and manpower are largely, if not predominantly, of Russian origin. The revenues from the oil industries go into the wide pockets of the state budgets. From there some of it may return to the enterprises of the Soviet Government in the Turkish Moslem parts of the Union.

The Russians, too, have looked round for oil concessions outside their frontiers. Economic and political motives unite in the Russian desire to exploit the oil reserves believed to exist in northern Persia. The oil of northern Persia belongs to the countries whose geographical centre is the Caspian Sea. It is the only part of that complex that is not controlled by the Soviet Union. The oil wealth of the Caspian provinces of Persia is a very nebulous matter, but the question of its exploitation is brought up with steady persistence from time to time in Russo-Persian relations. In 1896—before the first concession was granted to the British—the Shah of Persia had granted the Russians certain rights in regard to oil. On these was later based the concession given in 1916 to Akaki Khoshtaria, a Russian citizen of Georgian origin. Nothing ever came of that concession except romantic stories of backstairs intrigue. British and American efforts to secure oil rights in northern Persia were unsuccessful. Probably Teheran would not have been too willing to see Russians and Anglo-Saxons in such close contact. In spite of their renunciation of all concessions and their propagandist condemnation of "oil imperialism," the Russians have always kept an eye on the oil reserves of northern Persia. In 1878 there was a small oil concession in the neighbourhood of the north Persian town of Semnan. In 1925 the Soviet Union acquired a capital participation of sixty-five per cent and founded a Persian company to exploit the oil. The Semnan concession, in itself unimportant, still exists. In 1944–7 the Russians went energetically to work to acquire an oil concession for the north Persian provinces. They proposed to the Persians the form of a mixed company, familiar in the satellite countries of eastern Europe. This Russo-Persian oil company was to continue for fifty years. During the first part of that period the Soviet was to hold 51 per cent and the Persians 49 per cent of the capital. In the second half the Soviet majority was to give place to equality of holdings. The capital investment of the Persians was to consist of the oil reserves, the Soviet providing the technical equipment. The Russian pressure for the concession was frustrated by Persian opposition, and the oil of north Persia remains to this day below ground.

CHAPTER TEN

Conclusion: The Moslems and World Peace

LACK of stability characterizes the world of Islam. That is the outward sign of a historical process. Its causes lie in the great shiftings of power that have come in the outer world, and in the profound changes that have taken place, in the course of decades, in the peoples of Islamic civilization. But the occasions for the outbreak of open crises lose relative importance as the development with which they are connected extends. Events like the assassination of the Persian Prime Minister Ali Razmara, or the denunciation of the Anglo-Egyptian Treaty, merely removed the last weak barriers to long-accumulated forces of change. Even where the surface is relatively smooth, the same forces are to be found beneath it which elsewhere in the Moslem world have broken through.

It is difficult for Europe to define the Moslem unrest in familiar terms. The peoples of the Orient are blamed for lack of common sense, for inconsistency, for ill will. It may be that the grandfathers and great-grandfathers of the Europeans of today would have understood it all better. But it is not enough to point to the different mentality of West and East. There is also, if the phrase may be permitted, a difference of age between the "young" nations of the Moslems and the "old" nations of Europe. We should think ourselves back into the stormy youth of the European nations, to recover the sense of what it is that today moves the peoples of the Orient. In the annals of the French Revolution of 1789, in the stormy year 1848, in the efforts of the Germans and the Italians for unity, in the rise of socialism, in the formation of a religious democracy (in this case Christian) and a religious socialism, there are enough striking parallels to the events in Teheran and Cairo, in Karachi and Tunis. In Europe all these changes had a century to a century and a half in which to succeed one another organically; in the world of Islam they are crowding together and making their appearance almost simultaneously. It is largely for that very reason that the picture is so confused and complex. It is not the Moslems' fault: it was the West (including Russia) that with missionary zeal shook out over the peaceful, static civilization of Islam the cornucopia of its dynamic, revolutionizing ideas.

Until the eighteenth century Europe and the Moslems remained virtually on the same footing in regard to social and economic conditions and in technical advance. It was the industrial revolution in the West that destroyed that level position of the civilizations. After that the nations of Europe rapidly forged ahead of the rest of the world. But the Europeanization of the world resulted in the same process of development that had taken place among the peoples of Europe taking place also, at different times and with differences of intensity, among the other civilizations. That has ended the pre-European order in the Orient. Islam—here in the sense not only of a religious dogma but of a community of peoples—is struggling on a new plane for its position in the world of the twentieth century. It is the same struggle as in Hindu India and in the Far East, except that the region is not more or less compact as in those places but widespread and geographically and ethnically widely ramified. The common process is therefore more difficult to detect, but it exists.

In the unrest of the Islamic peoples there are three main currents: nationalism, a renaissance of Islam, and the demand for a change in social conditions. All three are to be found in the utmost variety and often in association. The bourgeois nationalists, the Islamic puritans, and the social reformers and revolutionaries of every shade have one thing in common: their determined opposition to foreign rule and foreign influence. Among the peoples of the West, nationalism has largely fulfilled its task; there are many who consider the unrestricted sovereignty of the national state as out of date, and the effort is being made to achieve supranational union or "integration." It is not so in the world of Islam. Here differentiation between national states is still in full swing, and the nations themselves are still in process of formation, the supranational realms of mediæval Islam having disappeared from the map, with the one exception of Persia. Thus in the present phase of development of the Moslem peoples nationalism is a constructive, integrating force. Where it is strong and can develop freely, its functioning is obvious. The Turkey of Kemal Ataturk is the best example. Only where it suffers from internal weaknesses and is unable to overcome outward obstacles does nationalism degenerate into an agitated flicker—as in Persia and in parts of the Arab world.

Twenty and thirty years ago it seemed that nationalism would take the place of Islam as the regulative principle of the community. That assumption has not proved correct.

On the contrary, the recent past has witnessed an astonishing revival of "political" Islam; it must only be borne in mind that Islam is much more closely concerned with the state and society, with the things of this world, than is Christianity. The "separation of church and state" is made more repugnant to it. Consequently all of the new national states are more or less occupied by the differences of view of laicists and puritans. Islam is supranational; in its strict form it denies the "sovereignty of the nation," which it regards as an alien production of the "materialist" West. The puritans are filled with the idea of the renewed union of the Moslem community—across the frontiers of the national states. Where nationalism tends to separate the peoples of the Moslems, the Islamic renaissance is once more a uniting factor.

National and Islamic tendencies affect social change. What has happened to the Young Turks right down to Naguib might be regarded as the "bourgeois revolution" of the Islamic Orient. The feudal social order is giving place to the sovereignty of the people, as in Europe between 1789 and 1848. Time has been too short, however, for the middle class to spread widely enough to become the permanent basis of democracy as in the West. It remains to be seen whether it will ultimately do so in the Orient. The demands of the great propertyless masses are finding their way into the "bourgeois revolution": the fellah is gradually emerging from his existence of unhistoried passivity. The formation of nations with a healthily integrated social order takes time; the new should be able to grow and ripen slowly. But as things are, the civilization of Islam does not exist in undisturbed isolation. It has the misfortune to find itself at a nerve centre of international politics.

The crises in Egypt, Persia, Palestine, and elsewhere were not of recent origin. In most cases their origin dated back many years. But before 1939 there was little reason to fear that these Oriental conflicts involved dangers to world peace. The events were generally confined within localized limits and involved no risk of seriously affecting the balance between the Great Powers. The system of rule of the colonial powers—above all, Britain and France—had scarcely been shaken, and firmly embraced the greater part of the Islamic world. In short, the Moslem Orient was a very important arena of international politics, but still on the whole a secondary one. A single decade has changed all that. Today the Islamic unrest directly affects world peace and the balance of world power. Today it is no longer an internal affair of European colonial empires. European hegemony is at an end in that part of the world, though French and, still more, British influence continues to hold positions that must not be underestimated. The might of Europe is disappearing, and leaving behind it no real successor. The new state system of the Islamic intercontinent is not yet sufficiently established to be able to bear unaided the burden of stability and security.

But at present there is forming between the dying age of European tutelage and the stabilization of the new and still vaguely outlined Orient a danger zone. Into this vacuum is streaming the high tension of the Cold War. Every change in North Africa, in the Nile valley, in Persia, in Pakistan, affects the relative strength of the two Great Powers.

The Islamic region is in a unique geographical situation. Neither Europe nor the Far East is situated on the tongue of the strategic and political world scales in the same way as the Moslem-inhabited "Inter-East." Anglo-Saxons and Russians have their interests fairly well marked out in Europe and the Far East. We may speak, at least in the main, of definite and permanent conceptions of American and Soviet policy in Europe and the Far East. It is not so easy to say the same in regard to the world of Islam. The Near and Middle

East, in particular, are a terrain on which, for various reasons, the two antagonists have operated so far only with hesitation. The Russians have had centuries of experience with the Moslems. They are a colonial power, and will remain so at present, on the soil of the intercontinent. The Russia of the czars was one of the three main participants, with Great Britain and France, in the division of the Islamic world. The change in the outward forms of Russian imperialism has brought no difference in that respect: Communist Moscow continues to hold the conquered regions with a firm and heavy hand. The struggles of the subjected Moslem peoples for political emancipation are met by the Soviet central administration with even more severity than under the czars.

Turkistan, Caucasia, and the Volga and Ural region are of vital importance to the Soviet Union. Without these Moslem colonial territories the Russian Empire would cease to be a Great Power. Almost the whole of the oil output and the cotton crop, and a high percentage of the ores, come from the parts of the Soviet Union inhabited by Moslems, quite apart from their growing share in industrial production. It is believed, moreover, that the main centre of all that is connected with atomic energy is to be found in Central Asia. It may therefore be said without exaggeration that the Moslem territories are the Achilles' heel of the Soviet bloc. This shows how overwhelming is Moscow's interest in a complete isolation of its twenty-odd million Moslems from the dangerous tendencies that are creating unrest in the Islamic world beyond the Soviet frontiers.

As a colonial power the Soviet Union is bound to look with suspicion upon nationalism, the Islamic renaissance, and similar movements. The isolation, however, of its own Moslems from the outer world permits it to manœuvre with elasticity outside the Russian borders—in so far as a dogma-bound regime like that of Communism can be elastic.

So far as the Orient is concerned, the Kremlin has inherited and taken over the historical Russian aims in the directions of India, the Persian Gulf, and the Straits. The diplomatic documents of the last decade show in detail that those aims have not been abandoned. In the course of the widespread development of the Cold War, however, they seem to have been subordinated to a wider aim, the neutralization of as extensive a buffer region as possible in front of the gates of the Soviet Union. While Stalin's policy succeeded not only in neutralizing buffer regions of this sort but in bringing them under direct Soviet control in Europe and in the Far East, the Soviet frontiers in the Near and Middle East have no such protection. Efforts at expansion in that direction have failed. How can the Soviet secure it there by cold means, without the risk of a great war?

The answer is plain. It must be in the Soviet interest to further all developments that may serve to keep out the West (especially the Americans) and isolate the Moslem world on all sides. So far as the nationalist and Islamic rising in the Near East confines itself to that negative aim, it runs in line with Soviet interests. That is no longer so, however, once the emancipation of Islam turns to the positive tasks of stabilization and union. In the present stage the Soviet glacis policy seems to aim at a weak, neutralized system of states, torn by internal dissension. The Soviet Union is thus pursuing, if the phrase may be permitted, a negative Orient policy: removal of Western influence, and prevention of internal stabilization and of regional collaboration between the Moslem states. It has not itself intervened either militarily or economically. It is relying on what under the Marxist-Leninist theory are supposed to be the irreconcilable differences between "imperialism" and "nationalism" and between the "imperialist powers."

There are many indications that the Communist theorists

regard the so-called revolutionary maturity of the Moslem Orient as not yet complete. It is difficult to gain a clear picture of the strength of Communism in the Islamic world. We must differentiate between organized cadres and fellow-travelling tendencies in general. Almost all Moslem states have prohibited the Communist Party; Islamic territory, moreover, is no easy soil for openly Communist propaganda. For these reasons there are no important legal Communist parties as in western Europe or south-east Asia, but only illegal cadres whose importance is difficult to estimate. Even the Persian Tudeh, though a pliant tool of Russian foreign policy, cannot be compared with the Cominform parties.

Open and secret partisans of Soviet policy make their appearance in the most varied guises. They extend from Left-wing intellectuals, many of whom have only a superficial acquaintance with the Communist social doctrine, to nationalist circles which, though outwardly anti-Communist, would have no great objection to Soviet support in the struggle against "Western imperialism." The fact that such fellow-travelling is widespread and notorious does not imply "revolutionary maturity" in the Marxist-Leninist sense. On the other hand, such currents of opinion offer the Soviet a serviceable instrument for the promotion of neutralist tendencies, and it would be in accordance with the view of Moscow's present Moslem policy expressed above if this, and not the seizure of power, were regarded as *at present* the principal task of the Communist cadres of the Near East.

In the negative phase of the Soviet buffer policy the Communist emissaries work more or less as the agitators at the back of the anti-Western, neutralist currents. This sort of thing has been observable in Teheran and Cairo, in Iraq and Morocco. From it may be inferred the Soviet effort to direct the unrest of Islam into paths that should lead to an irrevo-

cable breach between nationalism and the West. The aim is
to compromise the nationalists in the eyes of the West, and
particularly of America. And it has not been pursued without some success. One may sometimes hear the view expressed in the West that the Moslem peoples' struggle for
freedom is simply the work of Soviet agents, and that the
nationalists are nothing but Moscow's underlings. Needless
to say, such simplification brings grist to the mills of Soviet
Near East policy.

The Americans are newcomers in the Islamic world. Any
direct strategic and political interest of the United States in
the Near and Middle East dates only from the great shiftings
of power that followed the Second World War. The decline
of British world power compelled America to step into the
breach, first in the Turkish Straits with the Truman Doctrine
of March 1947. Before that, American activity in the Near
East had mainly been in the field of cultural policy—as, for
instance, in the famous American University in Beirut, now
nearly one hundred years old—and in the care of general
commerical interests. The Moslems habitually regarded the
Americans as the representatives of a great remote country
that was free from the stigma of colonialism and, indeed, enjoyed the reputation of a paladin of the right of self-
determination of peoples. So far as it is possible to speak of
any Near East policy of Washington before the Second
World War, it consisted in occasional interventions of the
State Department in favour of the principle of the "open
door" in commerce.

To this was to be attributed the minority participation of
American firms in Arabian oil. Only during the Second
World War did the United States, at the instigation of its own
government, interest itself in the large-scale exploitation of
Middle East oil. Today, as the result of a development not
yet ten years old, the Americans are the leading oil power by

the Persian Gulf. Arabian oil has become one of the chief of America's world-wide interests. Thus, oil plays a prominent part in the relations both of the Americans and of the Soviet Russians with the Moslem world. But there is a difference that must not be overlooked. The oil supply of the Soviet Union depends almost entirely on the fields round the Caspian Sea. The dependence of the United States on Moslem oil is, at all events at present, indirect. Even without the oil of the Persian Gulf, America herself is a great oil-producer. Her own rich resources, together with the surpluses of Latin America, assure the supply of her own market. But the oil of the Orient is the principal source of supply for the European allies of the United States. Before very long it will probably be their only source of supply.

A great change in the world's oil trade is at present taking place: western Europe, the principal consumer in the world market, is shifting its purchases from the Western Hemisphere to the Near East, while the oil of North and South America is gradually being taken up by the growing requirements of the Western Hemisphere itself. A partition of the sources of supply is taking place. The Atlantic Alliance as a whole cannot dispense with the oil of the Moslems. Under these circumstances the United States is closely interested in the continued working of the oilfields round the Persian Gulf and in their accessibility to the West; or, to put it negatively, in not letting the Soviet bloc gain any form of control of those fields. If it did so, the relative power of the two blocs in the field of oil supply would undergo an important change, with consequences to the balance of political power impossible to estimate.

These views have reference at present only to peacetime economics. In an armed conflict the Moslem oil—from the Persian Gulf to the southern Urals—would probably be largely neutralized. Each side would probably be able, with

the aid of the air arm, to prevent the other from making full use of the oilfields, or at least to hinder it in doing so. The Caspian Sea and the Persian Gulf are within convenient reach of the air bases on both sides.

The more the United States comes to a world policy adjusted to its situation and its strength, the less can it afford to neglect the political and strategic importance of the Islamic intercontinent in its conception. "The place where peace might be upset most readily is where the number of inter-power frictions is greatest. That is precisely why the Near East is in the process of replacing Europe as the world's center of gravity and breeding place of fresh conflicts." (E. A. Speiser: *The United States and the Near East,* page 122.) An American Islam policy is at present only in process of formation. Its guiding principle might perhaps, if we accept the view just quoted, be defined as that of the *stabilization of the intercontinent,* bearing in mind that the existing situation cannot be the basis of a genuine stabilization. The averting of Soviet infiltration into the Near East is only one side of the problem, the negative side. In the long run it will be impossible to be content with stopping up the holes found in one place and another. While the Soviet Union is awaiting the political isolation and social decay of the Moslem peoples, the initiative rests with the Americans. What is needed is the establishment of a system of Near East states which would gradually, as part of a policy of regional collaboration, be placed in a position to take largely upon its own shoulders the defence of the intercontinent. To harmonize this aim with America's commitments in other parts of the world may prove one of the most difficult tasks of American foreign policy.

First of all, the United States must take into consideration the situation of their European allies. France's strength depends largely on her colonial position in Arab and Islamic

North Africa. The same may be said for Great Britain with regard to the Near and Middle East. There is thus a direct connexion between the progress of Islamic emancipation and the existing equilibrium in western Europe. The Americans are faced with a serious question. If they decide to support the British and French positions, they will be forgoing their freedom of action in relation to the Islamic peoples. If they resolve on a gradual revision of the *status quo* in the Orient, then sooner or later the *status quo* in western Europe will be affected. A similar dilemma was to be observed again and again in British world policy in the past; it may suffice to recall the significance, in regard to the Islamic world, of the British alliances with France and Russia.

Israel touches a second and very sensitive point in American relations with the Moslems, and particularly with the Arabs. President Wilson's administration did a good deal in 1917 toward bringing the Balfour Declaration into existence. In 1948, under President Truman, the United States contributed largely to the coming into existence of the independent state of Israel. The reasons for the American support of Zionism lie much more in considerations of home policy than of any foreign policy connected with the Near East. With their millions of supporters at the polls, the American Zionists have always formed a powerful pressure group in Washington. They have sought support mainly from the Democratic Party, and less so from the Republicans. The interests of the state of Israel naturally find strong support among the American Zionists. What Israel wants is the maintenance of economic and military equilibrium between itself and the whole of the Arab states. Obviously this is not to be easily reconciled with an American initiative in the Arab-Islamic East. This explains why the course of American diplomacy in relation to the Arab-Israeli tension has often shown signs of hesitation and indecision.

The stabilization of the Islamic intercontinent, indispensable for the lasting peace of the world, is inconceivable without foreign aid. If foreign aid is not forthcoming, there is a danger that most of the Moslem states will slowly fall into a condition of economic and social weakness that will be bound to increase their susceptibility to revolutionary germs of every sort. The military security of the region may be an urgent problem; but in the long run it will not be enough to spread the slender shelter of a regional defence pact over the Near East if beneath it the problems of constitutional and social reform remain unsolved. A redistribution of the wealth flowing from the oil resources might do much to help. The oil boom gives reason for anticipating more and more ample benefit from this source. This alone might seem insufficient even if a Near East oil pool were brought into existence. As things are, the United States is the only power in a position to render aid on a large scale. But this would depend on the emergence in Washington, out of the conflict of interests, of a clear conception of the aims to be pursued in the Islamic Middle East.

The map of the Moslem world reveals three strong positions: Anatolia, the Nile valley, and north-west India (that is, the Indus valley and the Hindu Kush). Thus Turkey, Egypt, and Pakistan may be regarded as the main pillars of a new Moslem state system. Between these pillars lies the Persian Gulf with its oil wealth. It would seem, on the other hand, that Persia, beneath the deep shadow of the conflicts between Russia and the Anglo-Saxons, must remain a zone of instability; and the island republic of Indonesia, though the second among the Moslem states in order of population, is far away in the Pacific region.

The Turkish national state has long emerged from the disturbed initial period of decades ago. The Turkish Republic has thus been able to choose its definite place in international politics without inhibition or hesitation. It forms the bridge between the Moslem Orient and south-east Europe. As master of the Bosporus and the Dardanelles, it guards the gateway into the Mediterranean, which in past history has been the subject of the most violent rivalry. With her geographical situation, her political stability, and her military striking power, Turkey has been a valuable member of the Atlantic Alliance. So far she has been the only one of the Moslem states to be associated in this way with the West and to be the recipient of large-scale American economic and military aid. The example here offered of a new sort of partnership on the basis of entire equality of rights might provide a precedent elsewhere. The Turkish Republic is also represented in the Council of Europe, and it should be remembered that the Ottoman Empire was accepted in the nineteenth century into the "concert of Europe." In the course of their westward orientation the Turks have, indeed, turned their backs on the Moslem world; there has been a coolness between the Kemalist Republic and the rest of the Moslems, and Turkey is sometimes spoken of as simply a sort of outpost of Western security. But can Moslem Turkey really be excluded from active association with its Moslem neighbours in the east and south-east? The reaction of the Turkish nationalists to the policy pursued at heavy cost by the sultans was understandable and, no doubt, necessary. Today the Turks seem to be turning once more to the role in store for them in the Orient. The modern house of Islam now under construction cannot dispense with its Turkish-Anatolian cornerstone.

Egypt stands only on the threshold of genuine national statehood. The true picture of an Egyptian nation is still to some extent veiled by uncertainty. The Egypt of the khedives, and the monarchy of Fuad and Farouk, were no more than preludes. It is true that the history of Egyptian nationalism began long ago in the nineteenth century, but its energies have almost been monopolized by the struggle against the British occupation. Circumstances have thus prevented Egyptian nationalism from approaching the positive responsibilities of building up a state and nation. Does the seizure of power by General Naguib and the revolutionary officers mean that the Egyptian nation is at last emerging from the shadows of alien control and feudalism? So it would seem. But it is probably too soon to form a final judgment on the Egyptian Revolution. Egypt has much the same population as Turkey. In economic potential it is at least the equal of Turkey, though it will be a good deal more difficult to solve the social problems of the overpopulated Delta than those of Anatolia. The international highway of the Suez Canal makes Egypt more than ever, by its geographical position, the hinge of the Islamic world. Through Suez goes the only land connexion between the Eurasian continental mass and Africa; the Nile valley—from Alexandria and Suez to Khartoum—thus forms the great gateway of the Dark Continent. Moreover, Cairo is the centre of the Arab world that extends westward to Morocco and eastward to the Persian frontier. This central position of the Nile valley will become still more evident if in the course of time further Arab states in Africa should join the Arab League. In Egypt, therefore, lies the key to the solution of the very complex Arab question, which may justly be regarded as the cardinal point in the relations between the West and the Islamic world.

Here again comes into the front rank an issue often denied due recognition in the West, the Arab-Israeli tension. Israel is a small state with a population of about one million and a half, an island in the sea of Arabs and Moslems. In the long run the existence of Israel may depend upon its ability to fit into the system of the states of the Near East. It cannot continue indefinitely to exist as an island in a world of hostile neighbours. It is very doubtful whether it is doing this young state a real service when it is contrasted, as is sometimes done abroad, with its Arab neighbours as an "outpost of Western democracy." Leading Israelis are well aware of the dangers of isolating the country in this way. Israel, writes an Englishman well acquainted with the affairs of the Orient, must be regarded "as part of the body of South-Western Asia, and the claim of Israel as requiring definition, not in relation to domestic issues in Western lands, but in the first place to world interests in that region of Asia as a whole, and secondly to [its] Muslim neighbours." (Sir Olaf Caroe: *Wells of Power,* page 156.)

Pakistan is largely still an unknown quantity in the family of the Moslem states. The outer world has as yet scarcely realized that the connexion between the nucleus of the Moslem world and the Indian subcontinent, broken by the arrival of the Europeans, has been restored, and that the frontiers of the Islamic "inter-East" have been pushed far into north-west India. With the founding of the Indian Moslem state in August 1947, the so-called Middle East no longer comes to an end in Afghanistan and Persia, but extends east of the Indus. Only the future will show what national forces are developed among the Indian Moslems, the largest compact body in the world of Islam. The start has given the promise of healthy growth. After Egypt, Pakistan counts most in relation to the spiritual and social orientation of modern Islam. West Pakistan—that is to say, the Indus valley—forms the eastern cornerstone of the Islamic house; Bengal (East Pakistan) is the connecting link with the endangered south-east of Asia. At the same time the Indian Moslem state is a bridge to the great republic of the Hindus, who number not much less than the whole of the world of Islam. Or, rather, Pakistan could be that bridge, were it not for the acute difference with

Hindu India over the mountain land of Kashmir. So long as these two heirs of British rule in India are unable to secure tolerable relations with each other, Pakistan has no freedom of movement and cannot make anything like the contribution to the stabilization of the intercontinent that would correspond with the country's power.

But what is the relation of the India of Pandit Nehru to the Moslems in general? Hindu India has, after all, thirty to forty million Moslems within its borders, and it is the protagonist of the emancipation of Asia and Africa. To that extent there is a united front between India and the Moslem states in many fields—for instance, in that of the Asian and African block of votes in the United Nations. But the common defence against imperialism will lose its uniting force sooner or later; the national interests of the new Asian and African states will find stronger expression. The further that development proceeds, the nearer we shall come to the day when India must take her stand with regard to the questions of the intercontinent as a Great Power, and not merely as the standard-bearer of an idea. Thus even the relations of Pakistan with Hindu India are one of the uncertain factors in the future of Islam.

A restlessly flickering light shines today over the world of the Moslems. What tendencies will ultimately gain the upper hand, what the state system of the intercontinent will look like, how the Moslems will settle their relations with one another and with the outer world, all this is as yet entirely uncertain. It will probably remain uncertain for some time to come. Processes as profound as these do not reveal themselves clearly in a few years.

Let me conclude with what the rector of the Azhar University at Cairo has said about the relation of Islam with the world: "Islam has taught its faithful to live in peace with the adherents of all other religions, and, where necessary, to co-operate with them." If understanding is shown on both sides and is not frustrated by overbearing arrogance, the road will be clear for partnership between the West and the world of Islam.

Bibliography, Appendixes,

AND

Index

Bibliography

ISLAM, GENERAL

Enzyklopädie des Islams. 4 vols. Leyden.
ERNST DIEZ: *Glaube und Welt des Islams.* Stuttgart, 1939.
S. M. ZWEMER: *Heirs of the Prophet.* Chicago, 1946.
——: *A Factual Survey of the Moslem World.* New York, 1946.
LAURA VECCIA VAGLIERI: *Islam.* Naples, 1946.
H. A. R. GIBB: *Modern Trends in Islam.* Chicago, 1947.
——: *Mohammedanism.* London, 1949.
ROGER LE TOURNEAU: *L'Islam contemporain.* Paris, 1950.
F. M. PAREJA: *Islamologia.* Rome, 1951.
MIDDLE EAST INSTITUTE: *Islam in the Modern World.* Washington, 1951.
LOUIS MASSIGNON: *Annuaire du Monde musulmán.* 3rd issue, Paris, 1929.

NEAR AND MIDDLE EAST, GENERAL

HANS KOHN: *Geschichte der nationalen Bewegung im Orient.* Berlin, 1928.
——: *Nationalism and Imperialism in the Hither East.* London, 1932.
——: *Die Europäisierung des Orients.* Berlin, 1934.
PAUL HERRE: *Weltgeschichte am Mittelmeer.* Potsdam, 1930.
HUMMEL and SIEWERT: *Der Mittelmeerraum.* Heidelberg, Berlin, 1936.
HERMANN ONCKEN: *Die Sicherheit Indiens, ein Jahrhundert britischer Weltpolitik.* Berlin, 1937.
MARGRET BOVERI: *Vom Minaret zum Bohrturm, eine politische Geographie Vorderasiens.* Leipzig, Zurich, Berlin, 1938.

297

CONRADI OEHLRICH: *Das politische System der orientalischen Staaten.* Leipzig, 1940.

AMEDEO GIANNINI: *L'ultima Fase della Questione orientale (1919–1939).* Milan, 1941.

CARL BROCKELMANN: *Geschichte der islamischen Völker und Staaten.* Munich, Berlin, 1943.

D. D. WARRINER: *Land and Poverty in the Middle East.* London, 1948.

GEORGE E. KIRK: *A Short History of the Middle East from the Rise of Islam to Modern Times.* London, 1948.

KERMIT ROOSEVELT: *Arabs, Oil and History, the Story of the Middle East.* New York, 1949.

Geschichte Asiens (Weltgeschichte in Einzeldarstellungen). Munich, 1950.

ROYAL INSTITUTE OF INTERNATIONAL AFFAIRS: *The Middle East, a Political and Economic Survey.* London, 1951.

MIDDLE EAST INSTITUTE: *Nationalism in the Middle East.* Washington, 1952.

GEORGE LENCZOWSKI: *The Middle East in World Affairs.* Ithaca, N.Y., 1952.

Il Medio Oriente, special number of the weekly review *Relazioni Internazionali.* Milan, July 1952.

ERNEST JACKH: *Background of the Middle East.* Ithaca, N.Y., 1952.

THE GREAT POWERS AND THE ISLAMIC WORLD

HALFORD L. HOSKINS: *British Routes to India.* London, New York, 1928.

RAYMOND LACOSTE: *La Russie soviétique et la question d'Orient.* Paris, 1946.

E. A. SPEISER: *The United States and the Near East.* Cambridge, Mass., 1947.

WILLIAM REITZEL: *The Mediterranean, Its Role in American Foreign Policy.* New York, 1948.

DOMENICO CENSONI: *La Politica francese nel Vicino Oriente: Siria e Libano dal mandato all'indipenza (1919–1946).* Bologna, 1948.

M. V. SETON-WILLIAMS: *Britain and the Arab States, a Survey of Anglo-Arab Relations (1920–1948).* London, 1948.

GENERAL CATROUX: *Dans la bataille de la Méditerranée.* Paris, 1949.

The Security of the Middle East, a problem paper. Washington: The Brookings Institution; 1950.

ROYAL INSTITUTE OF INTERNATIONAL AFFAIRS: *United Kingdom Policy, Foreign, Strategic, Economic.* London, 1950.

MIDDLE EAST INSTITUTE: *Americans and the Middle East.* Washington, 1950.

SIR READER BULLARD: *Britain and the Middle East from Earliest Times to 1950.* London, 1951.

LEWIS V. THOMAS, and RICHARD N. FRYE: *The United States and Turkey and Iran.* Harvard University Press, 1951.

The Near East and the Great Powers, ed. Richard N. Frye. Harvard University Press, 1951.

GEORGE KIRK: *The Middle East in the War.* Oxford: Royal Institute of International Affairs; 1952.

THE ARAB WORLD

SIR BERTRAM THOMAS: *The Arabs.* London, 1937.

T. E. LAWRENCE: *The Seven Pillars of Wisdom.* London, 1935.

PHILIP HITTI: *History of the Arabs.* London, 1940.

GEORGE ANTONIUS: *The Arab Awakening.* 2nd edition, London, 1945.

FRANZ TAESCHNER: *Geschichte der arabischen Welt.* Heidelberg, 1944.

CARLO ALFONSO NALLINO: *L'Arabia Saudiana.* Rome, 1939.

GISELHER WIRSING: *Engländer, Juden, Araber in Palästina.* Jena, 1939.

FRITZ GROBBA: *Irak.* Berlin, 1941.

REINHARD HÜBER: *Der Suezkanal, einst und heute.* Berlin, 1941.

——: *Die Bagdadbahn.* Berlin, 1943.

A. H. HOURANI: *Syria and Lebanon, a Political Essay.* London, 1946.

K. S. TWITCHELL: *Saudi Arabia.* Princeton, 1947.

H. ST. JOHN B. PHILBY: *Arabian Days.* London, 1948.

Memoirs of KING ABDULLAH *of Transjordan.* London, 1950.

J. C. HUREWITZ: *The Struggle for Palestine.* New York, 1950.

MAJID KHADDURI: *Independent Iraq, a Study in Iraqi Politics since 1932.* Oxford, 1951.

MUSA ALAMI: *Ibrat Filiatin (The Lesson of Palestine).* Beirut, 1949.

ROY LEBKICHER: *Saudi Arabia.* New York, 1952.

A. E. CROUCHLEY: *The Economic Development of Modern Egypt.* London, 1938.

CHARLES ISSAWI: *Egypt, an Economic and Social Analysis.* London, 1947.

J. SPENCER-TRIMMINGHAM: *Islam in the Sudan.* Oxford, 1949.

A. M. GALATOLI: *Egypt in Midpassage.* Cairo, 1950.

JAMES HAYWORTH-DUNNE: *Religious and Political Trends in Modern Egypt.* Washington, 1950.

MARCEL COLOMBE: *L'Évolution de l'Égypte 1924–1950.* Paris, 1951.

ABBAS MEKKI: *The Sudan Question.* London, 1951.

Documents on the Sudan Question 1899–1953. Cairo: Egyptian Society of International Law; 1953.

F. TAILLARD: *Le Nationalisme marocain.* Paris, 1947.

JEAN DESPOIR: *L'Afrique du Nord.* Paris, 1949.

JACQUES KLEIN: *La Tunisie.* Paris, 1949.

JEAN CÉLÉRIER: *Maroc.* Paris, 1948.

E. E. EVANS-PRITCHARD: *The Sanusi of Cyrenaica.* Oxford, 1949.

H. E. HIRST: *The Nile.* London, 1952.

F. S. R. DUNCAN: *The Sudan, a Record of Achievement.* London, 1952.

JOHN HYSLOP: *Sudan Story.* London, 1952.

PERSIA

WALTHER HINZ: *Iran, Politik und Kultur von Kyros bis Reza Schah.* Leipzig, 1938.

WILLIAM S. HAAS: *Iran.* New York, 1946.

DONALD N. WILBER: *Iran, Past and Present.* Princeton, 1948.

FRITZ STEPPAT: *Iran zwischen den Weltmächten 1941–1947.* Europa-Archiv, 1948.

Bibliography

GEORGE LENCZOWSKI: *Russia and the West in Iran 1918–1948.* Ithaca, N.Y., 1949.

INDIAN MOSLEMS

ABID HASSAN: *Der Islam in Indien; Indien im Weltislam.* Heidelberg, 1942.
WILFRED CANTWELL SMITH: *Modern Islam in India.* London, 1946.
H. FISCHER-WOLLPERT: *Indien und Pakistan.* Europa-Archiv, 1948.
RICHARD SYMONDS: *The Making of Pakistan.* London, 1949.
LIAQAT ALI KHAN: *Pakistan, the Heart of Asia.* Harvard University Press, 1950.
SIR KERR FRASER-TYTLER: *Afghanistan.* London, 1950.
HANS STECHE: *Indien und Pakistan.* Berlin, 1952.

THE TURKS

DAGOBERT VON MIKUSCH: *Gazi Mustafa Kemal.* Leipzig, 1929.
KURT ZIEMKE: *Die neue Türkei.* Stuttgart, 1930.
GERHARD VON MENDE: *Der nationale Kampf der Russland-Türken.* Berlin, 1936.
GOTTHARD JÄSCHKE: *Der Turanismus der Jungtürken.* Leipzig, 1941.
——: *Der Turanismus und die kemalistische Türkei.* Leipzig, 1943.
——: *Der Islam in der neuen Türkei.* Leyden, 1951.
R. OLZSCHA and G. CLEINOW: *Turkestan.* Leipzig, 1942.
A. ZEKI VELIDI TOGAN: *Bugünkü Türkili (Turkistan).* Istanbul, 1942.
HERBERT W. DUDA: *Vom Kalifat zur Republik.* Vienna, 1948.
M. W. THORNBURG: *Turkey, an Economic Appraisal.* New York, 1949.
URIEL HEYD: *Foundations of Turkish Nationalism.* London, 1949.
ELEANOR BISBEE: *The New Turks, Pioneers of the Republic 1920–1950.* Philadelphia, 1951.
KARL KRÜGER: *Die Türkei.* Berlin, 1951.

EDIGE KIRIMAL: *Der nationale Kampf der Krimtürken.* Emsdetten (Westfalen), 1952.

ETTORE ROSSI: *La Leggenda turco-bizantina del Pomo Rosso.* Rome: Studi Bizantini; 1936.

FRIEDRICH VON RUMMEL: *Die Türkei auf dem Weg nach Europa.* Munich, 1952.

THE MOSLEMS' OIL

A. T. WILSON: *The Persian Gulf.* London, 1928.

RAYMOND MIKESELL and HOLLIS CHENERY: *Arabian Oil, America's Stake in the Middle East.* University of North Carolina Press, 1949.

A. M. STAHMER: *Erdöl, Mächte und Probleme.* Kevelar, 1950.

OLAF CAROE, *Wells of Power, the Challenge to Islam.* London, 1950.

H. HASSMANN: *Das Erdöl der Sowjetunion.* Hamburg, 1951.

ROY LEBKICHER: *Aramco and World Oil.* New York, 1952.

ANTON HANTSCHEL: *Baku.* Berlin, 1942.

PERIODICALS

The Middle East Journal. Washington (from 1947).
Oriente Moderno. Rome (from 1922).
Journal of the Royal Central Asian Society. London.
Cahiers de l'Orient contemporain. Paris.
Affrica. Rome.
The Middle East Institute—Newsletter. Washington.
Al-Ahram (daily), Cairo.
Die Welt des Islams. Leyden.
The Muslim World. New York.
Islamic Review. Woking, London.
Commerce du Levant. Beirut.
Le Monde Arabe. Paris.

Appendix I

STATES AND COUNTRIES OF THE MOSLEMS

	FORM OF STATE	CAPITAL	AREA IN SQ. MILES	POPULA-TION IN MILLIONS
Turkey	Republic	Ankara	296,184	20.9
Persia (Iran)	Empire	Teheran	634,413	19.0
Afghanistan	Kingdom	Kabul	251,000	11–12
Pakistan	Dominion of the British Commonwealth	Karachi	364,737	80
Indonesia	Republic	Jakarta	583,000	70–75

STATES OF THE ARAB LEAGUE

Egypt	Republic	Cairo	386,110	20.5
Jordan	Kingdom	Amman	37,100	1.3
Syria	Republic	Damascus	66,063	3.3
Lebanon	Republic	Beirut	3,475	1.3
Iraq	Kingdom	Baghdad	168,043	5.1
Saudi Arabia	Kingdom	Riyadh	597,000	6.5
Yemen	Kingdom	San'a	75,000	3.5
Libya	Kingdom	Tripoli, Benghazi	679,183	1.2

ARAB COUNTRIES IN NORTH AFRICA

Sudan	Anglo-Egyptian Condominium until 1951	Khartoum	967,500	8.1
Tunisia	French Protectorate	Tunis	48,300	3.5
Algeria	French General Government	Algiers	80,919 (without the Sahara region)	8.0
Morocco	French Protectorate	Rabat	153,870	8.7
	Spanish Protectorate	Tetuan	17,631	1.1

ARAB COUNTRIES BY THE PERSIAN GULF AND
INDIAN OCEAN

	FORM OF STATE	CAPITAL	AREA IN SQ. MILES	POPULA- TION IN MILLIONS
Kuwait	Principality under British protection	Kuwait	9,000	0.5
Bahrein Islands	Principality under British protection	Manama	213	0.1
Qatar	Principality under British protection		4,000	0.02
Oman and Muscat	Sultanate	Muscat	65,000	0.6
Aden	British Protectorate	Aden	113	0.7

FEDERAL REPUBLICS OF THE SOVIET UNION WITH
MOSLEM POPULATION

Uzbekistan	—	Tashkent	153,000	7.0
Turkmenistan	—	Ashkhabad	182,000	1.4
Tadzhikistan	—	Stalinabad	58,000	1.7
Kirghizistan	—	Frunze	75,000	1.6
Kazakhstan	—	Alma-Ata	1,033,000	6.8
Azerbaijan	—	Baku	33,000	3.5

Autonomous Soviet Republics within the Russian Federal Republic
(R.S.F.S.R.): Tatar (capital, Kazan), Bashkir (capital, Ufa), Daghestan
(capital, Makhachkala). The Autonomous Republic of the Crimea was
abolished in 1946; the Crimean Turkish population was compulsorily transferred elsewhere.

Eastern Turkistan	Province of the Chinese People's Republic	Urumchi	641,000	4.5

In the Republic of India there live 30 to 40 million Moslems; in British
south-east Asia some 3 millions; and in colonial Africa and Ethiopia some
35 millions. The number of Moslems in China is entirely unknown. In
Europe the Balkans (Yugoslavia and Albania) have 3 to 4 million Moslems.

Appendix II

THE MOSLEMS IN THE WORLD

1. ASIA AND EUROPE

Turkey, Persia, Afghanistan, Arabia, and Asia Minor }	70 millions	
Pakistan and India	100 "	
South-east Asia	65 "	
Soviet Union and Eastern Turkistan	30 "	
Balkans	4 "	Total 269 millions

2. AFRICA

Nile valley (Egypt and Sudan)	25 millions	
Maghrib (north-west Africa)	20 "	
Negro Africa	35 "	Total 80 millions

From *Islamologia* (Rome, 1951) and other sources. The available information permits only of rough indications, with no claim to statistical accuracy.

Appendix III

THE PROPHET'S LINE

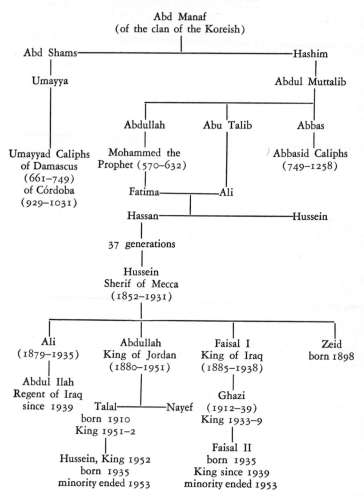

Abd Manaf
(of the clan of the Koreish)

Abd Shams ———————————————— Hashim

Umayya   Abdul Muttalib

Abdullah   Abu Talib   Abbas

Umayyad Caliphs   Mohammed the   Abbasid Caliphs
of Damascus   Prophet (570–632)   (749–1258)
(661–749)
of Córdoba   Fatima ———— Ali
(929–1031)

Hassan ———————————————— Hussein

37 generations

Hussein
Sherif of Mecca
(1852–1931)

Ali   Abdullah   Faisal I   Zeid
(1879–1935)   King of Jordan   King of Iraq   born 1898
           (1880–1951)   (1885–1938)

Abdul Ilah
Regent of Iraq   Ghazi
since 1939   Talal ———— Nayef   (1912–39)
          born 1910   King 1933–9
          King 1951–2

                            Faisal II
Hussein, King 1952   born 1935
born 1935   King since 1939
minority ended 1953   minority ended 1953

Appendix IV

THE EGYPTIAN DYNASTY

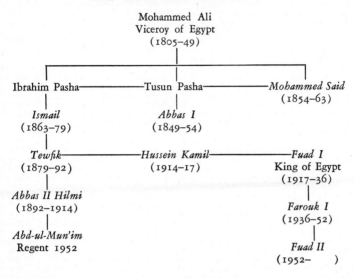

Mohammed Ali
Viceroy of Egypt
(1805–49)

Ibrahim Pasha————Tusun Pasha————*Mohammed Said*
(1854–63)

Ismail
(1863–79)

Abbas I
(1849–54)

Tewfik————*Hussein Kamil*————*Fuad I*
(1879–92)　　(1914–17)　　King of Egypt
(1917–36)

Abbas II Hilmi
(1892–1914)

Farouk I
(1936–52)

Abd-ul-Mun'im
Regent 1952

Fuad II
(1952–　　)

NOTE: In 1805 the Sultan of Turkey conferred the title of Viceroy of Egypt on Mohammed Ali (born in the Macedonian town of Kavalla), an officer who had come to Egypt with the Ottoman forces sent against Napoleon I. In 1841 a decree of the Sultan conferred on Mohammed Ali the hereditary dignity of a "Vizier of Egypt and Governor of Nubia, Sennar, Kordofa, and Darfur."

In 1867 the fourth Viceroy, Ismail, was raised to the rank of a "Khedive."

When Ottoman Turkey entered the First World War and Great Britain declared a protectorate over Egypt, the title of the Khedive was altered to that of Sultan of Egypt, implying the end of Ottoman suzerainty.

On March 15, 1922 Sultan Fuad proclaimed himself the first "King of Egypt."

On June 18, 1953 Egypt was declared a republic.

Appendix V

THE OIL OF THE MOSLEMS

1. WORLD EXTRACTION AND MOSLEM OIL

Extraction in million tons	1938	1945	1950	1951	1952
World	271.6	372.0	522.9	594.0	641.0
Near and Middle East:					
Persia	10.4	17.1	32.3	16.7	1.3
Saudi Arabia	0.1	2.8	26.6	37.1	40.4
Kuwait	—	—	17.3	28.2	37.6
Bahrein	1.1	1.0	1.5	1.5	1.5
Qatar	—	—	1.6	2.4	3.3
Iraq	4.4	4.7	6.7	8.6	18.9
Egypt	0.2	1.3	2.4	2.4	2.4
Near and Middle East, TOTAL	16.2	26.9	88.4	96.9	105.4
(Percentage of world extraction)	(6)	(7)	(16.9)	(16.3)	(16.4)
Soviet Union (90–95% in regions with Moslem population)	28.8	21.4	37.6	42.4	48.0
Indonesia and British North Borneo	8.3	1.7	10.7	12.6	13.6
Total extraction in Moslem countries	53.3	50.0	136.7	151.9	167.0
Percentage of world extraction	19	13	26	26	24
Western Hemisphere	221.4	310.4	376.0	433.6	
Percentage of world extraction	78	84	72	73	

2. REGIONAL CENTRES OF MOSLEM OIL

(a) *Persian Gulf:*   *Extraction 1950 (mill.t)*

Persia	32.3
Saudi Arabia	26.6
Kuwait	17.3
Bahrein	1.5
Qatar	1.6
Iraq	6.7
	——
	86.0

(b) *Caspian Sea and Urals:*   *Extraction 1950 (mill.t)*

    Caucasus:

Baku	17.0	
Grozny	1.8	
Maikop	1.5	
Other centres	0.6	
	20.9	
Ural – Volga region	10.6	
Turkistan	3.8	
		35.3

(c) Other regions (Egypt,
    East Indies)   13.1

             TOTAL   134.4

3. CONTROL OF MOSLEM OIL (1951 OUTPUT)

	Mill.t	*Mill.t*	%
Soviet*		42.4	28
United States:			
Gulf Exploration Co. (Kuwait)	14.1		
Standard Oil, New Jersey (Saudi Arabia, Iraq, Qatar)	12.4		
Standard Oil, California (Saudi Arabia, Bahrein)	11.9		
Texas Oil Co.	11.9		
Socony-Vacuum (Saudi Arabia, Iraq, Qatar)	5.0		
Standard N. J.-Vacuum (Indonesia)	3.4		
		58.7	38
British and Anglo-Dutch:			
Anglo-Iranian Oil Co. (Kuwait, Iraq, Qatar)	16.7		
Royal Dutch-Shell (Egypt, Iraq, Qatar, Indonesia, Borneo)	14.2		
Anglo-Iranian in Persia (nationalized in spring 1951)	16.7		
		47.6	31
French:			
Cie. Française des Pétroles (Iraq, Qatar)		2.6	2

* From this must be deducted the output of Sakhalin, the Ukraine, and the northern Urals. This amounts, however, at most to 6 to 7 per cent of the total Soviet output of 42.4 million tons.

4. INVESTMENT IN THE OIL INDUSTRY IN THE NEAR AND MIDDLE EAST
AT THE BEGINNING OF 1952

By Branch of Industry	Mill. dollars	By Country	Mill. dollars	%
Extraction	230	Persia	735	35
Refineries	840	Saudi Arabia	525	25
Transport	690	Iraq	315	15
other	340	Bahrein	168	8
		Kuwait	147	7
		others	210	10
Total investment	2,100		2,100	

	%
Share of total capital	
British and British-Dutch companies (after Persian nationalization only 14%)	49
American companies	42

Source: Mohammed Yeganeh: "Investment in the Petroleum Industry of
the Middle East"; *Middle East Journal,* spring 1952.

The table has been compiled from the actual extraction in 1951. It therefore
gives the relative strength of the great oil powers in the Islamic region at
the moment. A different picture results if instead of the output the amount
of the oil reserves below ground is taken as a basis. But in this regard the
details vary too greatly to enable a reliable judgment to be formed.

(Persian oil is still credited in the table to the British share. Without
Persia, the share of the British oil companies falls to 20 per cent. The
National Iranian Petroleum Company, formed after nationalization, has so
far shown no sign of any output worth mentioning. The further development
of Persian oil cannot at present be foreseen.

(It may be expected that there will be some changes in the relative position
of the powers as soon as the construction of the new pipeline enables the oil
of Iraq to be marketed more quickly and on a larger scale. But whatever the
future developments, the American oil companies are likely to remain in the
front rank.)

Country	Company	Ownership	%	Date and Duration of Concession
Saudi Arabia	Arabian American Oil Company (Aramco)	*American*		May 29, '33
		Standard Oil, Calif.	30	66 years Suplement of Aug. 21, '39
		Texas Oil Co.	30	66 years
		Standard Oil, N.J.	30	
		Socony-Vacuum	10	
Bahrein Islands		*American*		June 19, '40
	Bahrain Petroleum Co. Ltd.	Standard Oil, Calif.	50	55 years
		Texas Oil Co.	50	
Kuwait		*British-American*		Dec. 25, '34 75 years
	Kuwait Oil Co.	Anglo-Iranian	50	
		Gulf Exploration	50	
Neutral Zone (Saudi Arabia-Kuwait)	Kuwait-half	American Independent Oil Co.		Aug. 6, '48 50 years (a)
	Saudi-half	Pacific Western Oil Corp (Am.)		March 4, '49
Iraq	Iraq Petroleum Co. (I.P.C.)	*International Consortium*		March 14, '25 75 years
and subsidiaries:		consisting of:		
(a) Mosul Petroleum Co.		Anglo-Iranian	23.75	
(b) Basrah Petroleum Co.				
		Royal Dutch-Shell	23.75	Nov. 30, '38 75 years
		total British holding	47.50	

Country	Company	Ownership	%	Date and Duration of Concession
Iraq (cont.)		Socony-Vacuum	11.37	
		Standard Oil, N.J.	11.37	(b)
		total American holding	23.75	
		Cie. Française des Pétroles	23.75	
		others	5.00	
Qatar	Petroleum Development Co. (Qatar)	IPC Group (see Iraq)		1936 75 years
Persia	Anglo-Iranian Oil Co. Ltd.	British Government	56	May 29, '33 60 years*
		Burma Oil Co.	22	
		others	22	

* Nationalized by the Persian Government in the spring of 1951. Plant transferred to the National Iranian Petroleum Company.

Index

i

Index

iv

A NOTE ON THE TYPE

This book is set in GARAMOND, a modern rendering of the type first cut in the sixteenth century by Claude Garamond (1510–1561). He was a pupil of Geoffroy Tory and is believed to have based his letters on the Venetian models, although he introduced a number of important differences, and it is to him that we owe the letter which we know as Old Style. He gave to his letters a certain elegance and a feeling of movement which won for their creator an immediate reputation and the patronage of the French King, Francis I.

Composed, printed, and bound by H. Wolff, New York.